BOSWORTH FIELD

BOSWORTH FIELD

and the Wars of the Roses

A.L.Rowse

WORDSWORTH EDITIONS

First published in the United States by
Doubleday in *The Crossroads of World History Series*,
edited by Orville Prescott, 1966

First published in the United Kingdom in 1966
MACMILLAN AND COMPANY LIMITED
Essex Street, london

This edition published 1998
by Wordsworth Editions Limited
Cumberland House, Crib Street, Ware,
Hertfordshire SG12 9ET

ISBN 1 85326 691 4

Reprinted 1999

Wordsworth® is a registered trade mark of
Wordsworth Editions Limited

Printed and bound in Great Britain
by Mackays of Chatham plc, Chatham, Kent.

To
David Treffry
and
Raleigh Trevelyan

whose ancestors
fought in these campaigns

CONTENTS

PREFACE

I am very grateful to my old friend Mr. Orville Prescott, the editor of this series, for his invitation to step aside from my chosen field of Tudor studies to undertake this subject. Without his persuasion and encouragement I should not have thought of it—though it is, after all, the immediate prelude to that period. Since my undergraduate days I have been interested in the fifteenth century, and in the years since I have enjoyed the suggestive conversation of those eminent authorities Professor E. F. Jacob and Mr. K. B. McFarlane. I hope I have made good use of the instruction that they—perhaps not always consciously—have provided.

The subject of the Wars of the Roses has recently shown that it has not lost its power to fascinate the large TV public in Britain, as it exerted its spell upon people in the sixteenth century, especially the Elizabethans. With them it called forth ballads, laments, narrative poems, narrative prose, histories, biographies, chronicle plays. Shakespeare devoted to the subject a unique canvas—in breadth, depth and extent—with his eight plays covering the whole century from Richard II to Richard III.

Thus it has been a great advantage to be able to make so much use of the reflection of historical events in the mirror of literature—the book is in some sense a bridge between these two disciplines, too much divorced in this age of specialisation. It is not only that literature is part of the material of history, but history is—one should need no reminding—an important branch of literature.

I am much indebted to Professor Jack Simmons for his scholarly help and for guiding me around Leicestershire, in particular around Bosworth and the site of the battle; and to Mr. Peter Lewis, of All Souls College, for reading my typescript and correcting some errors. I am grateful to Dr. John E. Pomfret, Director of the Huntington Library, for his constant encouragement, to the Library service for procuring books from neighbouring Californian libraries when necessary, and to all the staff there—where this book was written—for their unvarying and obliging kindness.

A. L. ROWSE

Oxford,

Independence Day, 1965

The Houses
of
Lancaster and York

The Houses of Lancaster and York

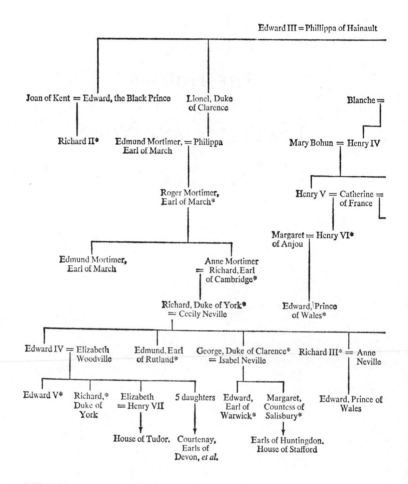

*Killed in battle, executed or murdered.

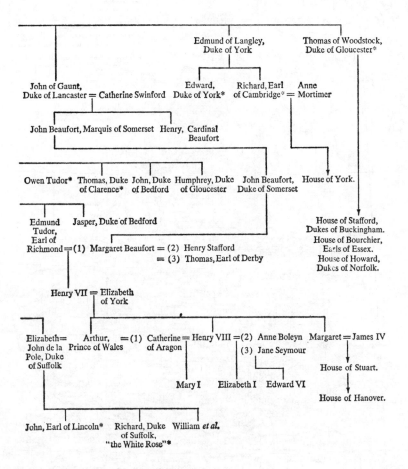

England in the fifteenth century.

PROLOGUE

What was settled at the field of Bosworth in 1485? Well, it ended a long dynastic struggle that filled so much of the fifteenth century with alarms and excursions, battles, feuds, the deaths of kings and princes, noble murders. The story of that century, which achieved a kind of culmination and received its quietus at Bosworth, was so dramatic that it inspired a prolific literature in prose and verse in the next century, reaching its summit with the history-plays of Shakespeare, a full canvas covering it all, from the Revolution of 1399 to Bosworth. That victory ended the rule of the male line of the Plantagenets and brought in the new dynasty of the Tudors. It altered the story of England, changed the succession of its kings.

Bosworth Field was all the more dramatic in that the victor, Henry Tudor, had hardly ever been seen in England, was "a figure totally unknown to almost all of his suddenly acquired subjects."[1] While Richard III, who was defeated and killed there, had taken a leading part in the government of England for more than a decade under his brother, Edward IV, before usurping the throne that was his brother's son's. Richard had long been a well-known, a too well-known figure on the public scene.

The year 1485, therefore, is one of the decisive dates in English history, along with 1066, the year of the Norman Conquest, or 1688, that of the Whig Revolution. Professor Chrimes, in his book *Lancastrians, Yorkists and Henry VII*, tells us that "no serious historian today would subscribe to the old-fashioned idea that the year 1485 in itself marked any particular turning-point in English history."[2] An idea is none the worse for being old-fashioned, and this is precisely what the year 1485 did do. Years in themselves are historical markers and, to the sensitive observer, have their distinctive character, even atmosphere. In our own lifetime, for an Englishman, what about the difference between 1939 and 1940; or, for an American, the difference between 1940 and 1941? What about the sinister character of the year 1933 for a German, or the meaning of the year 1945, that of an almighty deliverance from an evil thing, for us all?

The year 1485 was one of those years.

Even Professor Chrimes allows: "nonetheless the battle of Bosworth Field undoubtedly, as it turned out, did mark an important turning-point in dynastic history." It was, of course, the end of a long dynastic conflict, a brutal and fratricidal power-struggle. But more than power was involved. Kingship, monarchy of one kind or another, was the linch-pin of medieval society. It was not only a question of government, though "government is always a vital matter, upon which the life of the people and realm depends; in those days, and for centuries thereafter, the king *was* the government."[3] More than that, monarchy provided the sacred bond keeping society together; the king was a sacramental person, sometimes almost a sacrificial victim. (Historians should see these things in terms of anthropology.) The overthrow of a king upset society itself—this remained true as late as 1649, with the execution of Charles I. Any doubt about the monarchy disturbed something fundamental.

This was what the Revolution of 1399 did, in wresting the succession out of its rightful course. The precedent of 1327 was much in mind, but then Edward II's son and heir succeeded as Edward III. In 1399 Henry of Lancaster, son of John of Gaunt, Edward III's third son, captured the throne from his unsatisfactory cousin Richard II. It was true that this was done by the will of the magnates, the Church and Parliament—the will of the nation, so far as it could be expressed. Thus Henry IV held the throne, if unquietly, for the rest of his short life, and his son Henry V after him. But when the kingship failed with the grandson, Henry VI, the whole dynastic issue was opened by Richard of York. People were forcibly reminded that this was the heir of Edward III's second son—Lionel of Clarence, senior brother to Gaunt—if in the female line.

Which then was the rightful line, Lancaster or York?

Lancaster had been recognised in possession again and again

by all the institutions of Church and State—by crownings and anointings, by oaths of obedience and fealty, by acts of Parliament and recognition in Parliament, in three generations. Then force, through the military ability of young Edward of York, decided the issue against Henry VI. It looked as if the Yorkists were in for good, with the successful rule of Edward IV. And so they would have been if it had not been for the crime of Richard III against his own house. It was only that that gave Henry Tudor his chance—the Lancastrian heir through his mother and through only the Beaufort line. Otherwise the Yorkists would have held it; there would have been a different succession in England, a totally different surface-pattern to our history. It is hard to realise that we should never have had Henry VIII and Elizabeth I.

This prolonged struggle at the head of English society—and for its headship—gave an opportunity, as we shall see, for all the strains and tensions, the local feuds and conflicts, to break into the open. It was very distracting; it meant the breakdown of order in some areas at times. Enjoyable as it must have been to fighting types, presenting welcome opportunities to thugs along with the spirited and disorderly, it must have been a confounded nuisance to sober citizens, to the commercial middle class and to churchmen. Nevertheless, underneath the troubles at the top, the life of the country went on: the cloth trade expanded, as we can see from the evidences left in the clothing areas—the splendid Perpendicular churches of East Anglia, of the Cotswolds, of Somerset and Devon. It was, indeed, the age in which the Perpendicular style achieved its grandest expression with King's College Chapel at Cambridge, and Henry VII's at Westminster—those Lancastrian works, and St. George's at Windsor—a Yorkist offering. The age of Towton and Tewkesbury and Bosworth was also the age of the founding of Eton and All Souls and Magdalen, of Duke Humphrey's library at Oxford, the Lady Margaret's colleges at Cambridge. It was the time of Caxton's introduction of printing into England and of Henry VII's patronage of the Cabots and the early voyages to America.

Before the end of the century sensible middle-class folk, and not they alone, were heartily sick of the endemic strife and anxious to see an end to it. Bosworth put an end to it. "It is tolerably certain," Professor Chrimes says, "that if Henry Tudor had happened to be a man of lesser calibre than he was (as he might so easily have been), then Bosworth . . . would not in fact have been the end of the civil wars. But as it turned out, Henry was the very man for the job. He took over the Yorkist monarchy, used its methods and institutions, extended them, improved them, instilled into them the spirit and energy of a new efficiency. He thereby ensured that the realm of England should not lack a vigorous and, in the then sense of the term, a modern government."[4] In short, we are in at the transition from medieval to Tudor England.

Let us retrace our steps, and move out with Richard on his last march along the road westward from Leicester to the field of Bosworth. It is late August, towards the end of summer, the tracks dusty, the hedgerows thinning out as one gets farther from the town and its arable, for the country was more open then. From the higher country of the approach, along the spur that reaches its highest point at Ambien Hill, one sees the spire of Stoke Golding church pricking the horizon. Two armies are converging for a struggle that proved decisive and changed the course of history. For in the low-lying ground beneath the hill, that was more marshy then, Henry of Richmond's heterogeneous army was approaching, made up of French mercenaries, Welsh contingents, English recruits that had gone over to the stranger. King Richard's army was twice that of the unknown invader in size: why was he so easily and so completely defeated, after a contest of only a couple of hours?

To understand this last and decisive round in the conflict, the grounds of the conflict as a whole must be made intelligible; otherwise this is merely a tale of the battles of kites and crows. It all goes back to a revolution—the Revolution of 1399.

CHAPTER I

The Character and Reign of Richard II

To understand the Revolution of 1399, with all its consequences for the century after it—deposition of a rightful king, insecurity of tenure of the throne by his successors, dynastic wars, constant domestic turmoil—we have to portray the character and the reign of Richard II, of which the revolution was both consequence and culmination.

Richard II came to the throne, on the death of his old grandfather Edward III in 1377, when he was only a boy of ten; he succeeded to a heritage of troubles, which he was naturally incapable of handling. Some decades are disastrous in a people's history—like the 1930's in our own time—and the 1370's formed one such, which culminated in the revolutionary movement that convulsed south-eastern England in 1381 and shook society like an earthquake, the Peasants' Revolt.

We have to see so much of this period we are going to portray against the background of the seemingly endless war with France. The Hundred Years' War, which Edward III had initiated, may have begun as a family quarrel but it ended as a war between nations: it engendered acute nationalism among both English and French, and a legacy of hatred of each other that went on through the centuries. The very triumphs of Crécy and Poitiers, unexpected as they were against a far richer and more powerful nation, made it all the harder to make concessions later, when the war was going badly, in the interest of a moderate, sensible settlement. The war dragged on and on, and was popular among nobles and the knightly class who profited from it. The people at large had to pay.

Edward III, growing senile and in the hands of his mistress, Alice Perrers—as much of a gold-digger as royal mistresses usually are—had been incapable of giving leadership in his last years. His son and heir, the Black Prince, who had all the prestige that the age gave to the most famous soldier in Europe, was sickening to his premature death, aged only forty-three, in 1376. The King's third son, John of Gaunt—the most intelligent of the lot—was not a successful soldier, lacked prestige and popularity in consequence and was suspected in these years of having designs on the throne. Edward III had had a record brood for an English king: there was the trouble of providing for them and their progeny in the present, and in the future all the internecine conflict that the deposition of Richard II gave rise to among their descendants. Indeed, to be descended from Edward III came to be something like a death-sentence all through the next century and well into the Tudor age.

At that moment, the early years of Richard's reign, the clue to the popular discontent—as so often in the history of peoples—was the burden of taxation. How to pay for the war? *There* was the chief demand on the government. The people themselves did not want to see the end of the war—that was unpopular. And they could hardly be expected to understand the very real dilemma that that imposed on the administration, at its wit's end for cash. What the people could see, or hear talk about, and understand very well was the extravagance of the Court, the depredations of an Alice Perrers, the ostentation of a John of Gaunt—richest of all the magnates, with his vast dukedom of Lancaster and his splendid palace of the Savoy—the immense wealth of a prelate like William of Wykeham, Bishop of Winchester. "An overtaxed and leaderless people, at once war-weary and bellicose, was becoming ripe for revolt."[1]

This was what faced the boy-king's government at his accession, with all the added dangers—the lack of authority, of unified leadership, of confused counsels—of a minority.

For government in the Middle Ages, and for long after, was intensely personal—nothing impersonal about it, as with so much of modern government. There was the crucial importance of the Crown: everything depended upon the person of the monarch. Such was the aura of the monarch, "the divinity that doth hedge a king"—serving the profound purposes of keeping society together, answering to even more profound anthropological impulses—that it had taken twenty years of misrule on the part of the witless

Edward II before he was eventually deposed, and then there was a rising son and heir to take his place as Edward III. The events of 1327, the procedures of the magnates of the realm against Edward II, his deposition and subsequent murder at Berkeley Castle, were never very far away from the minds of people half a century after, in the troublous reign of Richard II. Most of all were they present to the mind of the young king himself, Edward II's great-grandson. Just as the Empress Eugénie had a cult of Marie Antoinette and feared a similar fate, so Richard II made a cult of his great-grandfather, Edward II. He once and again paid a visit to Edward's tomb at Gloucester to collect evidences of the miracles wrought at it—for of course a martyred king could work miracles with simple folk—and he pressed forward the canonisation at Rome, as a saint, of this luckless, kindly homosexual. Richard might have reflected on the moral of his great-grandfather's reign to more rational purpose. But humans in history, or anywhere else, are rarely rational.

Richard was crowned with great pomp at Westminster, 16 July 1377, the ceremonies presided over by John of Gaunt, the King's senior living uncle, who bore the sword Curtana beside the boy, "fair as another Absalom" to the beholders. In front of them walked the King's other two uncles, Edmund of Cambridge and Thomas of Woodstock, subsequently Dukes of York and Gloucester, with the young Mortimer, Earl of March. The characters, and the ghosts, of our tragedy walk in procession before us. For that young Earl of March married the daughter and heiress of Lionel of Clarence, who died young, but was elder brother to Gaunt, Duke of Lancaster. And through that heiress descended the senior claim of the house of York to the throne; they possessed in addition a junior claim through Gaunt's younger brother, the Duke of York—the house of York drew its titles, York and March, from both descents. Was this senior but female descent inferior to the male Lancastrian descent from Gaunt? But in England there was no Salic law against the descent of females. These open issues later became open wounds and crimsoned the course of history with the blood of Yorkists and Lancastrians alike.

The law of succession to the throne was not an absolutely settled matter. There was an element of election in it that was not devoid of reality, and might come to the surface in an emergency.

Even in the coronation service today, when all is so many shadows of the past, there is a vestigial element of election: when the archbishop presents the monarch before crowning to the people for their assent, the people politely, faintly, answer (in Latin). At the coronation of King John, in 1199, Archbishop Hubert Walter advanced the view, in John's interest—for the son of his elder brother was alive—that any suitable member of the royal family might be elected king. Now in 1377 the Archbishop's question to the people asking their assent was placed after Richard swore his oath as king, instead of before, thus giving the people's assent the character of a recognition of his right *de jure* and robbing the element of election of any significance. It was taken at the time, as several other hints were too, as a discouragement to any thoughts Gaunt might have to his nephew's throne. Everything seems to have conspired together in Richard's youth to give him exalted notions of his prerogative, of himself as king, as a unique person with a *mystique,* outside the bounds of ordinary rules and sanctions.

In politics, nothing succeeds like success, and nothing fails like failure. Much would depend on the personality of the young king, his character, upbringing and environment; the rest would depend on the circumstances he met with, the forces and factors welling up from below that are the material of politics, upon which judgment has to be exercised, decisions made.

On his father's early death, Richard was brought up by his mother, and was much with her. This must have been important in his make-up: there is no doubt that he was spoiled—all his adult life he behaved like a spoiled child. His mother, Joan, the Fair Maid of Kent, seems to have been a beautiful, good-hearted, easy-going woman, no political intriguer. When the Black Prince married her, she was the widow of the Earl of Kent, her sons by him, the Hollands, were thus Richard's half-brothers to whom he was attached. His education had been entrusted to two companions of the Black Prince: Sir Guichard d'Angle, whom Richard made Earl of Huntingdon at the coronation, and Sir Simon Burley, who became an important figure in the administration.

Richard was always emotionally attached to his personal friends —more than a ruler can afford; he had the unwisdom to identify himself with his underlings and to make their quarrels his quarrels. Too loyal and confiding when young, the harsh experiences of the world of politics and rule ended by making him suspicious and mistrustful, resentful and vindictive, a psychotic type with more than a touch of persecution-mania. It was very understandable and one is sorry for him: he was not a politic type. His companions spoiled the boy who was a king, especially de Vere who led him on ill courses, was gay and irresponsible, and whom Richard adored. The minatory, hectoring magnates—especially such a person as the Earl of Arundel, a harsh and aristocratic fighting tough—Richard had no liking for, and let it be seen. He could indeed usually be seen through, for he was wanting in that self-control necessary if a man is to control others.

Richard's appearance was attractive, though of a distinctly feminine cast. He had the pink and white complexion of a girl, with masses of fair hair, and flushed easily. When he grew to his full height he was rather tall, but slender and willowy. His face was rather hairless: the double-pointed beard of his portraits really two tufts on the chin, with small weak moustaches at the corners of the mouth. These accentuated the nervous and drawn look that began to show on his face as early as his middle twenties. In speech he had a slight stammer, though when roused he was eloquent enough and the passionate words—he was often in a rage—poured forth helter-skelter. Above all, he was no fighting soldier, and this in itself was a serious drawback in medieval military society, when so much of life was fighting.

The life of a medieval king was apt to be a fierce struggle for survival. This was not a personality to inspire confidence, much less to keep order in the nursery.

In the circumstances of medieval society and government, and for long afterwards, minority rule was sufficiently difficult and dangerous in itself. In the wonderful poem that was being written at this time, *Piers the Plowman,* with its vivid portrayal of the ills of the age, spiritual and material, this crucial weakness at the head of society is concisely expressed:

> There the cat is a kitten, the court is full ailing.

In the first years of the reign Richard's eldest uncle, John of Gaunt, was the leading figure in the government and had to bear not only its unpopularity but an additional load on his own account. For he had alienated the three most powerful groups, especially where raising money was concerned—the prelates of the Church, the rich bourgeois of London and the Commons in Parliament. As himself the most conspicuously rich magnate in the kingdom, with all the dukedom of Lancaster and more at his disposal, he was a vulnerable target, especially with his palace of the Savoy so obvious on the banks of the Thames, stuffed with rich furnishings, tapestries, jewels, precious objects—for Gaunt was something of a collector. To get his own back on the churchmen and as a propaganda weapon in the conflict, Gaunt publicly supported Wyclif with his increasingly radical criticism of the Church, its position in society, its wealth and doctrines. This added a bitter and acrid element in the revolutionary situation that was fermenting.

It is fairly clear that political discontents and tremors were to some extent seismological indications of profound disturbance in the society of the time. The full effects of the Black Death a generation before, with the subsequent visitations of the plague, were now felt. The population of England was reduced by one third—gone was the happy expansion, the comparative prosperity, of which we still have evidences in the splendid outburst of thirteenth- and early fourteenth-century architecture, such glories as Westminster Abbey, Lincoln Minster and Salisbury Cathedral. The whole economic ordering of labour was upset: labour was scarce, prices rose, attempts were made to peg wages at pre-plague rates and to regulate prices—both ineffective. The system of villeinage upon which an agrarian society rested was breaking down; the bonds that bound the villein to the soil were everywhere loosening, prospects becoming freer with a more fluid status, the fracturing of the cake of custom. In Richard's first years resistance to the labour statutes and attempts to enforce the *status quo* were quickening.

What brought everything to the boil and perilously fused the rural and urban discontents into the revolutionary movement of 1381 was the successive and inequitable demands for taxation. In 1377 a poll-tax of 4d., i.e., 4d. a head, had occasioned much outcry. In 1379 a graduated tax, more equitable in intention, was denounced as unheard of and its yield was disappointing. So in 1380 the government clamped down a grievous tax of one shilling a head, heavy-handed and utterly inequitable, which was beyond the capacity of most peasants to pay. "The result was evasion on a large scale."[2] Collectors were attacked, resistance developed into mutiny; the areas that were hardest hit, Kent and East Anglia, rose up and took the lead. "By May, 1381, the South-East of England was on the verge of revolution."

In June the Kentish rebels moved on London under their leader, Wat Tyler, an unknown man of strong personality who imposed his leadership. They encamped outside the walled city at Blackheath. Their clerical leader, John Ball, a vagrant priest released from the Archbishop's prison, which may have given him ideas of the throne of St. Augustine for himself, exhorted the peasant horde with his sermons on a text never to be forgotten:

> When Adam delved and Eve span,
> Who was then a gentleman?

There now converged also upon the terrified city the Essex horde, which encamped at Mile End just outside Aldgate. King, Court and government, utterly paralysed, took refuge in the Tower, which was well garrisoned and should have been impregnable.

The London mob now joined in with the peasants to attack the residences of grandees and well-to-do. As usual with such mob-movements the prisons were opened, criminals let out to take part in the festive amenities, lawyers were made a special target, a number of them summarily dispatched, and bonfires made of legal documents wherever they could be found.

An orgy of destruction was set going. First to go was John of Gaunt's palace of the Savoy—sheer simple-minded destruction of its contents, plate, jewels, furnishings trampled or thrown into the Thames, the house then given up to the flames and left a ruin. The hospital of St. John at Clerkenwell burned for days; so too the Treasurer's town house and his new manor at Highbury. The rolls in the Archbishop's chancery at Lambeth were destroyed, as were those in the Temple along with houses there. The flames could be seen from the Tower, where the young king appeared at a turret to persuade the crowd to disperse and declared himself ready to go out and meet them at Mile End. It was a signal act of courage, and it paid handsomely. During his absence the mob penetrated into the Tower—either by collusion, or through the paralysis that seemed to grip everybody except the boy-king at this juncture—

and two of the leading ministers, Archbishop Sudbury and
Treasurer Hales, with others, were dragged out and summarily
executed on Tower Hill.

Meanwhile, at Smithfield the young king, accompanied by
Walworth, the mayor, and a few lords, coolly confronted the
mutinous peasants. At his approach they all knelt—such was the
aura of kingship with simple people (not so with more instructed
persons later). "Welcome, King Richard. We wish for no other
king but you"—they did not impute their miseries to the boy, but
to his ministers. The King took the initiative in conciliation,
promised them pardon and that he would grant their requests.
They presented their not unreasonable demands through their
spokesman: the end of villeinage, for placing labour services on
the basis of free contract, for land to be let at a groat an acre.
Richard was free with his promises, provided that they would
disperse, and the Essex men, taking a king at his word, began to
go home.

There remained the men of Kent and Wat Tyler to be dealt
with next day. Murders continued in the streets, while Richard,
"extraordinary though it seems, apparently had been wandering
through the scenes of wild disorder in the city."[3] Such was the
magic in the name of king, that he moved about unscathed. Next
day, again with Mayor Walworth and a few lords, he met the
Kentish mob under Wat Tyler at Smithfield. Power had, inevitably,
gone to Tyler's head and he addressed the King insolently and
with more aggressive demands: not only the end of villeinage
and outlawry but the end of all lordship save the King's, all men
otherwise to be equal, the estates of the Church confiscated and
given to the laity, bishoprics to be abolished—in short, the end of
ordered government. Richard replied that all reasonable demands
would be granted if only they would go home. Tyler turned nasty
and demanded a written and sealed charter. Mayor Walworth
knocked him off his horse, and someone struck off his head.
It was a dangerous moment, touch and go, with the peasants
preparing to rush the royal party. But the boy-king had an
inspiration: he rode forward and offered to place himself at the
head of the commons: "Will you kill your king? I am your
captain. Follow me." The poor simpletons obediently followed him
away from the city, while Walworth hastily recruited a force of

volunteers, well armed, with which he returned to wreak vengeance on the dispersing rebels. Richard would not have any violence done to his sheep, declared them pardoned and off they went. In London the corner was turned—largely through the King and Mayor Walworth keeping their heads. But it had been a near thing.

The social earthquake rippled outwards, into counties where peasant leaders achieved immortality with their rebarbative medieval names: William Grindcob, leader of the Hertfordshire men, with their special grievances against the rich abbey of St. Albans; John Wrawe, who led the burning and pillaging in Suffolk and the attack on the abbey of Bury; Jack Straw and Litster; Adam Clymme in the Isle of Ely; John Hancchach in Cambridgeshire, where at Cambridge Great St. Mary's was sacked and the university archives burned in Market Square, to the shrieks of an old beldame, Margery Starre: "Away with the learning of clerks! Away with it!" Everywhere one comes across the instinctive dislike of the people for book-learning, the more understandable mistrust of legal rolls, deeds, and charters. Outwards and outwards the movement spread, to Norfolk where there were some murders, and some plundering, to feebler ripples at York, Scarborough, Beverley and in the south at Winchester.

When the movement was all over and the governing class had recovered its nerve, it became a case of the familiar distich:

> When the Devil was sick,
> The Devil a saint would be;
> When the Devil was well,
> The devil a saint was he!

Reaction set in, and the frightened governing class demanded reprisals. The King would not allow mass reprisals, however; repression was severe, but by due process of law. The impression in the country can be gathered from some verses of the time:

> Man be ware and be no fool:
> Think upon the axe and of the stool!
> The axe was sharp, the stool was hard,
> The fourth year of King Richard.

He accompanied his new Chief Justice, the Cornishman Tresillian, on a tour of the disaffected areas. It is said that when the men of Essex demanded the fulfilment of his promises at Mile End, he burst out, "Villeins ye are and villeins ye shall remain." Of course, the Rising had no perceptible effect on removing the disabilities of peasants and artisans—as is usually the case with such useless manifestations, almost always all loss. For that they would have to wait for the natural operation of economic forces making towards freer conditions of labour in both town and country.

For our particular purpose we should realise the effect this exciting and hazardous experience must have had on the young king. He was already surrounded by flatterers instilling into him exalted notions of his prerogative. His experiences in 1381 must have underlined, in a growing youth, his sense of his own uniqueness, the reverence accorded to the person of a king among the people at large—not so among the magnates; it must have reinforced a feeling of himself giving the law, the sense of being above the law. This was dangerous: it was not in accordance with received ideas of medieval English kingship as operating according to recognised rules of law and custom. On the psychological plane, it must have fed the young king's inner fantasy.

All these elements entered into his subsequent fate.

In 1382 a grand marriage was found for Richard: Anne, sister of Wenceslas of Bohemia, King of the Romans. Bringing off the match was a diplomatic score over the French, for Charles V wanted her for his own son. But the victory had to be paid for with a large loan to Wenceslas, and the new queen was provided with a splendid jointure. Hence the marriage was not popular: the English felt that as usual they had to pay, and the Queen's somewhat exotic entourage of Bohemians was not much appreciated. Actually she herself gave no trouble; she seems to have been kind and peace-loving, an influence for conciliation. Richard was undoubtedly attached to her, but he gave her no children—what was wrong with him?—and this in time added another weakness to his position.

His greatest weakness in these early years, when there was plenty of good will towards a young man coming into his inheritance, was his extravagant attachment to his personal entourage. This naturally aroused the jealousy of Richard's uncles and of the magnates, who considered themselves the proper counsellors of the Crown, as in the ominous case of Edward II and those who had brought him to book. Richard was even more extravagant in his dissipation of Crown lands to them, at a time when money was short and people overtaxed. Even the respectable Simon Burley, an intelligent man with a considerable library of his own, used his influence with the King to increase his patrimony from twenty marks to some three thousand. There were others, less worthy and respectable, to whom Richard handed out right and left. Like James I later, Richard had little idea of finance, often a sign of weakness of character, or at least another aspect of lack of self-control.

Most unpopular of all was his addiction to Robert de Vere, for this was a direct reminder of Edward II's doting on Gaveston, with whom de Vere had much in common, except for his aristocratic lineage. Neither of them was a sinister or a bad man, merely frivolous, light-headed and totally irresponsible—but that was enough to ruin a kingdom more than any amount of sinister ability. No doubt they found the heavy-handed, heavily cuirassed magnates, like Arundel, singularly humourless, and no doubt they laughed at them. It became no laughing matter either for them or for the King.

There was the horrid Thomas of Woodstock, for example, the King's youngest uncle, an ill-tempered, brash, rude tough. Not even John of Gaunt's avuncular advice, from his position of lofty grandeur, was always welcome. And there were always seeds of suspicion in Richard's mind as to Gaunt's possible claim to the throne, with his promising son Bolingbroke to follow it up. At Salisbury in 1384 there was a querulous, queasy session of Parliament, full of complaints; and a noxious friar, after celebrating Mass, informed Richard that Gaunt was plotting his murder. Richard was ready to believe anything. It is said that Thomas of Woodstock broke into the King's bedchamber in a rage, and threatened to kill anyone, even the King himself, who charged his brother with treason. Such were the amenities, the strains, within the royal family.

Naturally this kind of thing threw Richard back upon his own following of personal friends; this sinister dialectic is to be seen all through his reign. For the trouble was that he would not take telling. Two years before, when his Chancellor Scrope conscientiously rebuked him for the lavish grants Richard was making, he dismissed him out of hand. Like a spoiled teen-ager, any-body who attempted to interfere for his good earned his ill-will; and to this Richard added, in Swift's memorable phrase, "the long sedate resentment of a Spaniard." Deliberately flouting Parliament, the King appointed Michael de la Pole Chancellor in Scrope's place. This was a good appointment, for de la Pole was able and had hitherto been on good terms with the magnates. But when he became the brains of the King's party, they could not forgive him his middle-class origin—his fortune had come down to him from Eleanor Rottenherring of Hull, and I suppose the Pole (pronounced Pool) in that name to become so famous refers to the Pool there, whence their wealth came.

The quarrel within the royal family was patched up for an expedition against the Scots, the allies of the French enemy, later that year. If not so disastrous as Edward II's expedition to Bannockburn, it was an inglorious affair. Richard's heart was never in fighting, and he soon turned home, having wasted a large army on nothing better than laying waste the Lowlands. Characteristically he celebrated the show by creating his two younger uncles, Edmund of Langley and Thomas of Woodstock, Dukes of York and Gloucester, by which titles we shall hear of them later at sinister conjunctures.

Gaunt had had enough. He had spoken strongly to his nephew about the evil counsellors surrounding him, and been snubbed for his pains. It is clear that, whatever suspicions Richard entertained, Gaunt was moved by the desire to maintain the dignity of the Crown and to keep the royal family together in support of it: he was an honourable man. He was also an ambitious one, anxious to push his claim to the throne of Castile in right of his wife. Richard was equally anxious to be rid of him, and early in 1386 formally recognised his uncle as King of Castile. (In a fifteenth-century window in the ante-chapel of All Souls College at Oxford one sees Gaunt portrayed with crown and sceptre as such.) Now Richard betrayed his real affections by creating de Vere Marquis of Dublin, an unprecedented title, putting him ahead of all the other magnates, except for the royal dukes; and with it he was granted all the royal authority, lands and jurisdictions in Ireland. It was a provocative, and a silly, act. Gaunt was bought off by

Richard's support of a handsome grant for his Spanish expedition.

No sooner was Gaunt out of the way and involved in Gascony than England was threatened with a large-scale invasion from France. An immense subsidy of four fifteenths was demanded from Parliament that autumn, while Richard was so ill-advised as to choose this moment to elevate his favourite to a dukedom: de Vere was made Duke of Ireland, putting him on an equality with the King's uncles with the promise of an even larger palatinate than that of Lancaster. Lords and Commons, exacerbated, joined together to demand the dismissal of Richard's ministers, refusing to deal with either his Chancellor, Suffolk—Richard had elevated de la Pole to the earldom of Suffolk—or his Treasurer. Richard replied petulantly that he would not dismiss the meanest scullion in his kitchen at their bidding.

The King was thereupon visited at , Eltham, whither he had withdrawn, by a very ominous delegation. Without Gaunt to mediate and protect him, he now found himself face to face with his uncle Gloucester, who took it upon him to be spokesman for Parliament and the country at this juncture. He brought with him to speak for the Church Bishop Arundel, a very clever, smooth prelate, no friend of Richard's. At Eltham there was a showdown. They reminded the King, as spokesmen for Parliament, that he was bound to summon it once a year and to attend; otherwise it could disperse. (The implication was—no subsidy, no government.) Richard betrayed his inner thoughts in a passionate outburst: his people were plotting rebellion, and he would seek help from his kinsman, the King of France. This put him completely in the wrong, aligned him with the enemies of his country and of his own forebears. Gloucester was not slow to take advantage of this, and he drove it home intolerably: "a king who is guided by evil counsel, who withdraws himself from his people, neglects to maintain their laws, and is governed only by his own capricious impulses, can be removed from the throne and supplanted by some other member of the royal family."[4]

This direct reminder of his great-grandfather's fate broke the young man's nerve, and he was forced to agree to Parliament's demands. Suffolk was dismissed from office, made to disgorge his special grants, fined and imprisoned. A commission was appointed, which included both Gloucester and the Earl of Arundel, to supervise government and the King's household. Richard's minority was humiliatingly prolonged, when he was already older than some of his predecessors had been when they assumed their full regal powers. But bullying was no way to deal with him; he was growing into manhood with an exaggerated notion of kingship and his own sacredness, and in these circumstances humiliation was bound to breed a worse resentment. He had no intention of keeping undertakings with people who offended him, whom he regarded as worse than bullies, offenders against the sacred person of a king. Suffolk's fine was remitted and he was sent down to Windsor, where Simon Burley was his keeper; Richard joined them there, where they kept Christmas together in jollity.

Nearly the whole of next year, 1387, Richard spent away from London, touring the Midlands and the North, hoping to build up a personal party in support of himself. (It reminds one of Edward VIII's visit to South Wales before his abdication.) Richard's hopes rested upon Cheshire, a royal palatinate, and North Wales, where de Vere ruled. There they recruited a personal body-guard of rough and raw Cheshire archers and Welsh pikemen, who provided the King's main support—an unpopular one—for the rest of the reign. At the back of this royalist bastion was Ireland, also supposedly at de Vere's command—and he was adding to *his* unpopularity by repudiating his wife, Richard's cousin (and with his connivance), for a Bohemian waiting woman of Queen Anne's. Wales and Ireland as a fighting resource against the people of England!—it makes one think of that other *fantaisiste,* Charles I, and his hopes of Strafford.

That summer, while away gathering support, Richard procured a secret judgment from the judges which pointed against the legality of the commission imposed upon him and ruling in his name in London: a declaration which might lay them and their actions open to the charge of treason. It was probably the clever lawyer Tresillian who thought up this move: he was made to pay with his head for it shortly. Armed with the judges' declaration Richard returned to London in November, to be given a warm reception by the citizens. (More and more like Charles I, who was similarly led astray by the friendly reception he got from London on his return from the Scottish war in 1640.) Like Charles I, Richard was the victim of his own bad judgment: he completely misestimated the state of serious public feeling from the mob's welcome on the return of the prodigal.

The magnates were thoroughly alerted; Gloucester had learned the secret of the judges' declaration and realised the danger in which they stood. Each side was gathering its forces, resolved to appeal to force. The magnates withdrew from London and crowds of supporters flocked to what was undoubtedly the popular side. The lords appealed to Parliament against the King's friends—hence their name in constitutional history, the Lords Appellant. London now failed the King and showed that its sympathies were with the popular cause against the Court. The King's friends—de Vere, Suffolk, Tresillian and the rest—who were supposedly under arrest till the Parliament before which they were to be "appealed," or accused, Richard allowed to slip away into hiding or to escape. He had no intention of sacrificing his friends to his enemies. He had one more card to play: de Vere got through to faithful Cheshire, where he recruited forces with which he advanced bravely down the Fosse way, hoping to cut across the Cotswolds to the Thames and the King's rescue.

At Radcot Bridge de Vere found his retreat cut off by Gloucester, and ahead of him young Bolingbroke, Gaunt's eldest son, who now for the first time came out in open opposition to his cousin Richard. De Vere was never wanting in courage and he had been preparing to attack when he found his position hopeless. He escaped across the Thames at Bablockhythe—precursor of the Scholar Gipsy—and made for London and Richard in the dark days of December. It is said that the friends met once more, a last time, before de Vere got to his castle of Queenborough—of which he had been made keeper by Richard—and thence overseas.

The King lay at the mercy of the Lords Appellant.

Taking their tone from Gloucester and Arundel they had no mercy, either on the King or his friends, and the Parliament that followed well deserved its title of the Merciless Parliament. Entering the Tower with five hundred armed men at their back, in case of treachery—for they knew by now that they could never trust Richard—they made him yield to force. Walsingham, the chronicler, says that the lords threatened him that they would choose another king. He who had said that he would not dismiss the meanest scullion at their bidding had a hundred superfluous servants dismissed from his household—such was its extravagance and ostentation. All the judges who had supported Richard's constitutional rights were removed from office; all his courtiers of all ranks and degrees were dismissed. He was alone, face to face with his enemies.

Parliament met in February 1388, and the Appellants did their malign work well. Tresillian was dragged out of hiding in Westminster; no notice was taken of his plea that his sentence was illegal, as he knew it was: he was dragged on a hurdle to Tyburn and hanged, his estates confiscated. Next day Sir Nicholas Brembre, who was Richard's chief supporter in London and had been mayor, suffered the same fate there. Sir Simon Burley was a Knight of the Garter, had been a companion of the Black Prince, was a humane and honourable man: there was really nothing against him, except his devotion to the young king who had been left to his care. The Queen went down on her knees to Gloucester to intercede for him (Richard never forgot this); the King's uncle, York, his cousin Bolingbroke and Nottingham, the two junior Appellants, interceded for him. In vain: Gloucester, Arundel and Warwick had him beheaded; so too the King's intimate servants, Beauchamp and Berners, and Sir John Salisbury, Richard's diplomatic agent in his negotiations for a peace with France. Nothing was farther from these soldierly minds than peace.

"The Merciless Parliament well deserved its name," says our historian of the reign. "Never before in our history, not even in the dark days of Edward II, had legal sanction been claimed for the destruction on such flimsy pretexts of so many men of gentle birth. . . . The authors of these punishments must bear some responsibility for the long tale of violence and judicial murder which darkens so much of the parliamentary history, not only of the last years of Richard II, but also of the succeeding century."[5]

Undoubtedly this savagery was due to Gloucester and Arundel, backed by Warwick, as it completely reflected their spirit. Richard laid it up in his heart; he never allowed himself to forget.

Nor did the Appellants' rule prosper. That summer there happened, at the hands of the Scots, the crushing defeat of Otterburn—made memorable by the ballad of Chevy Chase—when

the Douglas took prisoner the young Henry Percy, Harry Hotspur. This put the North in danger and renewal of the French
war out of the question. A series of truces led to the suspension
of foreign war for the rest of the reign, little as this was to the
taste of the warrior class with their hope of ransoms and loot.
The Appellants dispersed on their knightly occupations: Bolingbroke on his well-publicised crusade against the heathen in East
Prussia, whither the odious Gloucester promised to follow; Arundel
considered a pilgrimage to the Holy Land, which he stood much
in need of. Peace was more to King Richard's taste—he was not
capable of masculine military leadership—and this became his
policy. At times the rumour came up that his purpose was to use
the French, if possible, against his internal enemies, and we know
that this was not remote from his mind. He was very conscious
of the kingly order being above that of ordinary mortals, and was
spurred to emulate his cousin, Charles VI of France, who had
just emerged successful from his struggle with *his* uncles and
declared his majority.

Richard took his opportunity. On 3 May 1389 he appeared in
full Council and asked the assembly how old he was. He was, as
all well knew, well over twenty-two. There was no reply to that
—his minority had been unduly, exceptionally prolonged; he now
assumed the full powers of government.

At the end of the year Richard ordered Gaunt home from
Gascony. Gaunt had had no military success with his Castilian
adventure, but it had turned out immensely profitable financially
and dynastically. Lucky house of Lancaster!—everything Gaunt
touched turned to gold. He had achieved a glittering settlement
for himself: a vast indemnity, a large annual pension, one daughter was married to the heir of Castile, another to the King of
Portugal—whereby Lancastrian blood ran in the house of Aviz,
recognisably in the personality of Prince Henry the Navigator,
religious, withdrawn, dedicated, like his cousin, Henry V. Gaunt
was no less lucky in bed: besides these useful daughters he had
the able Bolingbroke for son—these by his two wives—and by
his mistress, Katherine Swinford (the poet Chaucer's sister-in-
law), the clever brood of the Beauforts, one of them to become
the famous cardinal.

Gaunt took his natural place at Richard's right hand, if a little in the background. The next six years of relative harmony reflected Gaunt's conciliatory temper and moderation, his prudent advice to the King *suaviter in modo*—the right way, the only possible way, to treat him.

Even so Richard's psychotic temperament expressed itself very recognisably. In 1392 he had an explosive quarrel with London —perhaps nursing his resentment for the city's desertion of him at the crisis of his struggle with the Appellants—and imposed a heavy fine on it. This cost him the loyalty of the city in the final crisis, the Revolution of 1399, when the citizens passed over to Bolingbroke's side against their king. In the summer of 1394 Queen Anne died at Sheen (afterwards named Richmond, in honour of the victor at Bosworth). Richard's grief for her was sincere, but took an exaggerated form. Adam of Usk tells us, "which manor, though a royal one and very fair, did King Richard, by reason that that lady's death happened therein, command and cause to be utterly destroyed."[6] Surely the act of a neurotic—and also like Richard's extravagance! The odious Arundel failed to join the funeral procession, and insulted the King by turning up late at Westminster Abbey merely to ask permission to withdraw. Richard seized a baton from an attendant and struck the Earl to the ground; blood flowed on the pavement, so that the funeral ceremonies had to be postponed for the office of cleansing the church from the pollution of blood. Whatever Richard's faults, obvious enough, he certainly had a lot to put up with—and the treatment he received was just such as to aggravate the psychological trauma he suffered from. Everything shows that he was a *fantaisiste,* living in his own inner fantasy, with an inadequate grasp of external realities: a few years later we find him entering into negotiations with the fantastic idea of becoming Holy Roman Emperor!

That autumn of 1394 Richard went on his first expedition to Ireland. His cousin Edmund Mortimer, Earl of March, had achieved a great deal in his brief fighting career there, and then died there young. This Earl of March, we remember, had married the heiress of the dead Clarence, Richard's oldest uncle; her claim to the throne descended to the child of the marriage, a boy Roger, the young Earl of March, next after Richard in the senior line of succession. In Ireland, all was to do over again, as usual; and Richard's expedition was, also as usual, expensive. However, it was a personal success; it took his mind off his grief and it gave a much needed boost to his ego. The chiefs of the septs came in to give allegiance to the King; some of them were knighted; the rebel McMurrough, who had given so much trouble, surrendered and was well treated. Altogether Richard enjoyed his Irish experience; it gave him an impression which lured him on to his second, and fatal, excursion in 1399.

On his return Richard enjoyed his best and least troublous years. By 1396 his position was strong enough to negotiate a twenty-eight-year truce with France, with a marriage alliance with the French king's daughter by which he hoped to strengthen his position still further. It was a reasonable hope and it represented the fulfilment of a sensible, civilised, positive policy of peace. Alas for Richard's hopes!—like so much in his life it turned out to be merely wish-fulfilment. The alliance was unpopular: France was the enemy, and there were fears that the King would use the hereditary enemy against his own people. Himself no soldier, and possessing little foresight, he did not allow for the consideration that peace would leave a lot of fighting nobles with time on their hands, unemployed abroad. His marriage to the little Isabella, a girl of seven, of whom he became very fond, was a dangerous weakness; for there would be still no children for years, and this left the question of the succession wide open.

Richard was the victim of his intense personal affections. Robert de Vere, the quondam Duke of Ireland, had escaped the vengeance of the Appellants, to be killed while hunting outside Louvain. Richard now had the embalmed body brought home, to be buried grandly among the de Vere ancestors in Essex. Before the burial the King had the coffin opened to gaze once more in a passion of grief upon the features of the man he had loved and to take once more the jewelled hand in his.

For all his personal griefs, Richard was at the summit of his fortunes, with Gaunt at his side, the fortunate house of Lancaster with him. The semi-royal palatinate of Lancaster was still further enlarged, its liberties extended. Bolingbroke returned from his European travels—on which he had been treated like the prince he was—to support his father in supporting the King. Gaunt, on his second wife's death, married the mother of his Beaufort children—called after the castle in France where the future cardinal was born. They were now legitimised in everything except a claim to the throne—but it subsequently transpired that it was doubtful whether any such limitation could be made. So the Beauforts in turn transmitted a tenuous claim to that object of so much strife and endeavour.

Richard made the eldest Beaufort Earl of Somerset; the clever Henry got his first ecclesiastical preferment, his foot on the ladder that made him one of the richest prelates in Europe.

For himself Richard now felt strong enough to carry out his long-nursed, secretly cherished designs of revenge upon his enemies.

CHAPTER II

The Revolution of 1399

The Revolution of 1399 was really rooted in Richard's revenge, the completeness of it and the personal vindictiveness of it. It was understandable that Richard should seek revenge upon the enemies who had humiliated him and killed his friends. All the same, it was not right in a king: Richard should have contented himself with their defeat. He had no magnanimity—that quality so necessary in highest place—such as Bolingbroke showed when he sat in Richard's throne. If a king was more than a man then he had to rise above human littlenesses and weaknesses. Men looked to the kingship for justice above all, for impartiality so far as possible; they looked to the king to rectify their wrongs, not to take sides and certainly not to add further wrongs of a personal kind to add to the miseries of society. Richard was caught in the cleft stick of a psychotic personality: he demanded to be regarded as more than a man, but in his conduct he fell below the average standards expected of a man. The result was to be seen in the deep-seated sense of insecurity within himself, and the insecurity he spread all round him.

Now that Richard was in the saddle the leading Appellants, Arundel, Gloucester and Warwick, felt their insecurity and drew together again. Gloucester broke out angrily against the King's pro-French policy. Arundel remained irreconcilable, and both ignored the King's summons to come to Council. So Richard invited them to a banquet—like Herod's, said the chronicler Walsingham, at which the head of St. John the Baptist was served up. ("By St. John the Baptist" was Richard's favourite oath.) Warwick accepted, was cordially greeted by the King and after the banquet found himself led away to the Tower. Arundel shut himself up in Reigate Castle, but Richard secured him through his brother, now

Archbishop of Canterbury, swearing to him by St. John that the Earl should come to no harm. The King reserved to himself the pleasure of arresting his uncle Gloucester: "By St. John the Baptist, *bel oncle,* this will turn out the best for both of us." To Gloucester's plea for mercy Richard is said to have replied that he should have as much mercy as he had shown to Simon Burley. The Duke was led away to Calais to imprisonment and death.

Parliament met at Westminster in September and, since the magnificent hall that Richard was building was not finished, temporary buildings were put up in Palace Yard. The Appellants' actions of ten years before were condemned as usurpations of royal power and therefore treason. Arraigned before Parliament, Arundel showed that he was made of sterner stuff and defended himself with spirit. True to the man, he took the offensive and engaged in an altercation with each of his accusers, Gaunt, Gaunt's son Bolingbroke, the King's friend Sir John Bushy and finally with the King himself. When Arundel pleaded that he had obtained the King's pardon at the time, Bushy replied that it was not recalled by the King, lords "and us, his faithful commons." Arundel retorted, "Where be those faithful commons? . . . The faithful commons are not here."[1] The implication was, quite unjustly, that this was a packed Parliament. The King had not forgotten his faithful tutor and servant: "Didst thou not say to me, at the time of *thy* Parliament, in the bath behind the White Hall, that Sir Simon Burley, my knight, was for many reasons worthy of death? And I answered thee that I knew no cause of death in him." It was Gaunt who pronounced the death sentence, and Arundel was executed on Tower Hill, "no more shrinking or changing colour than if he were going to a banquet."[2] Arundel's brother, the Archbishop, was also found guilty of treason, and banished the realm. Warwick broke down and made a full confession, weeping and whining for mercy. Richard is reported as saying that this was more satisfying to him than all the lands of Arundel and Gloucester—and Warwick's sentence was commuted to banishment to the Isle of Man.

And what of Gloucester? A king's son could hardly be brought before Parliament: shorter shrift must be found for him. It was. A purported confession was read to Parliament, along with the news that Gloucester was dead at Calais. No one had any doubt at whose orders he had been made away with. Modern scholarship has corroborated the Tudor chronicler Hall: it appears that Gloucester was smothered in the Prince's Inn at Calais.[3] The responsibility rests squarely on Richard: he set the precedent for the murders and hackings within the royal family which made such a holocaust of the prolific progeny of Edward III for the next century and more.

Having stamped on his enemies, Richard rewarded those who stood by him in the exciting operation. Five of them, mostly within his family-circle, were made dukes. It was a cheapening of the title and rather absurd—the "duketti," as people called them. But two of them had been junior Appellants ten years before. Thomas Mowbray, Earl of Nottingham, was made Duke of Norfolk. Richard had given him the dirtiest work to do in the late proceedings: his father-in-law, Arundel, had been executed in his presence, while he must have been made party to the crime at Calais, of which he was captain and bore command—and responsibility. He was thus incriminated—a neat stroke on Richard's part. The second junior Appellant, Bolingbroke, now made Duke of Hereford—what was in store for him?

A singular opportunity to settle their hash, both of them, now came to Richard. Mowbray felt insecure and approached Bolingbroke with the warning that the King meant to destroy them both, for both of them had been in arms against him at Radcot Bridge; though he treated them at present with favour, he had not forgotten their offence and would do with them yet as he had done with the other Appellants. Subsequent events showed that this was no inaccurate reading of Richard's mind. Bolingbroke consulted his father, who advised, as in duty bound, that the conversation should be reported to the King. Richard had the matter laid before Parliament and, after a great deal of palaver that summer, it was decided that the dispute between Mowbray and Bolingbroke should be settled by the ordeal of battle at Coventry in September.

Thus the famous lists of Coventry opened—but the spectators were defrauded of their battle. For when all was set, the King ordered the disputants to lay down their arms saying that he resumed the dispute into his own hands. What were his calculations? He must have realised that he would be the loser whichever of them won. If Mowbray won it would be taken as justification of his charges against the King. If Bolingbroke, it would add to his already great prestige: Richard had never liked him and, with his mind gnawed by suspicion, must have feared him. But Bolingbroke was really the innocent party, and the King admitted that he had fulfilled his duty. He then banished him the realm for ten years, Mowbray for life. It was too good an opportunity to miss— to get rid of them both at one stroke; yet the obvious injustice of it did him no good. So far from redounding to his own credit, it added further to the general mistrust of him.

At the apogee of his power Richard became more obviously psychotic than ever. If only, having rid himself of his worst enemies, he could have followed now the path of moderation and conciliation! But that was precisely what he was incapable of. Evidently the life of a king, exacting and exhausting enough in itself, imposed too much of a strain on him. And undoubtedly he nursed a feeling of inner alienation from his people—as did that other tragic figure Charles I after the death of Buckingham. Richard's admiration for French civilisation, his desire to emulate the French Court, cut him off from his own too patriotic, too aggressively nationalist people. This in turn encouraged his love of luxury, extravagant ostentation in dress, feasts, tournaments, reckless expenditure on presents and grants to his friends. He could not contain himself. Culturally, Richard's reign was a brilliant, a dazzling, epoch, with the King's patronage of architecture and painting, the age of Wyclif and Trevisa, of Langland and Gower, of Chaucer, most Shakespearean of English writers. But that is not my subject.

Richard made his distrust of his people evident by surrounding himself by his Cheshire body-guard, wearing his personal livery with his badge of the white hart. Adam of Usk, an eyewitness, tells us: "the King meanwhile, ever hastening to his fall, among other burdens that he heaped upon his kingdom, kept in his following four hundred men of the county of Chester, very evil; and in all places they oppressed his subjects unpunished, and beat and robbed them. These men, whithersoever the King went, night and day, as if at war, kept watch in arms around him; everywhere committing adulteries, murders and other evils without end. And to such a pass did the King cherish them that he would not deign to listen to anyone who had complaint against them; nay, rather he would disdain him as an enemy. And this was a chief cause of his ruin."[4] No doubt this is exaggerated, but it shows how people felt. And people were not without ways of manifesting their feelings. When the young Earl of March came over from Ireland in 1398, "a youth of exceeding uprightness, who had no part nor share in such designs and wanton deeds of the King: him the people received with joy and delight, going forth to meet him to the number of twenty thousand, clad in hoods of his colours, and hoping through him for deliverance from the grievous evil of such a king. But he bore himself wisely and with prudence."[5] This was Richard's presumptive heir; he was killed the same year fighting in Ireland.

The King was certainly suffering from megalomaniac delusions. Surrounded by flatterers who assured him that he was the greatest of conquerors, for he had vanquished his enemies without a battle, on feast days Richard would sit in solitary state high on his throne, from dinner time to vespers, not speaking to anyone but watching. Anyone who happened to catch the royal eye had forthwith to kneel.

From this pinnacle of glory he proceeded to pillage his people. Large sums were extorted by way of pardons from all who had any part, however small, in the Appellants' doings ten years before. Special pledges, special oaths to maintain Richard's acts against his dead enemies were exacted. For the purposes of his absolute rule he was tampering with the appointment of sheriffs in the counties, and overriding the common law. This was not what the monarchy was for, but to govern justly in accordance with known law and received custom. Richard's rule had become plain tyranny.

At this juncture, 3 February 1399, Gaunt died. Since the last year's Parliament he had taken no further part in Richard's goings on—perhaps the ageing man was sickening to his death. Perhaps he was fearful for his house, for his son Bolingbroke had been, after all, an Appellant too and was now banished. Nevertheless, the old man's death—he was fifty-eight, elderly for a medieval royal personage—was a fatal loss to Richard in the events about to unfold; for Gaunt had always been loyal to the Crown, and was above all things a mediator, a skilled pacificator—he had plenty of experience at it.

Those whom the gods wish to destroy they first make mad. Richard proceeded to reward Gaunt's lifelong services to the Crown by an insane act. People generally expected that the opportunity would be taken to recall Gaunt's heir and let him succeed to his inheritance. Richard took the opportunity to extend his cousin Bolingbroke's sentence to banishment for life, and to divide up the great Lancaster palatinate among his partisans. This was serving notice with a vengeance on all landowners in the country that their most elementary rights, the rights of property and inheritance, were not safe in this king's hands. To this crowning act of injustice Richard now added a crowning act of folly: he left the country for Ireland. The young Earl of March—Richard's legitimist heir, so to say—had been killed there on his return from England. McMurrough, whom Richard thought he had settled, seized the chance to raise rebellion again. Furious, Richard determined on a large expensive expedition to chastise him.

With some forebodings Richard made his will. He desired that if he died his body should be buried beside his wife, Queen Anne, in the splendid tomb he had had made for them both at Westminster. With some forethought he took along with him on the expedition Bolingbroke's son and heir, the young Henry, of whom the King was fond. When the boy became a famous king, as Henry V, he did not fail to make reparation to Richard's memory. Richard appointed his one remaining uncle, the Duke of York, who had never done any harm or much good to anybody, to keep the realm in safety with a Council that contained three of his most unpopular familiars, Bushy, Green and Bagot. Having taken his measures, Richard departed, leaving the country wide-open to an invader.

Bolingbroke was not the man not to take his chance: for him it was now or never. He was waiting in Paris with Archbishop Arundel and Arundel's nephew, the young Earl; there was also a group of knights, fighting companions of Bolingbroke's campaigns in Eastern Europe, of whom the name of Sir Thomas Erpingham is still remembered by the fine gateway he built at Norwich leading into the cathedral close. It was said that when Bolingbroke heard the news of his disinheritance he betrayed no emotion. Here was a really politic type, in full control of himself and thus able to command others, unimpassioned and reserved, who did not betray his own counsels, inspired by tenacious determination, a man who would never give up, once he had committed himself. Unlike his cousin Richard he was a very masculine type, strongly built if somewhat thickset, a skilled jouster and hardened soldier, the secret of whose military, as of his political, success was his speed, his unerring sense of his opponent's weak spot, his cool strategy. It was not inappropriate that his favourite intellectual relaxation was moral disputation, hearing points of casuistry debated. His greatest pleasure was music, which always accompanied him. Here he was, ready: a chaste, conventional man, able and above all safe.

Richard landed in Ireland on 1 June 1399. Immediately Bolingbroke knew that the King was out of the way there, he made his dispositions, collected his following and early in July landed at Ravenspur on the Humber. He had chosen well to land in the North, for he was able to make contact with his duchy's officials, his Lancastrian retainers and following. There was hardly any opposition; the purpose of his coming was but to reclaim his own—justice and his right. This could be trusted to appeal to everyone, against an evidently unjust king. But at Doncaster more political considerations must have come into play, for there he was met by the greatest magnates of the North: the Percies, the Earl of Northumberland and his son Hotspur, the Neville Earl of Westmorland, Lord Willoughby and Lord Greystoke, a warden of the Marches. The adherence of the North was in the event decisive; it provided Bolingbroke with a large army, he realised that the country was looking to him for a change of government. A much wider game was open to him, indeed was forced upon him, for his own survival, if it was true that the King had vowed that "the Duke of Lancaster that now is would never come into England while he was alive."

Meanwhile Richard's Lieutenant, York, was pitifully ineffective. He could make no appeal to London, opposed as it was to Richard and ready at any moment to withdraw its allegiance. So he and the King's more active friends, Bushy, Green and Bagot, moved west to Bristol hoping to meet the King there. But York submitted to Bolingbroke, who then caused him to order the surrender of Bristol. Bushy and Green were summarily executed, Bagot later on in Cheshire whither he fled. With unerring instinct Bolingbroke now made for Chester, bastion (if that is the word) for what support there would be for Richard, whence best to catch the King.

The news of Bolingbroke's landing reached Richard belatedly in Ireland and he was further delayed by the treacherous schemes of his cousin Aumale—York's son, whom he had made a duke —who was bent on deserting a doomed cause. Richard now knew not whom to trust, and, instead of keeping his forces together, confusedly followed Aumale's advice to divide the army. The King sent the stronger detachment ahead to North Wales, and himself with the weaker landed in the extreme South-West. But his troops were weary and worn; Richard, making mistake after mistake with the fatality of a somnambulist, disbanded his forces and made practically alone, and slowly, up the west coast to Conway, to find his army had melted away in the North too. All this gave Bolingbroke the time to concentrate on closing the trap in North Wales.

He sent Northumberland and Archbishop Arundel to the King, offering reasonable terms: the restoration of the duchy of Lancaster to Bolingbroke along with his hereditary offices, the trial of five of Richard's councillors. It was the Appellants all over again, in the person of the youngest of them and the man most eligible to succeed him. Northumberland swore on the Host—so much for men's beliefs—that the King should retain his crown and that Bolingbroke would adhere to these terms. It does not appear that the Archbishop swore on the Host; no doubt he gave himself this dispensation. Discouraged and isolated, Richard accepted these terms—perhaps he hoped to take his revenge later, as he had done before, and then thrown it away. With this undertaking he left Conway, only to fall into the ambush that had been laid for him, be taken in custody to Flint Castle and on to Chester to meet his victorious cousin. The trap had closed: together the cousins journeyed southward to London, the King in some indignity, his entry jeered at by the people he had misgoverned and alienated.

There was no doubt that this time he had to go; the problem was how to get rid of him, the rightful, legitimate, crowned and anointed king. The revolutionaries had a precedent in the deposition of Edward II—only in his case there had been his rightful son

and heir, young Edward III, to take his place. The present situation was far more queasy and more dangerous—Bolingbroke was
not the rightful heir (a previous Parliament had named March as
the heir, but he was dead, leaving only a boy). From the drastic
yet necessary resolution of the dilemma rose the dynastic discontents and troubles of the century to come—our story.

The fact was that the law of succession to the throne was un-
defined—some ground for manoeuvre remained for an emergency
just like this. The first problem was to get an unsuitable king to
abdicate. There was no doubt that Richard had failed as king,
broken his undertakings, violated his coronation oath, undermined
all security, flouted law and custom, ruled not as an English
monarch but as a tyrant: no need to labour the point. That
constitutionalist, Archbishop Arundel, a premature Whig, wanted
Bolingbroke to ascend the throne by a Parliamentary title. Bolingbroke knew better than that: he would then not have the full
authority of the Crown to govern—a difficult enough job in all
conscience—and what Parliament granted Parliament might take
away. This was not doing justice to the Crown, the powers implicit
in it and indispensable to govern the kingdom. On his side Bolingbroke would have preferred to claim the right by conquest—as
William the Conqueror had done—and subsequent election and
coronation. This rather took the magnates by surprise, and made
trouble for the new king later.

In any case speed was the essence of the operation. The complete and sudden crumbling of Richard's position, no resistance
on his behalf, was evidence that a change was overdue, a revolution
expected. For the sake of the country the situation had to be
grappled immediately, or government would dissolve into chaos,
people would have second thoughts: that would mean civil war.
The problem for Bolingbroke was to succeed to all the powers of
the Crown unimpaired, and that speedily. He imposed a speedy
programme upon a somewhat dazed and breathless country; his
conduct was masterly. He showed that he had all the qualities of
a king that the rightful King was without.

Richard was under duress in the Tower; London had withdrawn its allegiance from him and commended itself to Bolingbroke. Adam of Usk was able to observe Richard's mood and
bearing in the Tower on St. Matthew's Day, having been expressly

taken there for the purpose. At dinner the King discoursed sorrowfully in these words: "'My God! a wonderful land is this, and a fickle; which hath exiled, slain, destroyed or ruined so many kings, rulers and great men, and is ever tainted and toileth with strife and variance and envy.' And then he recounted the histories and names of sufferers from the earliest habitation of the kingdom. Perceiving then the trouble of his mind, and how that none of his own men, nor such as were wont to serve him but strangers who were but spies upon him, were appointed to his service, and musing on his ancient and wonted glory and on the fickle fortune of the world, I departed thence much moved at heart."[6]

We now know that the official account of the proceedings as inscribed on the Parliamentary roll is not accurate, but the version put out for popular consumption—very understandable in our day—after the revolution was over. In fact Richard had been tricked by the undertaking given him by Northumberland and Archbishop Arundel at Conway. In fact he did not abdicate voluntarily, still less cheerfully, as the account states. In the Tower he seems to have resigned the Crown, under duress as he was, and to have resigned it not to Bolingbroke, but to God. That would have been in keeping with the mystique of monarchy that was the marrow of his being. His signet ring was taken from him.

In Westminster Hall, on 30 September 1399, the estates assembled, lords spiritual and temporal and the people. There was a vacant throne. Richard was declared guilty of having broken his coronation oath, a list of all the grievances against him was read out, he was declared unfit to govern and deserving to be deposed. It must have been at this point that the Bishop of Carlisle, with great courage, rose to protest on Richard's behalf and urged that the King should at least be heard in his defence. Nothing of this appears in the official account, and of course Richard was never allowed any defence. He was declared deposed, and Bolingbroke claimed the throne by right line of blood from Henry III—another untruth, for the implication was the legendary one that Edmund Crouchback of Lancaster had really had a senior claim to his brother, Edward I—in right of which "God of his grace hath sent me with help of my kin and of my friends to recover it." (All through history men will say "God" when they mean themselves or their own interest.)

Bolingbroke now, showing Richard's signet ring, mounted the throne and Archbishop Arundel preached on the text *"Vir dominabitur populo"*—a man shall be ruled by his people, or, as one might say, a man shall rule his people. For the Archbishop made a great point of the contrast between the manful Henry, with his manly career at home and abroad, and the childlike Richard— "Richard the Redeless" (or without counsel, would not take good advice). There is no doubt that the Archbishop scored there, and, by implication also, against the boy Earl of March, Richard's heir, though his claim was not mentioned. In any case, no one wanted another minority, the country had had enough of that. What it needed was a man, of full age and capacity, out of the royal family—and here was one.

It was necessary to hurry, for, in addition to other uncertainties, the French might at any moment intervene on behalf of their ally Richard and his French queen. The usurper, recognised and acclaimed now as Henry IV—he dated his reign from this day, 30 September 1399—proposed to accomplish his programme, deposition, election, coronation, in a fortnight—and did. Parliament was to meet on 6 October, though of course it was no regular Parliament without a king to constitute it: it was rather a Convention like that of 1688 which called William and Mary to the throne. The convocation of Canterbury met on the same date—under good Archbishop Arundel's guidance that would give no trouble. Henry at once showed his command, his prudence and wisdom. No persecution of Richard's judges, as the original Appellants had carried out twelve years before; Henry renewed Richard's judicature and kept many of his officials. Even Clifford, Richard's councillor and keeper of the privy seal, on his submission was allowed to retain his office—Henry was a magnanimous man, but this was a remarkable gesture. Of course everyone who had supported him expected to be rewarded, and a long list of annuities, grants, pensions, was put through. This shortly gave Henry much trouble, but at this juncture he could hardly help himself.

The coronation was fixed for 13 October, St. Edward's Day, for all the solemnity and sanctification that could give the new usurping King and his house. Adam of Usk was in the Abbey and saw Henry's eldest son bear the sword Curtana, representing justice, before his father; and just before the crowning the chronicler testifies, "I heard him swear to take heed to rule his people al-together in mercy and in truth."[7] Undoubtedly Henry intended to do all in his power to abide by his oath. At the coronation banquet the King's champion, Dymoke, rode into Westminster Hall to challenge any who denied the King's right, and Henry was heard to say, "if need be, Sir Thomas, I will in my own person ease thee of this office." He was, indeed, now king, by the three-fold claim expressed by Chaucer, now, like (almost) everybody else, transferring his allegiance:

> O conquerour of Brutes Albyoun,
> Which that by lygne and free eleccionn
> Ben verray Kynge . . .

What now to do with Richard? A full meeting of the lords, with Archbishop Arundel to the fore, condemned Richard to perpetual imprisonment in a secret place, no former member of his house-hold to have access to him. Once more there was to be no defence. At the end of the month he was taken from the Tower in disguise and transferred to the security of Pontefract, where he was in custody of those trusty Lancastrian officials Sir Thomas Swinford and Robert Waterton, whose fine family tombs, weepers and all, we still see in the church at Methley in Yorkshire.

The house of Lancaster completed its triumph with the annexa-tion of Richard's favoured palatinate of Chester to itself. The young Henry was now created Prince of Wales, Duke of Cornwall and Earl of Chester; shortly after he was made Duke of Lancaster and succeeded to all the lands and franchises of that palatinate, which the Lancastrian kings always regarded as their personal inheritance, and administered separately—as it is to this day—from the other lands of the Crown. Nevertheless, the joining of the great palatinate of Lancaster with the Crown meant that the latter was so much the richer. It would be necessary, for Henry had a likely brood of sons—in return an additional hope and strength to the new royal house—as against Richard's childless-ness.

Henry continued to exemplify his politic magnanimity, that was not to the liking of the more vengeful Londoners, and to a degree that still surprises. It was ill rewarded. The duketti were demoted to their former titles; but apart from that Richard's supporters,

Somerset and Rutland, were given high office, while Rutland and Huntingdon were shortly summoned as regular members of Henry's Council. It did not take long for these men to show their hand. By the middle of December the four Earls of Rutland (the former Aumale), Huntingdon, Kent and Salisbury, abetted by the Bishop of Carlisle and the Abbot of Westminster, concocted a promising conspiracy to catch Henry and his sons while spending their Christmas at Windsor.

Rutland, who does not seem to have been a very nice man, informed on his colleagues and later slipped over to the King's side. Once more Henry's speed and energy defeated his enemies. He immediately left Windsor for London; the rebels arrived and captured the castle, but no king. At this crisis London stood firmly by him and quickly raised an army. The rising was squashed, Kent and Huntingdon—Richard's Holland half-brothers—both lost their lives, so too Salisbury and Lord Despenser. The sacred person of the Bishop of Carlisle was untouched, though he was demoted, to lead later on a more useful life as a mere suffragan in the diocese of Salisbury. The Abbot of Westminster and Richard's Archbishop Walden, whom he had intruded into Arundel's see, were freed; Henry characteristically appointed the excellent Walden Bishop of London a little later. He bore him no malice, like a true king.

These events, however, settled the fate of poor Richard. The rebels put it about that he had escaped and was on his way to the rescue. It was probably considered too dangerous to leave him alive, and before January was out he was dead. It is not known precisely how—in these secret matters naturally no evidence was left, and it happened nearly six hundred years ago. Some said that he starved himself to death, others that he was deliberately starved to death; the tradition is that he was done to death by violence. That there should be no doubt that he was dead his body was brought to London and shown publicly through the city. There was then a solemn dirge for him at St. Paul's, Henry himself bearing the pall, and the body was removed for interment at the Blackfriars at King's Langley. Nevertheless, there were not wanting idiots all through Henry's reign to believe that Richard was still alive somewhere, somehow, and this added to the troubles that accumulated upon Henry when he sat in Richard's throne.

It was not until Henry's own son reigned in his place that reparation was made by the lad Richard had been fond of—now Henry V—and the poor king's body came to rest in the tomb he had built for himself and Queen Anne at Westminster.

His story was a true tragedy, with the unsteady hubris of his apogee followed so soon after by the nemesis of deposition and death. Politically, it was to be expected that he would be made away with, and this left Henry IV as the heir-male, i.e., the heir in the male line, a very weighty consideration to Henry and in itself. But, this being the Middle Ages, Henry as a man was undoubtedly weighed down by guilt and remorse; and this added to the well-nigh unbearable burden he had to carry.

CHAPTER III

Uneasy Lies the Head

Henry IV had attained "the world, the power and the glory" in taking his cousin Richard's throne; but he never knew any peace of mind or body again. His reign was full of trouble and anxiety, crisis after crisis, wearing down this strong energetic man, until well before the end he was prostrated with illnesses, when only in his forties a hopelessly sick man. And he had been so strong. Born in the same year as Richard, 1367, Henry was only forty-six when he died. It is as if the strain of kingship exhausted the strength of even the toughest.

We can see what medieval people thought, or rather how they reacted, from the ill omens Adam of Usk observed at Henry's coronation. "Three ensigns of royalty foreshadowed for him three misfortunes. First, in the procession he lost one of his coronation shoes: whence, in the first place, the commons who rose up against him hated him ever after all his life long. Secondly, one of the golden spurs fell off: whence, in the second place, the soldiery opposed him in rebellion. Thirdly, at the banquet a sudden gust of wind carried away the crown from his head: whence, in the last place, he was set aside from his kingdom and supplanted by Prince Henry."[1] Later on, the chronicler remembered further details. "One of the nobles [gold coins], at the time of his making the offering in the coronation Mass, fell from his hand to the ground; which then I with others standing by sought for diligently and, when found, it was offered by him." Adam adds that after the anointing "there ensued such a growth of lice, especially on his head, that he neither grew hair, nor could he have his head uncovered for many months." Perhaps the nits were in the sacred ampulla.

Magnificence and inefficiency, splendour and lice—there we have the Middle Ages.

First and last and all the time it was the circumstances in which he took the throne that raised up enemies to challenge him in turn, and constituted a constant weakness to his position. Then there were external enemies. Richard had been France's ally, married to the French king's daughter; renewed hostility took the place of alliance, and that brought the Scots down on the Border, where the doubtful Percies ruled like semi-independent princes. Next Henry was faced by a wholly unexpected national uprising under Glendower in Wales, which lasted for years and for which the King was in no way to blame (though the English were). A far better king than Richard, Henry was in a far worse situation.

Henry IV never had any respite. "There were years when Scotland, Wales, France (including both Calais and Gascony), as well as Ireland, called for a burden of military expenditure with which no English monarch had been faced since the end of Edward's reign."[2] That had been a century before. "In the country at large a government continually asking for money is bound to become disliked and, when the first enthusiasm for Henry had faded under the strain of taxation and the demand for loans to the crown, he was even less popular than his predecessor." Excellent politician that he was, Henry knew that the honeymoon would not last long; it was on account of that that he had been resolved to maintain the full powers of the Crown in taking over. "Tolerant and polite, Henry made what concessions he could, but was determined to uphold his own prerogative and to govern through the administrators closest to himself. . . . All these anxieties Henry met with courage and resilience. The prolonged effort cost him his nervous health and the house of Lancaster much political good will."

Anxious to exert all the powers of the English monarchy and to allow no diminution of its prestige, in his first year of rule Henry sought a showdown with Scotland—the perennial objective of English policy to break the Franco-Scottish alliance. All he achieved was a march across the Border as far as Edinburgh, which would not surrender, while Scottish guerillas harassed his communications, already stretched beyond the capacity of his commissariat. On his way back to London he heard the first news of Owen Glendower's rising in North Wales, a cloud no larger than a man's hand, which was to overcast much of the rest of his reign with all the consequences and troubles of a national resistance.

That Christmas, Henry had to entertain the Greek emperor, arrived to ask succour against the advance of the Turks. This also conferred an honour upon the new royal house and turned out expensive. Adam of Usk tells us that the emperor, Manuel II, was well entertained by Henry, "abiding with him at very great cost for two months, being also comforted at his departure with very great gifts."[3] It would seem that one of Henry's faults was that he was probably too generous. The chronicler was struck by the *outré* appearance of the Greeks, as the Greeks were struck by the *outré* appearance of the English. "This emperor always walked with his men, dressed alike and in one colour, namely white, in long robes cut like tabards; he finding fault with the many fashions and distinctions in dress of the English, wherein he said that fickleness and changeable temper was betokened."

With France, Henry hoped to maintain peace and even to extend Richard's alliance. He was not willing to return the little Queen Isabel, still less her dowry. Henry wished to retain both within the kingdom, and proposed that she might be married to his son and heir, Prince Henry. The French were hostile and would have none of it. In the summer of 1401 the girl, not yet twelve, had to be returned: Adam of Usk witnessed her departure from London, "clad in mourning weeds, and showing a countenance of lowering and evil aspect to King Henry and scarce opening her lips as she went her way."[4] Richard had certainly had the faculty of attaching those near him to himself.

Owen Glendower (Glyn Dŵr) was descended from the princes of North Wales, and held directly from the Crown considerable lands which his ancestors had ruled. He had been brought up a good deal in England, was a student at the Inns of Court and had been on one of the Scottish expeditions on which he was observed wearing the scarlet feather of a flamingo in his helmet. Glendower knew England and understood the situation there very well. He was a chivalrous squire, a gentleman of birth and breeding, an important landowner among his own people—and was treated with scant justice by Grey, Lord of Ruthin, a characteristically heavy-handed English magnate, an Easterner. Behind Glendower's protest there was all the pent-up feeling of the Welsh against English insensitiveness and disregard of their susceptibilities.

Driven beyond endurance, Glendower burned Ruthin and ravaged English settlements along the coast. He would have been content to be reinstated in his own lands: he understood the value of compromise, and it seems that he had the sympathies of the Percies—Harry Hotspur, Northumberland's son, was Justiciar of North Wales under the nominal rule of Prince Henry. But Glendower had gone too far; his estates were confiscated and himself declared a traitor. He thereupon widened his appeal, turned the struggle into a national resistance of the Welsh, held out year after year, and never did surrender. He outlived Henry IV, died, still uncaught, in a place unknown, a figure of folk-legend.

Naturally he appealed to the bards, who in turn whipped up Welsh sentiment all over the little country in his favour. They sang of the portents at his birth; undoubtedly the Welsh weather worked on his behalf. For three years in succession the King led an expedition into the fastnesses of North Wales without subduing the rebellion, or catching its leader or achieving much. In 1402 quite unusual weather conditions caused much hardship to the expeditionary force and held up operations. Meanwhile the rebellion made progress, broadened its base. Welsh students left Oxford to take part, Welsh labourers deserted English fields to go home and serve under Glendower's standard of the golden dragon. He made himself something of an international figure with his appeals for support to France and Scotland, fellow-Celts in Ireland and Brittany, his grandiose plans for a Welsh university and a separate archbishopric at St. David's, his claim to be regarded as Prince of Wales.

What we now know is that the Tudor family in Anglesey, cousins of Glendower, were his strong supporters and the backbone of the resistance. It was two Tudor brothers who captured Conway Castle in 1401. In 1402 Glendower appeared in South Wales, Glamorgan rose in revolt and shortly the whole of Wales was affected. In that same year Glendower captured Edmund Mortimer, younger brother of the late Earl of March, of the senior royal line of descent; what portended worse, Mortimer married Glendower's daughter. Henry's government, which had underestimated the seriousness of the rising at first, was at its wit's end to find the means to support campaign after campaign in remote, inaccessible Wales. Hotspur, a choleric, impatient, fighting type, grew dissatisfied with the inadequate means he was given, threw up his post and retired to the North where he was at home. To placate the too powerful Percies, Thomas Percy, Earl of Worcester, was made Lieutenant of South Wales and tutor to Prince Henry.

By contrast with the King's ill-success in Wales, the Percies won a resounding victory over the Scots in 1402 at Homildon Hill. A number of Scottish nobles were killed, but many more were taken prisoner. This further exacerbated the jealousies between the Percies and the King; for Hotspur refused to hand over the Earl of Douglas, whose ransom he meant to keep to recoup himself for the losses he had incurred in Henry's service. This was wrongful, for by custom the Crown had the right to the chief captures, and the King was just as much in want of money as those overmighty subjects, the Percies. Perhaps their triumph over the Scots went to their heads; they were beginning to have second thoughts about their support for Henry in 1399. Their support had been decisive, and they considered that Henry owed his throne to them. Now they had these further links with Wales: Hotspur's wife was Edmund Mortimer's sister—there was a direct contact with Glendower; Thomas Percy ruled, or was supposed to rule, in South Wales. All these dangerous elements came together in 1403 to constitute an almighty danger to the new royal house, a year of crisis and decision.

In 1403 Thomas Percy, Earl of Worcester, resigned his Lieutenancy of South Wales and Prince Henry was made Lieutenant of the Marches. Though only sixteen, henceforth he exercised actual command and took part in much fighting. The name of the (subsequent) knight, Sir John Oldcastle, which became familiarly connected with Prince Henry in tradition and legend, made its appearance at about the same time. Oldcastle came of a Welsh Border family owning land at the place of that name in Herefordshire.* In 1401 he was made keeper of Builth Castle on the

---

* A later poem when Oldcastle had become a full-blown Lollard makes great play with puns on the name:

> It is unkindly for a knight
> That should a king's castle keep
> To babble the bible day and night. . . .

> An old castle and not repaired,
> With waste walls and wowes wide . . .

> An old castle, draw all down,
> It is full hard to rear it new.

R. H. Robbins, ed., *Historical Poems of the XIVth and XVth Centuries,* 153–54.

Wye, in the next year he served in Carmarthen with a following of lances and archers. After the battle of Shrewsbury he was given powers to pardon or punish Crown tenants in Wales who had been in arms against the King; in 1404 he was knight of the shire for his county. He continued to serve in Wales in the following years and, as a companion in arms of Prince Henry, was treated with favour and made his way up.

In the summer of 1403 the Percies decided to strike against the house of Lancaster and to make common cause with Glendower. They published a manifesto declaring that Henry had broken his oath to them at Doncaster that he would not claim the kingdom but merely his own duchy of Lancaster. Northumberland remained on guard in the North, while Hotspur marched with his forces to Chester to join up with Glendower and cut off Prince Henry at Shrewsbury. The King heard of this new trouble when he was in the Midlands, at once appreciated the danger and, with his usual energy and decision, marched west to forestall the dangerous junction of Wales with the North that might have overwhelmed his house. At Chester, Hotspur had been joined by Thomas Percy; when they arrived at Shrewsbury they were surprised to find the King's standard flying from the walls.

Henry at once marched out to give battle before Glendower could arrive, though he was prepared to parley and give terms for the rebels' submission. This broke down, however, and in the afternoon the King led the assault, with Prince Henry in command on his left. The Prince was wounded by an arrow-shot in the face, but refused to give up; with redoubled courage his division attacked Hotspur's right uphill and rolled them back against the King's main battle. The struggle was a fierce one with little quarter given on either side, much carnage on both. In fact losses were equal, but Hotspur, fighting desperately, was cut down, the King raised the cry "Harry Percy is dead," and the rebels began to give ground. It was not until nightfall that the fighting ceased and the pillaging got under way. Thomas Percy was taken alive but sentenced and beheaded on the Monday after the battle: his head was sent to decorate London bridge, Hotspur's Micklegate at York. One would have thought a sufficient warning.

The genius of Shakespeare has implanted in our minds a conception of Hotspur as perennially young, a coeval and rival of Prince Henry. In fact he was three years older than the King; he was thirty-nine when he was killed at Shrewsbury—it is said that Henry shed tears over his body. For the rest, Shakespeare may have penetrated to the essence of Hotspur: there was something not grown-up about this fighting man, who lived in the saddle, no politic head—unlike Henry and his son—a simple type, headstrong and "intolerant of the shadow of a slight," with an impetuous stammer in his speech.

From Shrewsbury the King hurried to the North to deal with the head and fount of the rebellion, Northumberland himself. The Earl was preparing to reinforce his son, when he heard of his death; finding himself isolated, he surrendered to the King's mercy. His life was spared, but he was condemned to perpetual imprisonment, his wide lands and offices sequestrated. His office of Constable was given to the King's third son, Prince John, along with all Hotspur's estates in Cumberland. Such were the penalties of losing out.

Nevertheless, in spite of his hard-won victory at Shrewsbury, the King could make no progress in Wales. Glendower had now recruited West Wales to his cause and penetrated as far as Pembrokeshire, with the general support of the Welsh people. In September Henry marched an army into South Wales, but again had to withdraw for lack of means to supply it; the guerillas melted into the hills and could not be brought to battle. Lack of means was the endemic trouble of the Welsh campaigns; henceforth Henry withdrew from campaigning in Wales and left his son to carry the burden as best he could. What a strain it was we can tell from the Prince's letters, one of which we will cite as an example of the way a fifteenth-century prince wrote to his father, the relations that subsisted between this father and this son:

> My very dread and sovereign lord and father, I recommend me to your high lordship as lowly and obediently as I can, desiring always your gracious blessing and thanking you entirely for the worshipful letters that your noble highness hath written to me from your castle of Pontefract the 21st day of this present month of June. I have heard of the fair prosperity of your high and royal estate with the greatest joy that could befall me in this world. . . . My very dread and sovereign lord and father, at your high command in your other gracious letters expressed, I have removed with my poor household to the city of Worcester. . . .[5]

Then comes depressing news of the Welsh, who have made headway and ravaged the county of Hereford. The Prince had taken what measures he could:

> I will do all that in me lies to withstand the rebels and preserve the English land to the best of my small power, according as God shall grant me grace, and trusting always in your most high lordship to be mindful of my poor estate. And forasmuch as I cannot continue here without further ordinance be made for my abiding, and since the charges on me are unsupportable, I pray you to so ordain for me in speed that I may be able to do you service here to your honour and the saving of my poor estate.

The King in turn did what he could and advanced as far as Worcester to his son's support. There he was forced to write to the Council in London: "We would have you know that we should have nothing to maintain us here had we not put in pledge our poor plate and jewels, and of them made provision of money. Even therewith we can continue but a brief space, and thereafter if you make no ordinance for us, we must depart with shame and mischief and the country will be undone, which God forbid. . . ."

What a strain it all was! Henry was less able to pay his creditors than Richard had been; no wonder people became disillusioned with the promise of Lancastrian government. And yet we cannot say that it was Henry's fault: the fault was in the situation in which he was caught.

In 1424 the castles of Harlech and Aberystwyth surrendered to Glendower, thus locking the southern end of the great mountain massif under his allegiance. Much of South Wales was at his bidding too; the widow of the dead Despenser plotted to take the boy Earl of March thither, which showed that "there was a harbour for the enemies of the house of Lancaster, if they could only reach it."[6] Meanwhile Glendower, as an independent power, was in alliance with the French, who sent him reinforcements: in 1403 their ships assailed the royal stronghold of Caernarvon, in 1404 they made raids along the West Country coast. In 1405 a French expedition landed at Milford Haven, captured Haverfordwest, assaulted Tenby, took Carmarthen, while Glendower made sure of Cardigan. Together they moved east through Glamorgan making for Worcester, and might have broken through into the Midlands at the moment when Northumberland had got free and renewed rebellion in the North.

Actually 1405 was the year of decision for the Lancastrian king, with Glendower at his apogee and the North in question once more. This was probably the year of the famous Agreement between Northumberland and Glendower to divide up the English kingdom. Northumberland was to have the whole of the North and well into the Midlands; Glendower all Wales with the Welsh Marches; Mortimer was to have what was left. This was not sense, but fantasy. However, it represented pretty well the spirit of the old intriguer Northumberland, who had renewed contact with Glendower and Mortimer and now brought the Earl Marshal, Thomas Mowbray, Lord Bardolph and Archbishop Scrope of York into the field against the King. During these two years of tense crisis, and intense strain upon everybody, the Archbishop had been balancing to and fro according to which side looked like winning. In 1399 he had been on Henry's side against Richard; now, the fact that he came out against Henry was so much evidence that the King had lost ground in York, the northern capital, where the Archbishop was popular.

Though the royal forces were outnumbered by the Archbishop's at Shipton Moor they managed to get hold of his sacred person, upon which his Yorkshiremen melted away, before the King arrived at Pontefract. (That grim fortress must have held reminders for him.) Henry was at last angry, and determined to make the most conspicuous example possible as a warning to all rebels. He sent for Chief Justice Gascoigne and directed him to pass sentence upon the archiepiscopal traitor. Meanwhile, wise Archbishop Arundel arrived to warn the King against sacrilege upon a consecrated person. Gascoigne refused to obey the King's orders: he urged that legally the Archbishop could not be sentenced by a secular court. Henry's latent obstinacy refused to be baulked or to listen to representations. He had had more than enough—like Richard before him: he ordered up another judge who obeyed his orders and Archbishop Scrope was executed outside the city.

Once more Henry had to pay the penalty. He generously, but mistakenly, allowed the Archbishop's body to be buried in his own cathedral. At once—humans being what they are—miracles began to be worked at his tomb like mad; and this nonsense continued for years, until in the end the Reformation put an end to it. But it is not surprising that York remained a focus of Ricardian sentiment, for long doubtful about the Lancastrians, and coming out later in the century in sympathy with the Yorkist cause. Even Richard III was popular in York.

Meanwhile the slippery Northumberland escaped to Scotland. This time there was to be confiscation of his vast inheritance, and there were the lands of the other noble traitors to divide up within the Lancastrian family. Prince Henry got noble Framlingham Castle in Suffolk; Prince John was further provided for, and he got the keepership of Calais. Henry's half-brothers, Henry and Thomas Beaufort, came in for something fat and goodly out of the Mowbray estates. (Mowbray must have regretted his equivocal relations with Richard and Henry, as much as the Percies.) A great stroke of luck now happened to Henry, and fortune turned in his favour. The heir to the Scottish throne fell into his possession: this was the beginning of an eighteen-year-long captivity for the young James I, poeticising at Windsor. Northumberland thereupon found Scotland unsafe, got away to France, whence he returned to his final defeat and death on Bramham moor in Yorkshire.

One thing one learns from history is that people never learn anything from history—though they might so easily.

These events were severe blows to Glendower's cause, and meanwhile Prince Henry was at last making headway against the hard core of Welsh resistance. Three defeats were inflicted upon Glendower's forces in 1406, in one of which his son Griffith was captured, in another his Chancellor. Inch by inch the Prince's forces moved into the mountains. In 1407 elaborate preparations were made for the reduction of Aberystwyth Castle; all the tried campaigners of the Welsh war were there, the Prince's companions in arms, the Earl of Warwick, the gallant Thomas, Baron of Carew, Sir John Greindor, the hero of Grosmont, Sir John Oldcastle.

These mountain strongholds were virtually impregnable and could only be starved out. It was not until the next year that Aberystwyth surrendered. Harlech Castle, one with the rock upon which it is perched looking out over the sands of the estuary and to the mountains of Caernarvonshire, took longer to reduce. Inside was Glendower's family, with the three daughters of Edmund Mortimer, who himself died in the siege. Not until 1409 did it surrender, starved out. Next year came Glendower's last attempt to take the offensive; in it he lost his three chief captains, including his cousin Rhys ap Tudor, put to death at Chester. Glendower himself disappeared into the mountain mists, outliving the King. When Prince Henry became king he offered the Welsh hero terms. All to no avail: nothing but silence from the mountains. Glendower's son was pardoned, but by then the father was held to be dead, and buried no one to this day knows where. He lived on in poetry and legend, and in the memory of the Welsh people.

The peace of desolation covered Wales—until an almighty reversal of fortune brought the Tudors to the English throne.

By now the King was a stricken man, exhausted by the strain of it all. His illness came upon him in the year 1405, the crisis of his fortunes and of the reign, with the Northumberland-Scrope treason. The credulous people said that Henry had been stricken on the very day of the Archbishop's beheading—it certainly was about that time—and that of course the King suffered for his execution of a consecrated person. This was the Middle Ages, and, since Henry was not exempt from the beliefs of his time, he probably suffered a further injection of guilt at his execution of a holy man, a consecrated person, if politically a goose. The people said that henceforward the King suffered from leprosy. Henry certainly seems to have had a stroke this year, and a succession of minor strokes later. The "leprosy" was probably a kind of nervous eczema from the overstrain he had endured.

And, indeed, what wonder? What a life! It seems hard to understand why anybody would go in for kingship; but of course, apart from ambition, he was caught in a cleft stick by his birth and position. It had been a question of survival for him: he could not have survived under Richard as king. He must have had some afterthoughts when he sat in Richard's place; he had reason enough, poor man, for repentance.

Even the ordinary strain of medieval government would have been enough, but with the unceasing burdens, the continuing crises of the years 1401–7—it was more than the strongest and most willing man could bear. "When the Duke of Lancaster seized the Crown he can have had little notion of the financial burden which was to weigh upon him for the rest of his life. . . . In the Hilary Parliament of 1404 the Chancellor, in enumerating the emergencies to be met, included Calais, the Isle of Wight, Guienne, Ireland and Scotland, the expenses of the Percy rebellion, and the Welsh revolt. In the October Parliament of the same year, when a grant of two fifteenths and two tenths was made, the wording ran: 'considering the East March and the West March of Scotland, the rebellion in Wales, the alliance of the Welsh, Scotland, France and Brittany, the safeguarding of the sea, the March of Calais, Ireland, the recovery of Guienne, and the defence of the country.' In the worst years, 1401–7, there were seldom less than four or five extraordinary demands upon the revenue, mostly concurrent."[7]

Henry had emerged—but he could never have emerged without the constant support of Parliament. Unlike Richard he ruled along with Parliament, in alliance with Parliament, careful to keep in step with both Lords and Commons. "Throughout the fifteenth century the Commons took the greatest interest in public finance" —particularly the knights of the shire, who took the lead. Fundamentally Henry may be described—though without anachronistic overtones—as a constitutional monarch, as Richard had not been nor wished to be.

But, then, Henry was all the more anxious to make a good king, to exercise, conscientiously and responsibly, all the powers of the English monarchy for the good of the nation and the Church, at home and abroad. Abroad, the most distracting issue was the Great Schism in the Church, which provides the background to these reigns: there were two popes, one at Rome, the other at Avignon, with their rival claims, courts, paraphernalia, with their conflicting demands for obedience, for some seventy years. Imagine the scandal to the faithful, the diminution of authority, the loss of respect: how could the seamless vesture of the Lord support two heads? No wonder the growth of Lollardy in England gave the authorities such a headache: it was the main internal problem of the Church in these years. No wonder the Hussite movement in Bohemia reached such proportions—and there were fruitful contacts between the Lollards and the Hussites. The movement of criticism within the Church, the movements of protest against the Church—these were a continuing legacy and offered premonitory symptoms of the Reformation.

Of course the Great Schism, which had originated in national feeling—French against Italian—was fed by national jealousies. "The French government, true to its traditional policy of a French papacy, gave its support to Clement [the Avignonese pope] against his Italian rival. That was sufficient to secure Urban's recognition [the Roman pope] in England and Flanders; whilst Scotland and the Spanish kingdoms followed the lead of their French ally. For a full generation Western Christendom was divided into two camps in accordance with the needs of national policy. When at last the situation became intolerable, the settlement was dictated rather by reascns of international diplomacy than from any motives of religious expediency."[8] Of course. The most recent historian of Henry's reign, however, tells us that he made "genuine efforts to restore unity in the Church and to achieve some measure of reform by a general council."[9] It was at least in part due to Henry's diplomacy that a general assembly met at Pisa in 1409—it all cost money and effort, successive missions and much ecclesiastical palaver.

At home Henry, who was pious and conventional, had always Archbishop Arundel at his side, Henry's staunchest support all the way along. The Church was determined to crush the Lollards, and in 1406 the statute *De heretico comburendo* was passed, with its evil legacy in burnings and persecutions, especially under the nefarious reign of Mary Tudor, when something short of three hundred persons were burned for their religion in three years. At one of the burnings in 1410 Prince Henry was present. The victim was a poor tailor, John Badby, who did not believe that in the Mass bread and wine were transmogrified into flesh and blood. For this piece of rational common sense he was, very properly— according to people's lights—to be burned. When the fire was already lit the Prince, thinking that Badby had made a sign of recantation, ordered the faggots to be taken away. The heretic lay on the ground; the Prince went to him and offered pardon and a livelihood if only he would recant. But the miserable tailor had no intention of denying the evidence of his senses to please fools —so the fire was relit and back to the flames he went. All must have been edified by this demonstration of their faith.

5

Archbishop Arundel was determined to extirpate the influence
at Oxford of its most brilliant and original teacher in the previous
generation, the last in the line of Oxford thinkers who had constituted its glory for more than a century and made it one of the
great universities of Europe. Arundel forced a visitation upon the
university, in spite of its papal exemption. Leading followers of
Wyclif were made to conform or at least to shut up; one of them,
Peter Payne, had got away to become the official responsible for
foreign affairs in the revolutionary Czech state. Oxford, robbed
of its brightest spirits, settled down into second-rate conformity,
and lost the immense ascendancy it had enjoyed over Cambridge,
which became notably more favoured by the patronage of the
Lancastrian house for its orthodoxy.

Nevertheless there was a strong spirit of anti-clericalism abroad
in the country and expressed in the Commons. Since the burden
of taxation was so heavy what about the greatest immunity of
all, the Church? True, the secular clergy were taxed through the
grants made in their Convocations; but what about the immense
riches of the episcopal sees, that of Winchester, for example,
which made Bishop Beaufort in time the financial support of the
Lancastrian house, the chief creditor of the Crown? What of those
religious houses that made no contribution to clerical taxation at
all? Once and again motions were made in the Commons to
expropriate the superfluous wealth of the Church for the benefit
of the Crown and the relief of taxation. Archbishop Arundel was
not standing for this, and Henry IV stood firmly beside him. The
alliance of Crown and Church, conservative in their view of society,
was far too powerful for any combination of critics or radical
pressures. But what would happen when one day the Crown deserted the alliance and went over to the other side?

With the King's illness and his liability to periodic incapacity
—though to his dying day he would never give up or cease to
exercise ultimate control—Prince Henry was more closely associated with government at the centre; we find him much more at
Westminster, or in the neighbourhood of London, regularly attending Council. The main interest of the last years of the reign
is to be found in the party conflict around the King, conflicts of

views with regard to policy reflecting conflicts between interests and persons. In the ups and downs, the ebb and flow, of power the King, in spite of his health, was no passive spectator. He held the ultimate authority and meant to exercise it.

Henry was to be found shoulder to shoulder with Archbishop Arundel, who represented the old baronial party, the constitutionalist tradition broad-based in the country. They were—after their experience of life—in favour of peace and therefore sought understanding with France, though this was difficult since France was distracted by dissensions between the Orleanist and Burgundian factions. Prince Henry was in favour of a militant, activist policy, taking advantage of these dissensions to make an alliance with Burgundy to push home against France—the policy he pursued when he became king. As yet he was not free to have his way, though he was a leading figure in Council. He was supported by his Beaufort uncles, who formed the nucleus of a princely "Court-party," much more popular with and attended by the young, than the King's Court itself. Since the Prince was a kind of Opposition leader—an anachronistic phrase, but a pattern subsequently found frequently enough between the monarch and his heir—Prince Thomas, the King's second son, sided with his father against his elder brother.

These differences and broils extended to domestic concerns and interests. Prince Henry managed once and again to foil Archbishop Arundel's beneficent intentions with regard to Oxford— the Prince may have been a *commensalis* at Queen's during the year when Henry Beaufort was Chancellor of the university. Moreover, Prince Henry was a friend of Sir John Oldcastle's, now becoming the secular leader of the Lollard interest. In 1409 Oldcastle made an advantageous marriage with a Kentish heiress, the Lady Cobham, in right of whom he was sometimes named Lord Cobham and summoned as a baron to Parliament. This can hardly have given Archbishop Arundel unadulterated pleasure. In 1410 Prince Thomas married the widow of John Beaufort; but the financier Bishop Beaufort, very keen on the money, withheld some of the Beaufort property which Thomas thought should come to him with his bride. Prince Henry supported his uncle, the Bishop; Thomas allied himself with Archbishop Arundel.

Arundel was Henry's leading minister from 1407 to the end of 1409. But the rising tide of anti-clerical sentiment, which reached a new crest in 1410 with demands for expropriation of the Church's superfluous wealth, along with Prince Henry's hostility, forced the Archbishop out. His place as Chancellor was taken by Thomas Beaufort, who was suspected of favouring the anti-clerical party, as his father, Gaunt, had before him. The government was really the Prince's, full of energy and zeal to govern. Parliamentary petitions were addressed to "My lord the Prince and the Council"; the King remained in the background, sickening to his death.

Prince Henry was now free to pursue his policy of active interference in the dissensions in France. He had this to be said for him, that the French king was the traditional enemy. Prince Henry was the traditionalist, the fighting prince. He entered into negotiations for a marriage with the Duke of Burgundy's daughter. He sent a small expedition to assist Burgundy in his struggle with the Armagnacs, under the command of those faithful Lancastrian captains the Umfravilles and Sir John Oldcastle. Henry IV had wanted to marry his son to a daughter of the French king and pursue a policy of peace. How time brings about its revenges!— here was Henry back on Richard's path, obstructed by his son in turn.

The ironical twist of events back to Richard might have gone further, the resemblance in situation become closer, for in 1411 there was a definite demand, on the part of the Beauforts, that Henry should abdicate in favour of his son. The ground for the demand was Henry's ill-health. But the King recovered, and reacted vigorously by dismissing the Prince and his friends from the Council, and completely changing the government. All was done in proper form: the Prince and his lords were thanked for their great labours and diligence. Prince Henry replied on behalf of his government that they had laboured according to their oath and to the best of their understanding. Public appearances were kept, though the King and his son kept separate Courts and saw little of each other. There was no doubt that the Prince had been dismissed. The unsinkable Archbishop Arundel came back in 1412, with Prince Thomas to support him; the Beauforts were out. For what remained to him of life the government was the King's.

There followed a reversal of policy. The Armagnac party in France around the French king offered to give up French claims to Aquitaine in return for an English alliance. The opportunity was taken and a treaty at once concluded. An expedition under Prince Thomas, now created Duke of Clarence and named Lieutenant of Aquitaine, crossed to Normandy to aid the Armagnacs. This faction, who had called the English in, now bought them off and allowed them, rather humiliatingly, to proceed to Aquitaine.

This fiasco redounded to Prince Henry's credit, who never had trusted the Armagnacs but remained solidly in favour of the Burgundian alliance. Nor did he allow his case to go by default: he sent messengers to leading personages throughout England stating his case and thus won many of them round to his point of view. When he came to London it was observed that he had a greater following, and greater resort made to him, than the King had. The Prince was thus able to hold head against his opponents and refute their charges that he had diverted moneys intended for the defence of Calais to his own use. He demanded an audience of the King; at last his father received him and promised that the charges should be examined in open Parliament. In September the Prince appeared in London again with a numerous retinue. He had no difficulty in producing proof that he was still owed a large sum of money for his outlay in both Wales and Calais, instead of profiting from his services. But he did not shake the King's government.

This is the place to discuss the relations between Henry IV and his son, the traditions of their discord and of the wildness of the Prince's youth. The whole subject became overlaid with legend and myth—the more so because Henry V became a famous hero, something of a mythical figure—before ever Shakespeare arrived to stamp the legend indelibly upon our minds with the most wonderful of all his history-plays, the two parts of *Henry IV*.

It is necessary to get back behind the legend to the truth of history. What we can say is that good formal relations between the King and his son always subsisted: there was never a public breach, disagreement as to policy was conducted with dignity and decorum, even the Prince's dismissal was managed with formal courtesy. But there must have been feeling underneath, especially with the Prince's appeal to public opinion and his demand for an audience with his father to justify himself. Nor is it unnatural to suppose, in the circumstances of the King's debility and his son's haste to govern—as the judicious biographer of Henry V does—"some natural jealousy between the reigning sovereign and his heir."[10] It is a familiar enough pattern.

As for the stories of Prince Henry's youth, the few touches that go back to the fourth Earl of Ormonde have a certain authenticity, for he was in a position to know.[11] There is no reason to suppose that Prince Henry had a wildcap, scapegrace youth, though there is reason to believe that on his accession to the throne he became a changed man, underwent a kind of conversion in confronting the burden of his office. (It must have been this that drew President Kennedy, youngest of the Presidents, to the person of Henry and made *Henry V* his favourite play. At one of his last assemblies in the White House, he had an English actor recite Henry's speech before Agincourt with its theme of the burdens of kingly rule and the penalties a ruler has to bear.)

It seems to be true that from the time of his accession to the throne until his marriage to Catherine of France, Henry V maintained entire continence, a dedicated man. The implication is that earlier he had not—and that would be natural enough; he was a young soldier, full of vitality and energy, who passed much of his youth in camp with other fighting soldiers. It is true that Sir John Oldcastle was a companion in arms who rose through the Prince's favour. When Henry became king he dissociated himself from the knight, but that was because Oldcastle was a Lollard —a very different kettle of fish from Sir John Falstaff, who was anything but a pious Lollard. Shakespeare may have derived a hint from the historic Sir John Fastolf's retreat at Patay—for the rest the East Anglian Fastolf was a good, hardy, veteran campaigner—but Shakespeare never needed more than a hint. And it is true that when Prince Henry resided at Coldharbour in East Cheap, in the City, he was just across the way from Oldcastle's house, Cobham's Inn, and neither of them very far from the Boar's Head—for what that portends. We know that East Cheap stood for good cheer from the contemporary poem "London Lickpenny":

> Then I hied me into East Cheap:
>> One cries, "Ribs of beef and many a pie!"
> Pewter pots they clattered on a heap;
>> There was harp, pipe, and minstrelsy:
>>> "Yea, by cock!" "Nay, by cock!" some began cry;
>>> Some sang of Jenkin and Julian for their
>>>> meed [reward].
>> But, for lack of money, I might not speed.

The rumours of brawling in the City probably go back to the "hurling in East Cheap" in 1410, in which Henry's brothers, Thomas and John, were concerned. No doubt they were all a high-spirited lot. After supper there seems to have been a brawl between the young princes' followers and other young courtiers, so that the sedate mayor and sheriffs had to be called in to appease the disturbance. No doubt the young men's doings would be reported to their father. There seems to be no foundation for the tradition of Henry V's chequered relations with good Chief Justice Gascoigne, though they must have known each other, and when he became king Henry treated him with favour. Perhaps there is a confused reminiscence here of Gascoigne's refusal to carry out Henry IV's order to sentence Archbishop Scrope to death.

There does seem reason to accept the story of the Prince's last sad interview with his father, when he came before him—remember, that he was out of the Council, kept out of office—clad in strange attire, his garments slit and sewn over with needles. This would have been intended to imply that his eyes were open to all that was going on and the needles would be emblematic of diligence in doing his duty, readiness to repair. More than a century later we have evidence of the use of such symbols in the entourage of Queen Elizabeth, appearing on a dress of hers, notably the symbols of open eye and tongue. Something of the truth between King Henry and his son can be represented in the account that has come down in Capgrave. There seems little doubt that at the end the King repented his usurpation of Richard's throne; but he could make no remedy, "for my children will not suffer the regality to go out of our lineage."[12] The French chronicler Monstrelet may not be exact but he has the essence of the situation when he makes the Prince say to his father, "my lord, as you have kept and guarded it by the sword, so do I intend to guard it all my life"; to which the dying King replies: "Do as it seemeth good to you; for myself I commit me to God, and pray that he will take me to his mercy."

The excitements and the strain of these last political struggles wore down the King's remaining strength. He could hardly walk or ride, but as his life ebbed he remembered his crusading days and his brief visit to Jerusalem, as a young prince of the house of Lancaster. He dreamed of leading a Crusade to deliver the Holy City from the infidels. At times he seemed to recover, and then to suffer another seizure. His last seizure took him on 20 March 1413 as he was praying at the shrine of Edward the Confessor, patron saint of the royal house and of England, in Westminster Abbey; he was carried into the abbot's lodgings, and there in the Jerusalem chamber he died—in Jerusalem at the last.

Shakespeare, with his understanding of the human condition, of the inextricable dilemmas in which historical circumstance of birth and time and place entwine the great, expresses what Henry must have felt contemplating the upshot of his life:

> God knows, my son,
> By what by-paths and indirect crook'd ways
> I met this crown, and I myself know well
> How troublesome it sat upon my head:
> To thee it shall descend with better quiet,
> Better opinion, better confirmation;
> For all the soil of the achievement goes
> With me into the earth.

CHAPTER IV

Henry V, the Hero-King

To the English of the fifteenth century and for long afterwards, certainly to the Elizabethans, Henry V was the very type of the hero-king. His achievement in itself was astonishing: the victory of Agincourt against such odds, the conquest of Normandy, the achievement of the French throne, and all in such a short time, a brief life. Then there was his personality that made an indelible impression; among all the ghosts and shadows of history he could never be forgotten. Already in his own lifetime he was a legend: people wrote ballads about him and songs in his praise, though he discouraged it. There is no doubt that he was a hero to his people: his personality, his life, his fame carried that special kind of aura.

We have to get back behind the legend and see him in more rational terms. His was a dynamic personality, driven by a relentless will. We have already seen what a hard life he had as a fighting soldier when young, inured to hardship, on close terms with danger, immensely energetic and vital, already very experienced. We shall now watch these qualities broaden into the field of European politics, diplomacy, statesmanship, until he has the whole chessboard of Western Europe in his mind; and all his powers trained on the objective of ending the age-long dispute with France on his own terms, uniting the kingdoms if possible in his own hands, with the ultimate dream of uniting Christendom for a last Crusade. (It might have been just in time to save Constantinople from the fate of 1453.)

There was something Napoleonic about such a man, such an achievement and such schemes. We cannot deny him genius— even in the literal sense of the word, he was possessed by a spirit that drove him. There was even something obsessive about him —particularly with regard to Normandy, his determination to reclaim it as his just right, the insistence, the fixation, on his "rights." This was not only very medieval of him, but good propaganda—of which he made the utmost use by every channel, secular and religious. He undoubtedly had a genius for ruling—everyone admitted as much. In this he was a dedicated, a devout, man. The strong strain of piety in the Lancastrian house, which reached its apogee in the saintly Henry VI, was already marked in his soldierly father. A famous conqueror, a recognised hero, his name was a legion in itself; his prestige grew to be such that people submitted or were daunted, as with Napoleon. There was not only the aura; beneath the just and disciplined ruler, the man himself had charm and cast a spell.

He had all the advantage of youth and was good to look at. He was tall and lithe, with the figure of an athlete. He had an oval handsome face with wide forehead and long straight nose; small ears, with well-formed lips and attractively cleft chin—a masculine trait. His complexion was good, hair brown and thick, gentle eyes of a hazel colour that could blaze when aroused. He was good at out-door sports, particularly running and jumping, and was so swift of foot that with one or two fellows he could run down a deer in the open. Everything about him was masculine. Then there came a difference. A French observer, meeting him with his brothers, noticed that the King did not look so much like a soldier as his brother Thomas did; Henry had the fine manners of a great lord and the gravity of a cleric. On second thoughts he seemed more suited to the Church. This was penetrating; for where the mind and ambitions of the King were intensely political, all geared to rule and government, with an eye for every detail as well as the largest schemes, his inner life was devotional. He was a dedicated man, and, on assuming the burden of kingship, had experienced a kind of conversion.

The night after his father's death he spent alone with a religious recluse at Westminster preparing himself for his ordeal. The interests of the Church were always present to his mind; he made the most conscientious choice of his clerics, his own confessors and the country's bishops. He took a detailed interest in the arrangements of his chapel; he ordered that, since Agincourt had been won on the day of St. Crispin and St. Crispinian, they should be commemorated every day at Mass as long as he lived. In the last

year of his life he told the Benedictines whom he wished to reform
—he was their patron—that he had relied on and benefited from
their prayers on the morning of Agincourt. He was responsible
for pushing forward the cult of St. George as a fighting patron for
England—even if he never existed. (The Middle Ages were not
very critical about such things.) Here was the kind of man Henry
was.

He had beside him to help him in his task three brothers.
Thomas, Duke of Clarence, was a good fighting soldier; the next
brother, John, Duke of Bedford, was the closest to Henry in
ability though without his genius—he was both excellent soldier
and sound politic head of good judgment; Humphrey, Duke of
Gloucester, grew up to prove that he was neither, though he did
some good as patron of the arts and letters—very little otherwise.
Then there were the able Beauforts, the King's half-uncles:
Thomas, Duke of Exeter, a good servant of the state, and Henry,
Bishop of Winchester, its ablest administrator and financier. Their
sister Joan, Countess of Westmorland, was an intelligent reading
woman; at the time of his death Henry had on loan from her *The
Chronicle of Jerusalem* and *The Journey of Godfrey de Bouillon*
—there is his insistent dream of leading a Crusade. His cousin
Joan Beaufort was the girl whom the imprisoned James I saw
walking in the garden at Windsor and fell in love with; he wrote
the *Kingis Quair* in her honour, they were married and she became
Queen of Scotland.

Henry had no difficulty in driving this variegated team and
making them serve his powerful will. He was undisputed master of
them all, from the day he took over to the day he died. The
administration worked with greater efficiency and co-ordination in
consequence; the taxes were collected, large sums of money raised
in subsidies and loans for Henry's large purposes. Society itself
operated more efficiently, at any rate its upper and middle ranks
moved more coherently, "under the determined direction of the
monarchy."[1]

On the very first day of the new reign Archbishop Arundel
made way for Bishop Beaufort as Chancellor, though this move
was balanced by the appointment of Arundel's nephew, the Earl,
as Treasurer. Henry wished his reign to open with general conciliation and peace. Even in Wales pacification had been achieved, an

offer was made to Glendower and, though no reply ever came, Welsh were once more employed in positions of trust in government. The results were reaped: a contingent of five hundred Welsh archers served at Agincourt, along with captains like David Gam, the King's Welsh squire, who laid down his life there defending Henry's person. Another of Henry's Welsh squires, marvellous to relate, became the ancestor of the Tudor dynasty.

There was one notable exception to the mood of euphoria: Archbishop Arundel's policy of repression of the Lollards had provoked a growing body of discontent ready to break into the open. Lollard sympathies were fairly widespread among the artisan classes of London and Bristol, among the weavers of the Chilterns, in the eastern Midlands and along the banks of the Severn. Lollardy also had its patrons and leaders among the knightly class, outstanding among whom was the King's old companion, Sir John Oldcastle, a man of great bodily strength and courage. He harboured Lollard preachers in Kent, and was himself at length exposed through a volume of Lollard tracts that belonged to him being discovered in an illuminator's shop in Paternoster Row.

Oldcastle was thereupon summoned to the presence of the King, supported by a number of prelates, at Kennington. Henry must have known Oldcastle's views, and it is said that the knight had attempted to convert the Prince to them. The orthodox Henry was proof against any subversion of the kind, though he wanted to steer a more moderate course than Archbishop Arundel had done. He expressed his horror at the sentiments expressed, while Oldcastle defended himself by saying that he had read no more than a couple of leaves of the book. But the prelates were now hot on his track and an open attack was made on him for his support of Lollard preachers in his and his wife's counties, Hereford and Kent. In view of Oldcastle's relations with the King, the bishops determined to lay the case before him before pursuing it further. Henry, out of old friendship, besought the Church Militant to stay its hand until he could see what he could do with his knight. He evidently had some confidence that he would get him to see reason. But at an interview that summer Oldcastle stuck obstinately to his opinions, was berated by the King, and went off in dudgeon to shut himself up in his castle at Cowling in Kent.

Archbishop Arundel served citation upon Oldcastle to appear
before him, but no notice was taken; there was a great deal of
sympathy abroad for the knight, who was, however, excommuni-
cated, arrested by royal writ and taken to the Tower. Brought
before the Archbishop's court, where it was evident that Bishop
Beaufort did not wish to push matters to extremes and urged
Oldcastle to submit, the knight submitted a moderate and orthodox
confession of faith in the Church's sacraments, merely drawing
the line at the worship of images and vain pilgrimages. But Arundel
was determined to pin him down on transubstantiation and the
necessity of confession, upon which depended the priesthood. At
this, Oldcastle said what he really thought: at the consecration
in the Mass the bread remained bread; as to confession, it might
be salutary but it was not necessary to salvation. This was shock-
ing. Arundel had gained his point: Oldcastle was declared a heretic
and handed over to the secular arm for punishment. The King,
anxious for moderation, and having compassion on his knight-
hood, granted Oldcastle a respite of forty days, hoping that he
would recant and save his life. That Henry was thought to be
overlenient to Oldcastle we can gather from a poem of the
time—its poetry comes to our aid in evidence:

> A man might be forborne [removed]
>   Far from a king's place,
> Would make a king to be forsworn
>   To let [hinder] the law it must not pass.
>   And make him ween that he [be in] grace
>   And holy in condition,
>   And maintain him in his trespass,
>   While he picketh the stones out of the crown.[2]

Before that time was up Oldcastle managed to escape from the
Tower, no one knows how. There were many Lollard sympathisers
in and around London; he seems to have had little difficulty in
hiding himself among them—the faithful never did betray him—
while he planned a demonstration in force of Lollards from various
parts of the country to converge upon the City and to coincide
with risings in the counties. The King was alerted, and under cover
of darkness on 9 January 1414 took up his position in St. Giles's
Fields outside the walls to surprise the insurgents. They walked
into the trap and a good haul of prisoners was made. Several

score were hanged, including leading Lollard knights who had fought with Oldcastle in the Welsh Marches, and some Midlands gentlemen. The risings in the Leicestershire and Derbyshire villages sputtered out. Oldcastle made his escape to the Welsh Marches, and lay concealed for the next four years mostly in his native county of Hereford; though he was outlawed and a large price put upon his head, no one would betray him.

The great problem before Henry V, now that he was free to devote his mind to it, as his father never had been, was the question of France, and what England's relations to France were to be. It is hard for a modern mind to follow the bewildering complexities and cross-currents of the Hundred Years' War, and especially the medieval terms of its diplomacy, to elicit from them the real objectives and expectations of the combatants.

We shall observe a similar rhythm in the second half of the war under Henry V and his son to that of the first half under Edward III—surprising victories at the outset, giving the English conquests in France out of all proportion to their strength to hold them, followed by a long wasting away of these gains and acute dissatisfaction and dissension in England in consequence. These two periods of prolonged warfare were divided by some decades of uneasy truce, punctuated by mutual raiding across the Channel, occasional restricted hostilities, even sometimes peace as in Richard II's last years. The French had never executed the terms of the Treaty of Brétigny (1360); in consequence Edward III's renunciation of his claim to the French crown was regarded as null, the issue of what lands the English were to occupy in Gascony and under what title was left to mutual friction and local scuffling on the spot. These issues, so many open sores, were carried over from truce to truce, but they remained to be settled.

Henry V, firm on his throne and with a united country behind him, was determined to settle them, if possible once and for all. The moment offered too good an opportunity to lose. Charles VI was intermittently mad; the French state was distracted by the dissensions and factions around him. These were complicated by regional jealousies and disputes: the Armagnac party that supported the Dauphin was solidly based on the South; the Burgundian party on the East and on Flanders. The prize in dispute was the Isle of France, Paris, the throne. We have already seen Henry as Prince pressing for the Burgundian alliance and active military intervention in France.

Henry was a very consistent man—in the end a man with an *idée fixe*—and there is no doubt that this was his policy from the first. The experience of the past decades had shown that there was no settling the issues, or getting satisfaction from the French, by the way of diplomacy. Henry must have decided on a showdown, to renew his great-grandfather's claims, though this would need strenuous diplomatic preparation. We cannot go into the complicated diplomatic manoeuvres here, but the upshot of them was that Henry was prepared for a marriage-treaty with France, to marry Charles VI's youngest daughter, Catherine, and on that basis to turn the truce, which came to an end in December 1413, into a permanent peace; but he would not surrender one jot of the rights and heritages belonging to him.

What were these?—that was the essence of the matter. The French insisted that the dispute was "essentially a feudal quarrel between a Gascon vassal and his French overlord."[3] Our English historian tells us that "Henry was determined to show them that it was more than that." He would revive his great-grandfather's claim to the French throne, which was a just one, if there were no Salic law. But did he mean this seriously? Or was it just a cover for his real objectives—a strengthening of the position in Gascony, the recovery of Normandy? It seems that the French did not take his pretensions, or his intentions, as seriously as he did himself— he was a profoundly serious man—and there may have been some scorning of the young king by the French Court. Hence the story of their sending him a tun of tennis-balls to play with, which he on his part would turn into cannon-balls against France, et cetera.[4]

For, of course, France from every point of view was very much the superior power, in size and resources, in population and agriculture, in culture and civilisation. France was three times the area of England, and her population must have been several times larger. It turned out, however, that she was at this time inferior in military efficiency and technique, in striking power, in organising her resources; this reflected the inefficiency of her less well-integrated society, less flexible and open to the new commercial currents of the English. Then too there was the fatal defect of lack of control at the centre, indeed disputed control, with a constant tug-of-war for power between the factions.

Henry, who never lacked confidence in himself, did not fear the odds. Preparations for war went on all through 1414 concurrently with intense diplomatic activity, embassies passing to and fro. When the French rejected his claim to the French throne, he fell back on the terms specified by the Treaty of Brétigny— Normandy, Touraine, Anjou, Maine, the full duchy of Aquitaine: the old Angevin inheritance mostly lost by King John. The French were prepared to make large concessions, but not to go so far as that. Very well: Henry claimed the crown. To this the Archbishop of Bourges is said to have replied that "Henry had no right to the crown of England, and that the French should be dealing with the heirs of Richard II."[5] The situation was now beyond argument.

It seems that at this point Henry intended to win back Normandy at least; the preparations he was making—a body of only two thousand men at arms with some six thousand archers—and the plan of campaign he followed indicate a reconnaissance of Normandy in force, as a preliminary to invasion in greater strength.

The forces were already gathered at Southampton when there broke the news of a plot which gave some point to the French ambassador's retort. This was a crazy conspiracy of Henry's cousin, Richard, Earl of Cambridge—younger brother of Edward, Duke of York, who had redeemed his earlier disloyalty to the house of Lancaster by good service and who was to die at Agincourt—to put the Earl of March, Richard's heir, on the throne. Cambridge was a light-headed fool, but his ingratitude was worse; for Henry had treated the people involved well, even generously. It was Henry who had given Cambridge his earldom. Henry had made Scrope, the second person in the conspiracy, Treasurer in his government in 1411; had made him his confidential agent in the negotiations with France and even shared his bed with him. Henry had done his best to pacify the North by restoring Hotspur's son to his great earldom; he had released March from his honourable confinement and treated him with confidence. In this case his confidence was rewarded, for it was March who resisted Scrope's temptations and divulged the conspirators' plans to the King. Ghosts of the past—Percy was to raise the standard of revolt in the North, bring in the Scots, and link up with Glendower and Oldcastle in the West. It seems that the Lollards were privy to the conspiracy. The time for all this was past; Henry made short work of these fantasies: Cambridge, Scrope and Grey were executed after an emergency trial. (When the Yorkists came to power a generation later the judgment was condemned as "erroneous"—so much for party spirit.) Henry continued his friendship to York and March as before. All was set for the expedition to sail.

As the ships made their way down Southampton Water the swans of the Solent turned out to see them off, swimming confidently among the vessels.* This was taken to be a good omen; it turned out to be so. The season was already late: Henry can only have intended a demonstration in force, an exploration of what might later be attempted. The expeditionary force embarked on Sunday, 11 August 1415, and landed in the Seine estuary on the 14th. At once Harfleur was invested, the key to Normandy. It was a strong fortress, strongly held, and could well have held out if only the Dauphin in Paris had come to its aid. Strong as were its bastions, its marshes were more deadly: dysentery got hold of the besiegers and it wrought havoc among them. Henry lost one of his closest friends, the talented young Bishop Courtenay, as well as other leaders and captains. The townsfolk also suffered, food was running out and no help came from their countrymen. It was not until 23 September that the town surrendered and Henry entered it barefoot to give thanks. No pillaging was the order— since Henry's claim was that he was but occupying what was his own.

There was a large haul of ransomable prisoners, knights and

---

* All the authorities say that there were some fifteen hundred vessels. I do not believe it. Medieval figures are almost always exaggerated, and yet modern historians, e.g., Kingsford and Jacob, accept this figure literally. Kingsford tells us that Henry's largest ship carried seventy-five men at arms and one hundred and forty-eight archers, the smallest barge four lances and eight archers. How many ships then would be needed to transport a force of only some eight thousand men? On Henry's second invasion in 1417 he had some ten thousand effectives; yet the number of ships to transport them is again given as fifteen hundred. It is evidently a conventional figure.

gentlemen: these were put on parole to meet him at Calais—
so Henry had already made his decision to march through the
country, at whatever risk. For his force was down by some two
thousand, as the result of the siege and the sickness. He left more
troops behind to occupy Harfleur, which he intended to keep as
another Calais, a base for further operations when the time came.
It was not until 8 October, and with a force of only nine hundred
men at arms and five thousand archers, that he began his hazardous and fateful march across French territory to Calais—some
hundred and fifty miles by the route he was forced to take.

For by this time, if belatedly, superior forces were collecting
to watch his route, bar it where possible and in the end attempt
to overwhelm him. From Harfleur he hugged the coast via
Fécamp, Arques (near Dieppe) and Eu until he got to the Somme
—that country so fought over and drenched in English blood in
our time. At the Somme he found the bridges down, the fords
rendered impassable or guarded, and had to turn upstream and
follow the river dangerously inland many miles to find a crossing.
On his way upstream at Corbie he had a man hanged for stealing
a pyx from a church—an incident Shakespeare made use of and
put down to his rascal, Bardolph. At last Henry found a crossing
and could turn north towards Calais and safety. But the weather
had turned nasty; in rain and mud they marched by Péronne and
along a route between Bapaume and Albert, some miles south of
Arras—those so familiar names—until, half-way between Arras
and the coast, he found the way barred by an immensely superior
French army. They were close to a little village called Agincourt.

Henry did not allow himself to be daunted by the vast superiority
of the forces opposed to him, though he must have been greatly
tensed up—a man of his temperament. His chaplain heard him
say to Sir Walter Hungerford, who wished that they had ten
thousand stout archers from England with them: "You speak as a
fool. By the God of heaven, I would not, if I could, have a man
more than I have. For this people which I have is God's people,
whom He hath thought it meet for me to have at this present.
Wot you not that the Almighty with this humble few can overcome yonder proud Frenchmen, who so boast themselves of their
numbers and strength?"[6] This was a familiar thought with Henry:
he had once written to his father from the fighting in Wales that

strength did not consist in the multitude of the people but in the courage of the few. (This sentiment much appealed to William Shakespeare when he came to write about it.) It was now to be put to the test on the field of Agincourt.

Like Churchill in 1940, Henry had reasoned grounds behind his confidence: it was no mere foolhardy courage. He knew the lack of unity in the French command, indeed the disunity and disputes that nullified France's great superiority in resources. Indeed the technical superiority lay with him—that of the long-bow, the proficiency of the English archers, of whom his force mostly consisted, against the inefficiency of antiquated feudal cavalry supported by sectional units of men at arms inadequately integrated. A conservative estimate of the French army would rate its strength at twenty-five or thirty thousand—there have been many higher estimates. Its numbers turned to its own destruction; for it was drawn up on a narrow front between two woods, and was therefore disposed in depth, of which no use could be made: it turned out a chief cause of the disaster that ensued. Henry drew up his force, with maximum efficiency and unity of command, in a front consisting of a half-circle of archers, protected from cavalry attack by sharpened stakes, and in wedge-formation for more deadly fire-power and effective defence; two wings thrown out for further protection, one under the Duke of York, who was killed in the action.

The French cavalry attack floundered, and the centre gave way. This was disastrous, for the masses of men behind them pushed forward and the resulting mêlée offered an inescapable target to the English archers and light troops on their flanks. There ensued a fearful butchery: the floundering mass could not move and were slaughtered "like sheep." At the crisis of the battle the cry went up among the English that the baggage in the rear was being plundered, there were so many prisoners; fearful of the danger, Henry gave the order to kill the prisoners, before moving on to attack the second French contingent, which was so demoralised that it gave little resistance. Those who could fled from the scene of carnage.

The French suffered terrible losses, particularly in the highest ranks of chivalry. Among the dead were the Dukes of Alençon and Bar, two brothers of the Duke of Burgundy—namely, the

Duke of Brabant and the Count of Nevers—d'Albret and Châtillon, respectively Admiral and Constable of France—numerous counts, over a thousand knights and, it is estimated, some four or five thousand men. Among the prisoners were more members of the French royal family, the Duke of Bourbon and the Duke of Orléans, who was to spend the next quarter of a century as a prisoner in England, where he had the leisure to make himself one of the most accomplished poets of the age. In addition there were Boucicault, the Marshal of France, the Counts of Eu and Vendôme, and Arthur, brother of the Duke of Brittany. On the English side there fell York and Suffolk, and scarce a hundred men besides.

It was an astonishing performance; Henry emerged, still a young man, the most famous ruler in Europe. However, as politic as he was religious, all the glory was ascribed to God; for Henry, the event merely proved the justice of his cause.

Prestige brought diplomatic gains even more important than victory in the field. Henry now engaged in a strenuous diplomatic offensive to bring pressure from every quarter to bear upon France. At this point he was willing to forgo his claim to the French throne for the positive acquisitions of Brétigny—Normandy, Maine, Anjou and all Aquitaine. No French government could possibly agree to this. Very well, his reply was to raise his claim to the French throne itself. His diplomatic aims were to keep the unwieldy bulk of France divided between Burgundians and Armagnacs, and, though he was in constant negotiation with both to bid up one against the other, he ultimately settled for the Burgundian alliance as the better bet against France, and also on account of English commercial interests in the Netherlands. His second aim was to isolate France by taking away her allies and rallying his own. Thus he managed to detach the Genoese, on whom the French relied for help in the sea-war in the Channel and to bring a Portuguese fleet, from the friendly and related house of Aviz, to his own aid. Henry thus won complete supremacy in the Channel for the conquest of France, an ascendancy which lasted his reign and for some time beyond.

His greatest diplomatic triumph came in the next year, 1416, with the visit of the Emperor Sigismund to England and the conclusion of the Treaty of Canterbury. The German emperor made an offensive and defensive alliance with Henry, pledging mutual support for the recovery of their claims against France. This was more important diplomatically than for any active help it gave Henry in the field. For one thing it effected an Anglo-German concord against the hitherto dominant French at the Council of Constance, now engaged in the reform of the Church. The Anglo-German alliance completed France's diplomatic isolation and profoundly altered the balance of power in Western Europe—for the time being.

In England all was at Henry's disposition. He had rewarded Richard II's heir, March, and Richard's nephew, Huntingdon, with full restitution to their honours and estates for their good service in the war. Not a cat now mewed against the house of Lancaster in the person of its victorious king. However, Oldcastle was still at large; there was much sympathy for him among poor priests, and "no person or community had ventured to lay hand on him despite the enormous rewards offered."[7] For four years he had remained concealed on the Welsh Marches, though once he ventured with impunity within a few miles of London. In the summer of 1417 the Scots broke the truce to make the "Foul Raid" across the Border, though it did them no good and only provoked retaliation in the harrying of the Lowlands. It was fatal to Oldcastle, however, for the government was convinced that he was in touch with the Scots and redoubled their efforts against the Lollards and to run him to earth.

Oldcastle was at length caught, in the autumn of 1417, but not—it is pleasant to record—until his old knightly companion, Henry himself, was overseas in Normandy. To Henry's brother, Bedford, Lieutenant of the realm, there fell the honour of extinguishing this irrepressible spirit, this outsize monument of heresy. Four Welshmen betrayed him and ran him down in Powysland. "His arrest was not achieved without a violent struggle, for he was a man of great bodily strength; but at length he was badly wounded, overpowered and carried to the castle at Welshpool."[8] Wounded and bodily broken, though not in spirit, he was taken in a litter to London, thence to the Tower and brought before Parliament. Called upon to answer by the Chief Justice, he answered that he recognised no judge there, for his proper judge, King Richard,

was in Scotland. It was a sad end for the companion of Prince
Henry—no doubt his troubles and persecution had unhinged
him. He bore the torture of a slow fire at St. Giles's Fields with
great bravery: not a cry escaped him. Pathetically, he recognised
his old comrade, Sir Thomas Erpingham, among the large crowd
who had gathered to see him die. "In the eyes of contemporaries
his heresy bulked far more largely than his treason, and far worse
than his intrigues with the Scots and the puppet Richard was his
denial of the efficacy of prayer to the Virgin and the saints, of the
necessity or value of confession to a priest, and of the change of
the substantial bread into the body of God."

That may be true for the simple-minded; but it is unlikely to be
true for the rulers of men.

Henry embarked for the invasion of France in his flagship, the
Trinity, on 23. July 1417. This time he had an army of ten
thousand fighting effectives, three-quarters of them archers, with
perhaps a couple thousand more in support, siege-train, engi-
neers, miners, commissariat, the King's household and those indispensable persons the chaplains. The chaste Henry would allow
no female camp-followers. When the army was disembarked the
main fleet was sent back under the command of the Earl of March.
Henry's plan of campaign was the conquest of Normandy, securing
first the left bank of the Seine, from which to conquer lower
Normandy, thus drive a wedge between the duchy and Anjou and
effectively isolate Brittany, which would be reduced to neutrality.
In this strategic conception, as in the concentration of his forces
upon a spearhead, his archers—his equivalent to a panzer-division
—Henry showed his military mastery as against the dispersed
efforts and campaigning all over the place of his great-grandfather,
Edward III. Henry allowed no secondary diversions, no dispersal
of forces into Aquitaine. Indeed the story of the war shows upon
what narrow margins, what restricted resources, he accomplished
his prodigious achievement. He could not have done it but for the
discord of the French princes: "the two parties had but one thing
in common: they were equally ready to make terms with the
foreign invader, if thus they could gain some sufficient advantage
over their domestic enemies."[9] This gave Henry his grand opportunity: he made the maximum use of it.

In August, Clarence began the investment of Caen by the capture of William the Conqueror's foundation of St. Stephen's Abbey, where Henry took up his quarters. This was followed by the occupation of the sister foundation of Queen Matilda, the Abbey of the Trinity. In September, Caen was taken by assault, but Henry would allow no plunder—for this was his city by right. While he remained there organising the future government of his duchy, promising clemency and protection to his liege subjects, his brother Gloucester received the submission of Bayeux and its neighbouring towns and villages. The terror of Henry's name was a legion in itself: at Lisieux no one remained to submit. But the peasantry in general were prepared to live under whichever master proved stronger. Not so the towns or the upper classes—and this was ominous in the long run.

It was usual to suspend field operations in the winter and go into winter quarters: not so Henry this winter. He plodded on through rain and mud until, with the fall of Falaise in February, he could regard the conquest of lower Normandy—all that west of the Seine—as complete. The next three months he spent mainly at Bayeux and Caen organising the civil administration of his duchy. Since he claimed that it was his by right he disturbed the existing machinery as little as possible. As the representative of the old dukes of the line of the Conqueror he appealed to the ancient law and custom of the duchy; indeed—a significantly archaistic touch—he restored the annual *Rotulus Normanniae,* the yearly record of official acts as it had been kept in the days of King John—two hundred years before. From the first he regarded Normandy in a different light from his other conquests in France: this was a recovery of what was his own. The administration might be French, but the government was to be English, an overseas base like Calais. To this end he offered special terms to English subjects to come over and settle in the Norman seaports. Except for Harfleur, where there were as many as four hundred resident in 1435, he had little success. One cannot ultimately prevail against the order of nature. Except for a few buildings here and there, a few personal names and a mass of documents, above all the foundation of the University of Caen, the English occupation left few traces that it had ever been.

With lower Normandy firm behind him Henry was now free to

devote the summer campaign of 1418 to conquering upper Normandy on the north-eastern side of the Seine, with its strongly fortified capital, Rouen, the second city in the kingdom. The key to it was Pont de l'Arche across the Seine, which Henry seized in June without any interference from either Armagnacs or Burgundians. They were engaged in complicated manoeuvres around Paris; for the moment the Burgundians were in possession there, but to the south and east the Armagnacs held Melun and Meaux, controlling respectively the Seine and the Marne. Rouen was left to its fate. It was so strong that only blockade could reduce it; the siege lasted from 30 July 1418 to 19 January 1419.

The Earl of March and Thomas Beaufort, now Duke of Exeter, had been busy in England all winter raising fresh troops and in the spring they arrived with their reinforcements for the King. They gave good service in mopping-up operations, achieving the surrender of Cherbourg at last and Evreux. Meanwhile Richard Beauchamp, Earl of Warwick—who was to win a great name in these wars and whom we still see on his splendid tomb in his chapel at St. Mary's, Warwick—was investing Caudebec, below Rouen, on the Seine estuary to cut it off from sustenance on that side. The mouth of the Seine was blockaded by an English fleet, reinforced by a Portuguese squadron sent by King John, kinsman of the house of Lancaster. Rouen was starved out. No help came from either Burgundy or the Dauphin. The spirited and tenacious resistance put up was entirely that of the citizens themselves, and it only increased their sufferings.

In January 1419, to save further suffering, the surrender was arranged through the intervention of Archbishop Chichele—who had succeeded Arundel—and the mediation of the Norman clergy. Naming Thomas Beaufort governor of the city, Henry made his solemn entry in procession, more ecclesiastical than military, and characteristically went first to the cathedral to give thanks. He was received with the chant *Quis est magnus dominus*—the answer being, of course, their rightful lord and master. Henry had little to learn from moderns in the art of propaganda, and fulfilled the first requisite that he believed it himself. Only after hearing Mass and making his offering in the cathedral did he take up residence in the castle of his remote ancestors, the Norman dukes.

From this base Henry now entered upon an intense diplomatic

offensive. He had to keep negotiations going with both Burgundy and the Dauphin. At first it seemed that the Dauphin's party were more amenable and offered larger concessions. But they could not meet Henry's demand for either most of Northern France to be ceded, or else his claim to the French throne recognised. The Burgundians in turn demanded that the negotiations should be in French; Henry demanded that they should be in Latin, on the ground that neither he nor his Council could speak or understand French. This was surely mere diplomatic manoeuvring while the facts spoke for themselves. The Dauphin promised to meet Henry at Evreux, and failed to turn up. In May, Henry at last had a meeting with poor mad Charles VI, in the hands of his Queen Isabel and the Duke of Burgundy. He also had his first glimpse of the Princess Catherine, target of his marriage negotiations now over years. He was supposed to have fallen for her charm. Let that be as it may—politics were the thing.

Henry found the French claims considerably hardened, perhaps as the result of the negotiations between the Dauphin and Burgundy which were simultaneously going on at Pontoise and which achieved a treaty of peace and a formal alliance: no alliances with the common enemy. Henry determined to teach both parties a lesson. When the truce for his peace-talks expired he delivered an assault on Pontoise, key to Paris. The booty was enormous— enough to have lasted the garrison two years of resistance, it was said. The whole of the Vexin fell to him; Clarence raided right up to the gates of the capital, which was now denuded of supplies. The Duke of Burgundy, responsible for its defence, deserted the city for Troyes; opinion in Paris turned against him. In this emergency the Dauphin arranged to meet Burgundy at Montereau, and there on the bridge on 26 August 1419 the Dauphin's entourage hacked the Duke down and despatched him. This dastardly murder placed the whole game in Henry's hands, as he was quick to realise. Henceforth, the blood of Jean sans Peur ran for years between the house of Burgundy and the royal house of France, keeping the kingdom divided and letting the English remain.

With the house of Burgundy bent on revenge, both sides wanted the English alliance now on practically any terms. The situation transformed, Henry could afford to wait to impose his own. He spent the next four months in his Norman capital directing the course of negotiations and organising the administration of his new conquests. He seems to have been a glutton for government, to have had—like Napoleon—an insatiable appetite for rule. To aid him in his task Bedford was summoned over from England, while Gloucester took his place as Lieutenant of the realm. There all was quiet; all the chivalry of England was overseas, winning name and fame, ransoms and booty—for them war could be made to pay. In Normandy the lower classes were accepting the *fait accompli* of the conquest; nearly all the minor posts in government were occupied by Normans, only the top officials being English. Commerce was reviving in the Channel with security attained—an intermission from the endemic ding-dong raids from coast to coast.

Henry came to terms with Philip, the new Duke of Burgundy, first: they were Henry's own terms, high and intimidating, which Philip had no choice but to accept. Henry would marry Catherine, but her dowry was to be the French kingdom; Charles VI might nominally retain the crown—his rule was but nominal anyhow—but on his death Henry was to succeed him, and meanwhile to govern as Heir of France. During these negotiations Henry's headquarters were at Mantes—where William the Conqueror had received the injury from which he died. Meanwhile the remaining resistance in upper Normandy was sputtering out, castles surrendering, like Coeur de Lion's famous Château Gaillard in its impregnable position above the Seine. The whole country was alive with memories of the past. All the while Henry was drawing closer to Paris.

Charles VI, now completely dominated by Queen Isabel—who was only too willing to see the aggrandisement of her daughter at the expense of her son whom she detested, was with his Court at Troyes. Thither came the English envoys under Warwick; negotiations were easy, Queen Isabel was agreeable to the same terms as Burgundy had accepted. In effect it came to accepting Henry as ruler of France. It was an extraordinary consummation, really beyond all expectation. There were not wanting critics on both sides. To patriotic Frenchmen it was intolerable to set aside the male line of St. Louis for an Englishman. But discerning Englishmen could see that to accept the title of Regent of France gave away the English claim as of right, the ground upon which the war had been fought. If they had been able to see further into the future they would have had even greater qualms. For, apart from the immense loot that France offered to the chivalric class in booty and ransoms, what would England get out of the deal, for all the drain on man-power and resources put into the adventure? Henry would become King of France, England would take second place to the much larger and richer country; and even England's conquests, such as Normandy, would lapse back to the French Crown under Henry.

We have reached a point such as not seldom recurs in the history of conquerors and conquests, when the dynamic of conquest impels the conqueror to a point where he no longer serves the interests of his own country that gave him his base, but goes beyond to a point where he is overstraining his country's resources, draining its strength, in the interests of his own outrageous ascendancy. Louis XIV reached this position with the war of 1702. Napoleon reached it with the war of 1809 against Austria—Talleyrand saw that from that point he was no longer serving the interests of France but exhausting them, drew his own conclusions and left his service.

But conquerors sometimes cannot help themselves: they are drawn on by the logic of events, or rather the dynamic they have themselves set going. As with Hitler and the unexpected extent of the conquests of 1940—who said that it sometimes happened that people were led beyond what they originally intended. So we have observed Henry, who set out with the aim of recovering Normandy and, if possible, the territories acquired by the Treaty of Brétigny, led on by success after success opening the way before him, to the improbable, the unbelievable, consummation of the union of France and England. Events were to show that it was not possible; Henry had, in the short term, for the rest of his own brief life, achieved the impossible.

If Henry were asked to defend himself before the bar of history, he would no doubt do so in the terms of the clause to be put before the Estates of France and of England:

> From the time that we or any of our heirs come to the same, both realms shall be governed not severally but under one and the same person; keeping nonetheless, in all manner other things, to either of the same realms their rights or customs, usages and

laws. Also that henceforward perpetually shall be still, rest and shall cease all manner of dissensions, hates, rancours, enmities and wars; and there shall be for evermore and shall follow peace, tranquillity, good accord and common affection, and stable friendship and steadfast between the same realms.[10]

In other words, the justification of Henry's war, as of some other people's in history, was peace. If he had lived he might have achieved a period of peace between the two kingdoms under his rule. But perpetual peace between France and England, with all the history of the centuries to come before them!—the idea was a dream.

The peace of Troyes was made in March 1420—"one of the most fateful treaties upon which England has been induced to enter."[11] In April, Henry set out from Rouen up the Seine along the scenes of his conquests to St. Denis, burying place of the kings of France, then along under the walls of Paris where the citizens turned out to gaze on the splendid spectacle of his retinue. Nearing Troyes he was escorted into the city by the Duke of Burgundy. On 21 May 1420 the treaty was solemnly ratified and Henry betrothed to Catherine in the cathedral of Troyes, in the presence of his brothers Clarence and Bedford with forty nobles and knights; and on the other side, of Queen Isabel and Duke Philip of Burgundy, as commissaries of the mad King Charles VI, whom Henry was to displace and succeed. On Trinity Sunday, 2 June, Henry and Catherine were married and their nuptial bed blessed according to French custom—we shall see with what results.

After the ceremonies the business of fighting once more. Henry had taken on the immense obligation of reducing Armagnac France to submission, and in alliance now with Burgundy he set out to clean up Northern France of all resistance. Sens—with its cathedral built by the builder of Canterbury Cathedral—was garrisoned by the Armagnacs, but the townsfolk welcomed Henry. He had been married by its archbishop; as Henry entered his cathedral city the King paid him a courteous compliment: "you have given me a wife, now I restore you yours—your church."[12] Montereau had to be taken by assault, after which Duke Philip was able to give his father's body honourable interment.

The siege of Melun, a key-position on the upper Seine south of Paris, gave far more trouble and lasted several months. We must remember that cannon were as yet little developed and made not much impression on strong city-walls. Henry was opposed to the hazard of assaulting this town, and his judgment proved right. All that summer he and his brothers lay in their tents to the west, Burgundy, with Warwick and Huntingdon, in theirs on the east. Henry summoned over young King James of Scotland to command the withdrawal of the Scottish contingent in the garrison—in vain; on the other hand, Henry's brother-in-law, the Duke of Bavaria, arrived to lend a hand. France was like a corpse being carved up. No aid arrived from the Dauphin.

It is from the siege of Melun that comes a story, whether legendary or no, which testifies to the aura of Henry's personality and may have contributed something to a famous scene in Shakespeare later. The town had to be mined, and there was a dispute between two of Henry's captains which should have the honour of entering the mine first. To settle it the King went in. The French defence was gallantly led by Barbazan, who encountered Henry all unknown to him in the mine and fought with him hand to hand. In a pause, admiring each other's valour, they learned each other's identity; Barbazan withdrew, ordering the barriers to be closed. It may be only legend, but legend has its uses no less than truth.

During the siege Henry paid several visits to Paris, and had all the strong points placed in his hands, the Louvre, the Bastille and the castle of Vincennes to the east of the city, favourite residence of the Valois kings. On the surrender of Melun in November, the country all round Paris being now cleared, Henry made his state-entry into his capital, 1 December 1420, riding at the head of a grand procession with poor King Charles on his right, the Duke of Burgundy on his left. Henry went straight to make offering at Notre Dame, before taking up residence at the Louvre. Everyone marked the magnificence of the Heir of France in contrast to the poor estate of its king. But, after all, its king was a poor lunatic; Henry was the ruler.

Henry was welcomed by the Parliament, the university—the most famous in all Europe—and the burgesses. The main purpose of the visit was to have the Treaty of Troyes solemnly ratified by the Estates, which were summoned early in September. Henry and Charles VI presided in equal state, as again at a *lit de justice* at which Charles's son, the Dauphin, and his chief supporters were judged guilty of the murder of Burgundy, while royal letters declared them incapable of succeeding to any rights, prerogatives or estate. So far as law and public recognition could make him Henry was sovereign. With his appetite for government he exercised the power and made the decisions, reorganising administration, particularly the top-heavy, inefficient royal household, removing and appointing officers at pleasure. No lack of confidence in his new rôle and kingdom in Henry—he and Catherine kept magnificent state in the Louvre, while her father was laid aside with few in attendance. (Perhaps he was happier thus: he was certainly incapable of the cares of government.) Christmas was kept with splendour at the Louvre, after which the princes dispersed on the multiple affairs of the dual monarchy.

In England all was quiet, but Parliament had met in December and the general desire to have the King back in the kingdom was voiced. It was three and a half years since he had set foot in his own country. Even more pointed were references to poverty and distress, the scarcity of money—no doubt through the drain overseas. The country was well aware, perhaps proud, of the King's astonishing achievement and his elevation, but it was also apprehensive of its effects on England and its independent sovereignty. The Commons asked that petitions to the Lieutenant of the realm might be terminated within the kingdom without being sent abroad. Henry was not having this: even while abroad he was "determined to keep the reins of government in his own hands."[13] On the other hand, he was careful to have the Treaty of Troyes submitted to Parliament when he met it in May, rehearsing all that had been done in France and the treaty's ratification by the Estates there— thus associating England fully and representatively with his dual monarchy.

After Christmas he and Catherine set out for England, where he intended to have her crowned as queen. They stayed three weeks in the Norman capital, whither Henry summoned the Estates of Normandy; a subsidy was voted, ordinances for better government passed. The Duke of Brittany's brother was liberated in the hope that he might be useful in bringing Brittany, which had played an equivocal rôle, on to the English side. (In England, Henry's stepmother, Queen Joan, was held in confinement for her dealings with Brittany and the intelligence her foreign attendants had been sending abroad.) Two important nobles, key-figures in Gascony, who had deserted the Dauphin now came to pay fealty to Henry; they proved no more faithful to him than they had been to the Dauphin. In this brave new world, in which the old and tried obligations of feudal society had been profoundly disturbed and were in fact being transformed, everybody who was anybody was playing for his own hand.

Leaving Clarence as Lieutenant in France, Exeter as Governor of Paris, and attended by a grand retinue—the King of Scots, Bedford and Bishop Beaufort, the Earls of March and Warwick— Henry and Catherine progressed from Rouen to Calais and crossed over on 1 February 1421. At Dover, where they arrived on the morning of Candlemas, there were crowds to welcome them, so too at Canterbury and along the Pilgrims' Way so recently celebrated by England's great medieval poet in his *Canterbury Tales*. Catherine was crowned by Archbishop Chichele at Westminster on Sunday, 23 February, the Archbishop and Bishop Beaufort on her right, the King of Scots on her left. Etiquette forbade Henry to be present at what was her show.

After the coronation Henry and Catherine made a progress through the provinces. It was all carefully planned—politics occupying the first and last place in Henry's mind—to visit centres of old Lollard disaffection, Bristol, the Welsh Marches, Leicester, and so to the northern capital, York, to show his queen to his subjects. While Catherine paid a visit to her cousin, Charles of Orléans, at Pontefract, Henry went on pilgrimage to the shrine of St. John of Bridlington, patron of the Lancastrian house, and St. John of Beverley on the feast of whose translation Agincourt had been won. While on this northern tour two events of importance to the dynasty occurred. Henry's unfortunate son, to live a life of misery as Henry VI, was conceived; while in France in March there happened the disaster of Baugé, a bad portent for the future.

The disaster was all the worse for being superfluous. Clarence, who had been left as Lieutenant of France and should have been at his business in Paris, was raiding Armagnac territory in the Loire valley with a small force—apparently hoping to achieve some

feat of bravado that might compare with Agincourt—when he allowed himself to be surprised. It was no more than a skirmish, but
it was a disaster because of the quality of the English killed and
taken prisoner. Clarence was slain—and his want would be felt
in time to come when, of all the male progeny of the house of
Lancaster, not one was left save the feeble Henry VI. Along with
Clarence were killed those famous Lancastrian knights Gilbert
Umfraville and John Grey, Lord Roos and a dozen others. The
prisoners were hardly less important: Richard II's nephew, Huntingdon, Henry's cousins—the Beaufort Earl of Somerset (in time
to become father of Lady Margaret Beaufort, mother of Henry
VII, through whom he derived his title to the throne) and his
brother Edmund, Lord Fitzwalter and other notabilities. It was a
bad blow and must have given useful encouragement to the
Dauphin's discouraged cause beyond the Loire: it showed what
could be done by waiting and biding the chance.

Henry heard the news at Beverley, but with his usual self-control
the King said nothing to his entourage until the morrow. One of
his most kingly characteristics, everyone recognised, was his patience in adversity. The news made no difference to his plans: he
went on through his extended progress through the eastern counties, attending the enthronement of the bishop at Lincoln, and
back through Lynn, with a pilgrimage to Walsingham, to Norwich
and so to Westminster to meet Parliament in May.

And what was the purpose of this so admirably conceived and
extensive tour, so well spaced and with its devotional attentions
well to the fore? Politics, of course: to see for himself the state
of his English kingdom, to observe the conditions prevailing
within the religious orders, to impress upon English opinion his
achievement in France and to rally it behind the Treaty of Troyes,
and to raise the money to carry it out.

Since the treaty needed all the support he could muster, he
could hardly appeal to Parliament for the money it necessitated.
So the cash had to be raised by loans and this had been one of the
objects of the tour. (Since the money would be drained off to
France, the effects would be bound to be economically deleteri-
ous.) By far the biggest lender was Bishop Beaufort, with the
revenues of the see of Winchester as security and his own credit
to raise cash upon. At the time of the Council of Constance

Bishop Beaufort had temporarily been in his nephew's bad books. Beaufort had carried out Henry's policy at the Council effectively in 1417, had had a major part in the election of Martin V and in return had been nominated cardinal with a commission to act as legate—to advance papal policy—in Henry's dominions.

Archbishop Chichele had reported the plan to Henry in France. Henry was going to have no such invasion of his prerogatives, and impounded the offending commission. His uncle persevered, and procured a fresh bull from the Pope. By this he exposed himself to the penalties of the statute of Provisors—forfeiture of his goods and degradation from his see, the source of his wealth. This was brought home to him by Thomas Chaucer, who had been told off to watch his ambitious kinsman. There followed a hard-headed discussion between these men of business, with the clear alternative: leave the country and the fats of Winchester, or retain them and compound for the offence. The sensible bishop opted for the latter. Many years later Gloucester reported the King as saying, "he had as lief set his crown beside him as to see him wear a cardinal's hat."[14] So long as Henry lived there was no hat for Beaufort, nor, religious as Henry was and anxious to see reform in the Church, was there any recovery of papal power in his dominions: the facts of power were what they were. Having gained his point, Henry was too politic to bear his uncle any ill will. He continued to treat him with confidence, and the realist bishop coughed up loans to the prodigious extent of over £20,000 for the war.

On his last visit to England, Henry found time to push, what was very close to his heart, the reform of the monastic orders and to further his own religious foundations. The French war provided an excuse for a useful measure—the dissolution of the alien priories and the confiscation of their lands to the Crown: a good precedent for the Dissolution under a later Henry, Henry VIII. Some of these lands went to Henry V's pious foundations: the Charterhouse at Sheen, the royal residence which subsequently became Richmond and on the opposite bank of the Thames the Bridgettine house of Syon. In these he was to be prayed for perpetually; when the inmates of one went to their rest they were to ring a bell so that those of the other might take up the continuous round of prayer.

Having taken these steps for the benefit of the war and of his soul, Henry was ready to return to France. He left Catherine behind him, for she was expecting her baby. The child was born at Windsor on St. Nicholas's Day, and was baptised by Archbishop Chichele. Bedford, Bishop Beaufort and Jacqueline of Hainault —by marrying whom Humphrey Duke of Gloucester was to cause so much trouble—were the godparents. The characters in future tragedies were gathered around that cradle. When Henry, campaigning again in France, heard the news he sent a message to Catherine to hear a Mass of the Trinity and offer the child to God. It is ironical to think—in this period replete with the ironies of history—that subsequent kings of England descend from Catherine of Valois not through the blood of Henry V, but through a child she had by Henry's Welsh squire, Owen Tudor.

Henry's personal influence had had more effect in recruiting troops and cash than all the efforts of his faithful servants. When he left England for the last time on 21 June 1421, he took with him a thousand fresh archers and men at arms. Once more he engaged with all his vigour in his vocation of rule and in the endless task of conquering France. Since the Dauphin's forces would never meet him in the field, Henry was thrown back upon reducing what strongholds remained to the Dauphin in Northern France, fortress by fortress. At the same time he kept complex diplomatic negotiations going all the following winter, on the whole with discouraging results. The Emperor Sigismund, for all his promises, rendered him no aid in the field; in Northern Italy, Genoa and Milan were giving the Dauphin active support.

The siege of Meaux, in a position to command the Marne above Paris, occupied the whole winter and right up to May 1422. It is said that "as an example of scientific siege warfare, the leaguer of Meaux was probably Henry's masterpiece."[15] So much for the military art as such; a contemporary states that the siege was "the most harmful of all that Henry undertook."[16] Dysentery was rife from the marshes of the Marne and carried off numbers of the besiegers. It is not known whether Henry contracted the disease here, but certainly the strain of that winter took a heavy toll of his strength. However, the capture of Meaux markedly altered the situation in Northern France: Henry, in alliance with Burgundy, was now master of all Normandy, Picardy, the Isle of France, with most of Champagne, Maine and even into the Orléanais. The Dauphin now had no real authority north of the Loire. All looked promising; but all depended on Henry's life, and the Burgundian alliance.

Whitsuntide Henry and Catherine spent in state at the Louvre. One day they went to the Hôtel de Nesle with a grand following to see the mystery play of the life of St. George. This was followed by an important council: it seems that Henry was to go east to co-operate with the Burgundians. Then a demand came from the Duke to relieve him on the Loire. But Henry was already sickening to his death. He had to do all he could to help the Duke, and he made the attempt; he could not ride and had to be taken in a litter. Beyond Corbeil he could not go, though he made one more effort, being rowed down the Seine to Charenton. Brought back to the castle of Vincennes, he never left his bed and no one, it seems, entertained any hope of his recovery.

Though on his death-bed, all through August he was able to transact business: his mind was clear. He had his brother Bedford, his uncle Exeter, Warwick and his English intimates with him at the end. No concern apparently for Catherine on his part, or on her part for him: she remained with her parents at Senlis, he did not send for her. His mind was wholly given to politics and his soul. He might have said, as Napoleon said of himself: *"Je suis né un être tout à fait politique; je n'aime ni la femme ni le jeu."* What concerned him was the disposition of the dual monarchy he had—contrary to the course of history—won for himself. He hoped to keep it for his son, whom he left to the special care of Bedford, who was to be Lieutenant of Normandy and perhaps of France. Others say that the Duke of Burgundy was to be Regent of France, though no one can say whether he would have accepted it on English terms. The dying King enforced that at all costs the alliance with Burgundy must be kept: he well knew that that was the condition of English rule in France. In the event Bedford became Regent. His brother Gloucester was to be Protector of the realm in England, though subordinate to Bedford and to act by his advice. Henry is said to have sent a last message to Gloucester urging him not to prefer his private interest to the public weal.

At the end Henry was concerned to justify himself and his action in entering upon the war. He protested that his motive had been only to pursue his just title, to obtain "both peace and my own rights." His mind fixed on politic rule to the last he spoke at length to those that were with him on "the just and right ways they were to follow and the method of government they were to observe."[17]

When told that his end was near he called in his chaplains to recite the seven penitential psalms. When they came to the words *"Benigne fac, Domine, in bona voluntate tua Sion, ut aedificentur muri Jerusalem,"* he stopped them and said, "O good Lord, thou knowest that mine intent hath been and yet is, if I might live, to re-edify the walls of Jerusalem." It was the dream with which his father had died, in the Jerusalem chamber at Westminster.

Henry died in the early hours of 31 August 1422. He was aged thirty-five, and had reigned only nine years.

The French whom he chastised, even his enemies who followed the Dauphin, all recognised the exceptional quality of this personality. He had a genius for rule. What impressed them most was his zeal for justice, his desire above all—like St. Louis—to be a just ruler. Chastellain, a bitter critic of the English, said, however, of their King: he was "above all the prince of justice, both in relation to himself, for the sake of example, and in relation to others, according to equity and right. He gave support to none out of favour, nor did he suffer wrong to go unpunished out of regard for kinship."[18]

As to what he left behind him, a cliché of the historians is for once in place: it was a *damnosa hereditas*.

CHAPTER V
A Child-King: Henry VI

"The sudden removal of this powerful regal will," says a recent historian of Henry V's death, "is the dominating fact of English history in the Lancastrian period."[1] It was, indeed, for the next four decades. We may even say that had it not been for Henry V's early death the Lancastrian house would not have come to an end, as it did, nor would his son's reign have broken down in a welter of chaos brought on by the defeat and extrusion of the English at length from France, the attempt to carry Henry's impossible legacy abroad. Only that dominating powerful will, with all the aura surrounding his personality, could have kept it going, perhaps for a full lifetime. Even so, we cannot believe that English rule in France could have continued beyond that, contrary to the whole contemporary trends of history.

The Hundred Years' War itself had sharpened the antagonism between French and English, encouraged and nourished their respective nationalisms. They were caught now in a tangled web of mutual hostilities, memories of ill-doings on either side, recriminations, insults, dislike; each side would grow its own popular myth, with its heroes and fables—Agincourt and Orléans, Henry V and Joan of Arc, fighting Talbot with whose name French peasants frightened their children to bed and who still remained a hero to the Elizabethans, and on the other side brave Dunois and La Hire. Henceforth they were two peoples. Henry V's great ambition may have been "to settle once for all the question of France." It was hubristic of him, and also ignorant of the irresistible tides of history, to think that he could. It was an idea already out of date, if he had known it—France was France (that was what Joan of Arc saw with the simplicity of genius) and England England. However, as our historian soberly observes, "to the fifteenth century the inducement of immediate gain by successful warfare was always more compelling than remoter considerations of economic security or political achievement."

The extraordinary thing was that Henry V's legacy, the English dominion in France, held together as long as it did. That was in part tribute to the influence of the "powerful regal will" continuing after the death of the man—people felt themselves to some extent bound by his will, attempted to carry out his deathbed instructions and realise his intentions. (The will itself was much cited in the disputes that grew round Gloucester as Protector.) Still more, the English maintained their hold as long as the divisions within France continued and the Anglo-Burgundian alliance held good. *That* was the condition of English rule; when the alliance came to an end, and Burgundy made peace with the Dauphin (Charles VII), as came about in 1435—twenty years after Agincourt, it served notice on the English to quit.

It took them a long time, even after this, to realise fully that the game was up. And then, as the result of the exacerbated faction—fighting within England, all was lost. The consequences of Henry V's legacy were probably worse for England, in the long run, than they were for France.

The terms of Henry's will were, as we have seen, contingent and left scope for flexibility and manoeuvre. Bedford had precedence and remained in France, carrying on the endless war and governing in the name of Henry VI, until he died, only forty-six, in 1435. (This year was the decisive turning-point.) When Bedford visited England, which he did only for brief periods to compose growing dissensions, he took precedence. Meanwhile Gloucester was accepted by the Council as Protector, but with limited powers; the real authority lay, during the King's minority, with the lords spiritual and temporal, assembled either in Council or in Parliament. Parliamentary sanction was given to the arrangement and, little as Gloucester liked it, he accepted it in 1422 and that governed the situation. Until the King came of age it was really to be government by Council, with Gloucester enjoying precedence and such power as he could muster.

This led, as anyone could have foretold, to a power-struggle between Gloucester and his opponents. (The facts of power in politics do not in essence change from age to age—it is like the struggle for power that ensued upon the death of Stalin, or, for that matter, of Julius Caesar, with whom Henry V was in his own time compared.) Gloucester naturally fancied a strong prerogative and would have liked to exercise it; he was a Renaissance type with Italianate ideas—and a flavouring of Italianate culture; he preferred the Roman civil law to English common law, with its statutory limitations. But Gloucester's greatest limitations were his defects of character. He was irresponsible and self-seeking; he really had no idea of statesmanship, even his own personal career was wrecked by the sheer incompatibility of his aims. He contributed, as much as in him lay, to wrecking the alliance with Burgundy, and found compensation in the jingoism of the London mob—with whom, of course, he was always popular.

Gloucester's uncle, Bishop Beaufort—the child-king's great-uncle, was not only the brains of the Lancastrian house, but his financial ability and statesmanship were its chief support. Always, therefore, unpopular with the mob, and not much liked as a man. He was too able, to please other people; he was certainly ambitious and anxious to exercise power—as who, in his situation, would not be? In fact he represented the constitutional, English conception of government, in keeping with law and custom and representing, as far as possible, the bulk of the governing class, the lords spiritual and temporal, the knights, the Commons in Parliament. At the crisis of Gloucester's duel with his uncle in 1432, against whose massive figure he developed a perfect fixation, it was Parliament that supported Beaufort and saw him through, though at a price.

For Beaufort had a weakness in his position. Checkmated by his nephew in 1426, he accepted from Martin V the cardinalate which Henry V had refused to allow him to accept earlier and went off to preach the Crusade against the Hussites of Bohemia. It may be that, like Wolsey later, Beaufort had his eye on the papacy. When he returned Gloucester managed to defeat the exercise of the Cardinal's legatine commission—a foreign jurisdiction always unpopular in England, until Henry VIII put an end to such things for good and all. Martin V's aim was to use Beaufort, as later he brought pressure on Archbishop Chichele, to repeal the anti-papal statute of Provisors. In spite of the weakness of a royal minority the English would not have this. Beaufort's cardinalate made him an international figure with a European outlook, fortified by the marriage alliances of the Lancastrian house—Philip of Burgundy, for instance, was married to Beaufort's niece, Isabella of Portugal. Nevertheless, the real basis of his strength (like Wolsey's) was England, not Rome; in the end this prevailed, and with it his policy, which was in keeping with the interests of the country, against Gloucester's volatile jingoism. Beaufort's financial support proved indispensable to the conduct of the war in France, though himself came to favour a peace-policy. As the light-headed Duke declined so the weighty prelate enjoyed more and more power—until death claimed them both, after a duel lasting a quarter of a century, at about the same time in 1447.

What of the infant-king, in whose name and under whose formal auspices many of these scufflings and manoeuvres took place?

Henry was only nine months old when his father died, and was immediately proclaimed king. Two months later, 21 October 1422, his grandfather Charles VI died and Henry was proclaimed King of France. The child was normal enough in his early years and gave no promise of the fatal psychotic legacy he inherited from his grandfather and the talented, but neurotic and unstable Valois. In November 1423, a child of nearly two, he was brought to Parliament and shown to his future subjects. On the 14th, when the Court was leaving Staines, he "shrieked and cried and sprang," so that the day's journey was given up.[2] However, a couple of days later he was conveyed to London and made a public entry in his mother's "chair" seated in her lap. On 18 November he was taken into Parliament at Westminster and received an address. Next year Dame Alice Butler succeeded as his nurse, with "license to chastise us reasonably from time to time." We know that he was chastised a good deal as a boy—on the old English principle of "Spare the rod and spoil the child"—and that he was spirited enough to resent it.

Next year, in April 1425, he made a public appearance at St. Paul's, "led upon his feet between the lord Protector [Gloucester] and the Duke of Exeter unto the choir, whence he was borne to the high altar."[3] Afterwards he was "set upon a fair courser and so conveyed through Cheap and the other streets of the City."

Several times during the Parliament of that year the small child kept state within the Parliament chamber at Westminster. Next year he himself opened Parliament at Leicester, for which Bedford had been summoned home to allay the dissensions between Gloucester and Beaufort—the Duke virtually winning this first round against his uncle. Bedford dubbed the boy-king a knight, who in turn dubbed a number of young nobles. He kept the Christmas and New Year at Eltham, where among his presents were some coral beads that had belonged to Edward III (Henry in time became a good bedesman); among the games were the interludes of Jack Travaill and his companions, and there were portable organs to play.

The Council ordered that the young lords who were Crown wards should come to Court to be brought up with the boy-king. In May 1428 the grand Richard Beauchamp, Earl of Warwick, became Henry's governor, instructed to "teach him to love, worship and dread God, draw him to virtue by ways and means convenable, laying before him examples of God's grace to virtuous kings and the contrary fortune of kings of the contrary disposition." Henry grew up to be one of the most virtuous kings there have ever been, but that did not save him from a frightful fate, for he was no good as a king. Warwick was further to "teach him nurture, literature, language and other manner of cunning [kenning, or knowledge: Henry had regrettably no cunning in the modern, pejorative sense of the word], to chastise him when he doth amiss, and to remove persons not behoveful nor expedient from his presence."

He grew up to be quite well educated in French and Latin and was versed in history, his favourite study after the scriptures. Piety was indeed his foible; though he sometimes diverted himself with hawking and hunting, he preferred religious exercises. He would have been best off as a churchman, for that was where his heart really was—though even here not as a busy administrative bishop but a quiet contemplative, a monk. His most active intellectual interest was education, and with his grand foundations of Eton and King's he did more good for his country than many more successful monarchs as such. He took little enough interest in government, once he had grown up. He was more content to be a passive spectator of the exciting, deadly—and, it must be admitted, sometimes lunatic—game of politics, more lunatic than he. For, as the chronicler Hall correctly said, he was "neither a fool, nor very wise."

Perhaps we shall not do his memory an injustice if we describe him as "soft." He was merciful—and this was an almost useless quality in a king, whose duty it was to keep order in a tough, rough society. His confessor and biographer, Blackman, gives instances of his weakness towards transgressors, "and this is plain in the case of many to whom he was exceeding gracious and merciful; for he was become an imitator of Him who saith, 'I will have mercy.'"[4] He was also humble—this too was a mistake in a king, whose business it was to repress the high and mighty. Blackman describes his "humility in his bearing, in his clothes and other apparel of his body, in his speech and many other parts of his outward behaviour." He dressed very soberly, in a sad-coloured long cloak and round cape, "like a townsman"; instead of the long pointed shoes of his courtiers, he wore "round shoes like a rustic." It was absurd; he must have presented a ludicrous figure—when outward pomp was expected in a monarch, and was in itself an *instrumentum regni,* as Elizabeth I so well understood. When he had to don his robes of state for some state-occasion, he atoned for the sin by wearing a hair-shirt underneath. He was too good for this world; in the end he was put out of it.

Of his physical appearance we know that he was tall and slender, of no muscular strength, though his limbs were all right, and that the benevolence of his disposition shone in his face. This may mean that he looked a little daft, for in his portraits he looks weak about the chin. In 1453, when he was thirty-two, he had a complete and total breakdown, physical and mental, which lasted for some eighteen months until the beginning of 1455. At the end of that year he had a second breakdown, which lasted for three months; this time he was not completely prostrated but able to transact a little business. After the victory of the Yorkists and his imprisonment in the Tower he sank into melancholy decrepitude, though not permanently bereft of his senses. Sometimes he came to and said something to the point, as in the pathetic reply he made when reproached with usurping the crown: "My father was king of England, and peacefully possessed the crown for the whole of his life. His father, my grandfather, was king before him. And I, a boy, crowned almost in my cradle, was accepted as king by the whole realm, and wore the crown for nearly forty years, every lord swearing homage and fealty to me, as they had done to my forefathers."[5]

His trouble was not so much that he was a Lancastrian as that he was a Valois.

His mother, Catherine of Valois, had her jointure as queen to live on; Baynard's Castle was set aside for her London residence. The child-king was mainly at Windsor, Westminster, Berkhampstead or Eltham in winter, Wallingford or Hertford in summer. The queen-mother had her own household separate from her son's, and as Henry grew into boyhood they were more apart. In 1428 Gloucester promoted an act of Parliament prohibiting any person from marrying the queen-dowager without the consent of king and Council. This may have been intended to prevent her marrying Edmund Beaufort, the able soldier whom she is said to have fancied: that would have meant an accession of influence to the Beauforts whom Gloucester detested. There could be no such objection to her taking up with Owen Tudor, a mere squire of the late king who was now clerk of her wardrobe. This was a convenient post for rising at Court—as Richard Cecil, Burghley's father, found with Henry VIII. But the Tudors rose even higher than the Cecils, through Owen Tudor's affair with the Queen. It was kept very quiet, and no one knows when they were married. That they were married admits of no doubt, for the legitimacy of their children was not questioned, and they were recognised by their half-brother, Henry VI, who was very strict about such things.

It was not until Catherine retired to Bermondsey Abbey, perhaps for a childbirth, in 1436 and died there 3 January 1437—she was thirty-five, the same age as Henry V—that her second family came before the light of day. By Owen Tudor she had had three sons and a daughter. Two of these sons became important in history. The elder, Edmund Tudor, married Lady Margaret Beaufort, daughter of John Beaufort, Edmund's brother. Thus the Valois blood did come together with the Beaufort—the royal line of France with that of England—through the active agency of a Welsh Tudor, to produce Henry VII. Catherine's second son, Jasper, made it the chief care of his life to look after his young nephew, Henry Tudor, upon whom the hopes of the Lancastrian house came to rest.

Meanwhile the grandfather, Owen Tudor, was whisked off to Newgate in 1437, when his misdemeanour in marrying a queen was discovered. Thence he escaped to Wales, while his sons were placed in charge of Catherine de la Pole, abbess of Barking, and were well brought up, educated by priests. In time to come they were nobly provided for and made Earls of Richmond and Pembroke respectively by their half-brother, the King. Owen went back to live prosperously in Wales, remaining always faithful to the Lancastrian house, with which he had come into such unprecedented proximity, and for which he laid down his life after Mortimer's Cross, in the market-place at Hereford.

But this is to anticipate. We must go back to the conduct of affairs at the beginning of the child-king's reign, with Humphrey Duke of Gloucester as Protector. Jacqueline, Countess of Hainault and Holland in her own right, had taken refuge in England from her husband, to whom she was doubtfully married and with whom she was at loggerheads. This was the Duke of Brabant, who proposed to make his cousin Burgundy the heir to her territories. Gloucester, without much reflection, leaped at the chance of gaining a principality for himself, and married her. He proceeded to raise a force of some four thousand troops with which he and Jacqueline descended upon Hainault, to the indignation of Burgundy, who thereupon made a temporary truce with the Dauphin to chase them out. Contrast the behaviour of Bedford, who was doing everything to keep the Anglo-Burgundian alliance together, at this moment marrying Burgundy's sister to this end.

Gloucester's expedition was a complete fiasco, and therefore did not do as much damage with Burgundy as might have been expected—after all, it was all in the family. On its failure he ceased to be interested in Jacqueline and deserted her for her lady-in-waiting, Eleanor Cobham, with whom he had fallen in love. Some years later, when a papal decree conveniently freed him from Jacqueline, he married Eleanor, who had been living with him as his mistress. To marry her was thought worse than keeping her as a concubine and it certainly created more scandal:

from it arose "shame and more disgrace and inconvenience to the whole kingdom than can be expressed," says a contemporary chronicler.[6] However, Gloucester jogged along happily enough with her, until, towards the end of his life, the silly woman's dealings with sorcery—hoping to learn whether she would become queen—got him into more trouble than even Jacqueline had done.

While Gloucester was away in the Netherlands, Beaufort had taken the lead in the Council and governed the country. One observes the contrast between Beaufort, constantly raising money for the purposes of the state, and his nephew as constantly demanding increases of salary for his services as Protector or loans for building his palace of Placentia at Greenwich—in time to become a favourite residence with all the Tudors. On his return Gloucester was able to recoup himself with the custody of the vast inheritance of the Earl of March during the minority of his heir. March's illegitimate cousin, Sir John Mortimer, had been put in the Tower before Henry V's death on suspicion of treason. In 1423 he attempted to escape to Wales to incite a rising to place March on the throne—that old theme. It was a hare-brained scheme, and, as we have seen, March—though the second of his line to be heir-presumptive to Richard II—always abided by the country's decision in 1399 and was loyal to the Lancastrian house. However, he was ordered to his government in Ireland, where he died of plague in 1425. His heir was his sister's son, young Richard of York, to whom now came the vast inheritance of the earldom of March, in addition to the extensive domains of the house of York. It remained to be seen whether, when he grew up, he would be so quiescent about the claim of the senior line of descent to the throne as his uncle March had been.

In France during these years, 1424–26, the dynamic of Henry V's conquest continued, the co-operation with Burgundy to which Bedford adhered at all costs held, and the English dominion reached its fullest extent. Under the Treaty of Troyes the Anglo-French dual monarchy was to conquer the areas still in the possession of the Dauphin. Though the Dauphin was in control of most of Central and Southern France, a larger area, the territories under English control owning the allegiance of Henry VI were richer and better placed strategically. In 1423 the Dauphin

raised a new army with a strong Scottish contingent—surplus population from the hills and braes—and invested a key Burgundian
town, Cravant, the capture of which would enable him to link up
with his eastern supporters in Champagne. Bedford moved to the
rescue and wiped out the Dauphin's force.

Closely co-operating with Burgundy, Bedford felt able to move
next year over to the offensive and complete the conquest of Maine
and Anjou, reducing the territories north of the Loire. The Dauphin had collected a large army of some fifteen thousand, including considerable contingents of Scots and Italian mercenaries. The
older French leaders, who had learned from bitter experience, were
anxious to avoid a pitched battle; but the younger men with the
Scots were determined to push forward to the Norman border
where they encountered Bedford. Bedford, cool and deliberate, was
so confident that he sent away his Burgundian contingent for mopping-up operations, and proceeded to inflict a disaster on the
French at Verneuil after the conventional Agincourt pattern. The
losses fell hardest on the Scots, who were wiped out as a fighting
force, some five thousand of them. But the French lost their leaders—the Duke of Aumâle, the Counts of Narbonne, Ventadour
and Tonnerre killed, the Duke of Alençon and Marshal Lafayette
prisoners—as well as some fifteen hundred men.

"At this moment an advance on Bourges might have given the
best hope of ending the war."[7] There was the Dauphin's capital,
the strategic centre of his power. But Bedford was intent on finishing the conquest of Maine and Anjou, reducing everything north
of the Loire first. Then, in December 1425, he was summoned
back to England to deal with the crisis that had been reached
in the disputes between Gloucester and Beaufort, and there Bedford was forced to remain until March 1427. The chance of ending
the war on English terms was lost for good.

> There is a tide in the affairs of men
> Which, taken at the flood, leads on to fortune;
> Omitted, all the voyage of their life
> Is bound in shallows and in miseries. . . .

The English in France were now to experience the shallows and
the miseries.

The turning-point did not come at once, but with the siege of

Orléans, October 1428 to May 1429, which had been undertaken against Bedford's advice and at which Joan of Arc, incarnation of the spirit of resistance in the French people, made her apparition. For it seemed both to French and English alike more of an apparition than any ordinary appearance—this peasant-girl who dressed in soldier's clothes, who was without the weakness of her sex or indeed any sex at all, who regularly had visions of the saints and heard their voices, by which she lived, and was convinced that she was commanded by God to deliver the Dauphin, conduct him to be crowned at Rheims as King of France and send the English back to their own country. Her first success was in convincing the Dauphin that he was the true Heir of France, for his mother, Queen Isabel, had been no better than she should be and herself sown the seeds of doubt as to his paternity in her son's mind. Joan of Arc, once she penetrated to the Dauphin's presence, convinced him by some secret sign which she would never divulge, even under extreme pressure later.

She undoubtedly possessed extraordinary telepathic powers, with the magnetism of a saintly personality and all the power of a dedicated person with everything trained on one end in view. We have seen the astonishing results this kind of concentration could achieve, in a normal person, with Henry V; we are now to observe the less astonishing—for, after all, Henry had achieved the conquest of France against the direction history was to go; Joan of Arc was working with the course of history, it was in the logic of events that the English would be driven out of France. And hers was an abnormal personality, "a sexless woman, not as other women are"—as the Victorian historian says, and we might add, nor men either—"but subject to peculiar hysterical affections."[8] We understand the phenomena of psychosis, of abnormal psychological types, better nowadays. To her, her visions and voices had an absolute, an unquestioned, objective reality. They were, of course, the objectivisations of the inner promptings that came naturally, but exceptionally, to an exceptional temperament, a solitary peasant-girl brooding on the intolerable wrongs of France at Domrémy in Lorraine, border country torn between both sides, a location where they could be felt more acutely.

Then, too, hers was an activist spirit: she could not understand

the incomprehensible hesitations and doubts of politics. That gave
her power—power over other people, power to command.

> *Jehanne, de bonne heure née,*
> *Béni soit cil qui te créa!*
> *Pucelle de Dieu ordonnée,*
> *En qui le Saint-Esprit réa*
> *Sa grande grace. . . .*

So long as that power held, and so long as she was successful, her
spell held good—and its potency for her own side and for the
enemy alike. Nothing succeeds like success. Her motto might
equally have been *"De l'audace, et encore de l'audace, et toujours
de l'audace,"* like that other insurrectionary spirit inciting France
to victory centuries later. But the moment she failed, or was checkmated, her spell was broken. This was why it became a prime
necessity to the English, militarily and politically, to destroy her.

So often in the course of the war the Dauphin had failed to
come to the relief of his cities being besieged by the English.
Now, at the nadir of his cause, the Dauphin accepted Joan's mission and was impelled to undertake the relief of Orléans. She
managed to get inside the city, and early in May led an attack on
the fort of St. Loup outside. "The capture of the fort of St. Loup
was the turning-point of the siege and in a sense of the whole
war."[9] It stayed the rot—of confidence among the French. Nevertheless Joan nearly ended her mission at her next venture by her
rashness and precipitancy. It needed a tried soldier, Gilles de Rais,
to persuade her against a frontal attack on the English position
in favour of the detached forts of the Augustins and the Tourelles.
These were captured. No matter that the English were badly
outnumbered: it worked like magic. It was the moral impact that
counted: the English raised the siege and marched away. A thrill
passed through the Dauphin's France—he even began to believe
in his own cause. Bedford said later that the adversity of the
English in France all went back to the unlucky siege of Orléans,
"taken in hand, God knoweth by what advice."[10]

Joan's instinct for keeping the initiative, giving the enemy no
time and no rest, enabled her to rush the English out of Jargeau
and Beaugency in June. She then came up with an English force at
Patay; true, they were very inferior in numbers—as they had been

at Agincourt—but this time the French used their numbers to overwhelm their opponents. It was really Joan's battle: she had forced it on the reluctant Alençon. The English casualties were very heavy, and among the prisoners was the commander, the famous fighting Talbot. Sir John Fastolf, with the main body, managed to get away—hence the report of his cowardice, undeserved in fact, but which became a leading characteristic in the character of Falstaff.

Joan was now able to achieve the consummation of her desire: the way to Rheims was clear and thither she accompanied the Dauphin for his coronation, standing beside him at the altar with the sacred banner that had brought her victory, *Ou Nom Dé* (In the name of God). It was a great act of state, in medieval terms, for now Charles VII really was the crowned and anointed King of France; it was an act in complete defiance of the Treaty of Troyes, which Bedford regarded as a permanent settlement. It served notice on the English, and it undermined the status and confidence of the Burgundians, for the Duke of Burgundy was a liege man of the King of France.

Who was the King of France now, the child Henry VI or his adult uncle, Charles VII?

Joan of Arc's instinct was to settle the question by an attack on Paris, the Anglo-Burgundian capital. But she was not allowed to strike while the iron was hot. The French command, in particular her opponent La Trémouille, wasted its time on truces while "French national feeling was kindling in all directions: a breath would have fanned the sparks into general conflagration."[11] She could not get the French leaders to move on Paris till too late, then the attack was mismanaged and she herself was wounded. "The Maid, at last, had failed in an undertaking, and that was just what La Trémouille wanted." He took the army back south of the Loire and disbanded it for the winter. The incomparable value of her inspiration and leadership at critical moments was lost. "Those jealous of her authority and prestige would give her no chance";[12] they kept her in gilded inaction among the intrigues of the Court, until she felt the virtue and the power were going out of her. Her "voices," i.e., her intuition, told her that her career was coming to a close.

With the spring she leaped into action on her own, ill sup-

8

ported by the people whose cause she had saved. Compiègne was being besieged by the Burgundians. She entered it on 24 May 1430, and that afternoon led a sortie against the central position of the besiegers; her force was pressed back, with her fighting heroically in the rear, until she was surrounded and taken. The English were exultant at the capture of the witch. But the Burgundians had taken her: the Duke wrote agreeably to his friends that now the delusion of the Pucelle (the Maid) might be considered at an end. He expressed himself "more delighted than if a king had fallen into his hands." She was certainly worth a king's ransom. No move came from the miserable Court of Charles VII to ransom her. She was sold for ten thousand gold crowns to the English, who were glad to pay it.

It was a matter of supreme importance to them to arrest the tide that she had set going. How to account for the reverses that had been inflicted on troops victorious all the way from Agincourt to Verneuil? How to answer her triumphant conducting of the doubtful Dauphin to his sacring at Rheims as rightful King of France? The answer was to be the coronation of Henry VI, grandson of Charles VI, as King of France, and the public trial of Joan, given the widest reverberation possible, as a heretic and a witch. The reverberation has gone on ever since.

As a counter-move to the crucial event at Rheims the Council in France had pressed for Henry's coronation in England. This had taken place at Westminster, in the presence of Parliament, 6 November 1429. It was a clear and bright day; the child of eight was led by his governor, Warwick, to the high scaffold set up for him in the Abbey, where he sat "beholding the people all about sadly and wisely" and attending the service, as always, with great "humility and devotion."[13] With the spring he moved to Canterbury and on St. George's Day, 23 April 1430, he crossed the Channel to Calais in the care of Cardinal Beaufort. Later in the summer he was brought to Rouen, where he was present next year during the trial of Joan, himself as innocent as the Maid. There all the vultures were gathering.

Her friend the Archbishop of Rheims had accepted her capture piously as a judgment on her obstinacy and self-will. He was able to console the French Court with the news that an adequate successor had been found in a shepherd-boy—the idiot lad Guil-

laume le Patourel—who said "more or less" what Joan had said.
The learned University of Paris was of the opinion that she was a
disseminator of pernicious errors. The Vicar-General of the In-
quisition demanded that she be handed over to the care of the
Holy Office. The Bishop of Beauvais, on the ground that she had
been apprehended within his diocese, wished to have the honour
of constituting the court. Among his assessors were three of the
most eminent authorities from the Sorbonne.

There was no one to defend the peasant-girl.

Except for her native shrewdness, she was easy prey. She had
no wish to deny, she insisted that she "had seen St. Michael and his
angels as clearly as she saw her judges there"; she had not only
seen St. Catherine and St. Margaret but embraced them both and
felt the warmth of their flesh.[14] (For men she was without sex.)
They spoke French, good French, certainly not English. Certainly
she heard her voices—they were always with her at times of crisis,
telling her what to do. These phenomena went back to when she
was thirteen—evidently to puberty—and were first experienced
after a day of fasting. There was no denying her assumption of
men's attire (it is an offence in England today for men to wear
women's clothes, though not for women to wear men's)—her motive was obvious enough: convenience and self-defence, though it
might well have had other unconscious implications. During her
imprisonment attempts on her virtue were made by her keepers;
she had no trouble in resisting them.

Shrewd and spirited as her defence was, all these clever men
had no compunction in enticing her on to dangerous ground in-
tellectually—the distinction between the Church Militant on earth
and the Church Triumphant in heaven. Joan leaped into the trap:
her commission had come from God, she could only submit to the
authority of God. *"Je me actens à Dieu mon créateur de tout;
je l'ayme de tout mon coeur."* At this she was threatened with
torture, the instruments of torture exhibited to her. The articles of
her condemnation, with the learned opinions of the University of
Paris, were read over to her. "If she saw the faggots laid and
the torch ready she could say nothing else."

Offers were made to her to recant. The purpose of these was
obvious: a recantation would tell against the sacring at Rheims;
and anyone who relapsed after recanting could be burned with

satisfaction. On 24 May 1431 she was to be sentenced. A grand stage was set in the churchyard of St. Ouen: a platform for Cardinal Beaufort in his scarlet and three bishops; Joan alone and exposed on a scaffold opposite. She was preached at in a long discourse; confused by all these learned and good men, her certainty failed her. When the Bishop of Beauvais as judge was about to give sentence, she faltered and signed a recantation of her sins and false impostures. Remanded to gaol, she put on female garb.

Then her confidence returned to her. Her men's attire had been left in her cell, as a temptation; she resumed it. Her voices—her inner promptings—returned and reproached her for denying them to save her life. It was "treason" they told her: how could she deny that God had sent her when he had sent her?

She was a relapsed heretic now. She was taken to the Old Market, to be preached at once more and delivered to the flames. She asked for a crucifix to be held before her eyes: this was the only mercy. At the end she called on God and his saints to help her. No God came to her help. Her ashes were carefully collected and thrown into the Seine so that there should not be any mistake.

But it seems that the infallible Church had made a mistake. For, five hundred years later, when the poor heretic was turned into a saint, "evidence" was collected to show that her "voices" had been from God, after all, and not from the devil. The one pronouncement was as silly as the other.

If any human being ever was a saint, this poor peasant-girl was. One can only conclude from her story, though not from that alone, that people's convictions in the realm where there can be no certainty are apt to be at once the silliest and the cruellest thing about them.

The elimination of Joan was a great gain to the English; the situation in the field improved and a number of towns were recovered. In one skirmish the celebrated Poton de Xaintrailles was captured along with the idiot shepherd-boy the French thought a sufficient substitute for Joan of Arc. The road to Paris was at least clear, that to Rheims was not. So Bedford decided to have his nephew crowned at Notre Dame. The boy-king made his entry into Paris by the Porte St. Denis on Advent Sunday, 2 December

1431. A grand retinue of England attended him: Beaufort, Bedford and the young Duke Richard of York, the famous warriors Warwick and Salisbury, a bevy of bishops. The nobility of France were conspicuous by their absence. His reception by the city was hearty enough, for the sympathies of the populace were Burgundian. On his way past the Hôtel de St. Pol, Henry exchanged salutations with his notorious grandmother, Queen Isabel, who had been one of the chief instruments in making the Treaty of Troyes, by which he was there.

For the rest, the whole affair was English. Cardinal Beaufort crowned the boy in Notre Dame, 16 December. The event was not popularly managed; the state banquet was rather poor, and anyway rushed by the mob. There was no largesse—the occupation of France was too expensive—and not even the customary amnesty. The mercurial Parisians were displeased.

Henry returned to England early in 1432 to witness a new attack by Gloucester on his uncle, the Cardinal. The most important result of Henry's coronation had been to end Gloucester's Protectorate and his precedence in Council. Government came fully into Beaufort's more capable hands. This was more than Gloucester could stand; he called in the Crown lawyers to build up a strong case, based on precedents, against Beaufort presuming to act as a cardinal in England. Archbishops of Canterbury had had to resign their see on accepting the cardinalate; ought not Beaufort to resign Winchester? Beaufort appealed to Parliament which met in May, and the issue was thrashed out in the presence of the King. Finally the Cardinal was exonerated, but again at a price: he had to buy himself out with another loan for the purposes of government. We are told that at this time "the English government could in fact have gone on paying its way had it not been for the war, which could not be made to pay for itself."[15]

Warwick found that the boy-king now—he was not yet eleven —was "grown in years, in stature of his person, and also in conceit [understanding] and knowledge of his royal estate, the which cause him to grudge with chastising."[16] In his private circle "he hath been stirred by some from his learning, and spoken to of divers matters not behoveful." On Henry's next visit to London, therefore, the Council appeared before him to admonish him. From Christmas 1433 to Easter 1434 the boy paid a long visit to

Bury St. Edmund's, one of the grandest of English foundations—
a century later, just before its fall, Leland described it as a shining
city. It must have looked rather like Ely, with an immense nexus
of monastic buildings within those precinct-walls of East Anglian
flint and stone that still remain. Henry was admitted to the fra-
ternity and ever after it became a favourite resort with him in
the troubles of his life. It offered peace and quiet, meditation and
contemplation, in place of the self-seeking and jostling for position
of politics, the personal feuds and jealousies, the ulcerated hatreds.

Once more, on Bedford's last visit to England, the boy-king
had to intervene in a quarrel raised by Humphrey of Gloucester—
this time against his brother Bedford. It seems that Gloucester
expressed himself dissatisfied with Bedford's conduct of the war in
France. And this, Bedford, conscious that he had done his best,
much resented. Things were not going well in France. The Burgundians were opting out of the war, by a series of truces. Soon
the English would find themselves isolated, having to carry the
burden alone. In 1432 Bedford's wife, Burgundy's sister, had died
leaving no children—a link broken. Bedford, thinking always of
political duty, and anxious to shore himself up within the Burgundian alliance, then married Jacqueline of Luxemburg, of a
powerful Burgundian house. By thus doing he offended Duke
Philip, whom the Luxemburgs had not consulted. It is probable
that Philip was determined to be offended anyway: he was looking
for a way out of the war, without losing face—after all, he was a
signatory of the Treaty of Troyes.

In April 1434 Henry had had to preside over a Council at which
charges and counter-charges were made by his uncles against each
other—Gloucester, with his flair for popularity, making the easy
appeal to the jingoistic sentiments of people for a more aggressive
prosecution of the war. In the end the boy intervened as king to
declare both charges and counter-charges null and void, that there
was no prejudice to the honour of either Duke, and they both had
his confidence and affection. Later on, Henry's transparent honesty
and sincerity did give him considerable and unexpected successes
as a peacemaker. But now, only a youth, it may have gone to his
head. Gloucester, a perpetual nuisance, encouraged him to take a
precocious interest in mere politics. At the end of this year the
Council admonished him again, reading him a solemn warning

that he was not yet endowed with so great knowledge and discretion as to be able to decide in matters of difficulty, or to change the governance appointed for his tender age. Shortly there would be a change, when the wise Warwick went overseas to fill Bedford's place. Warwick had brought him up virtuously and well, had taught him the use of arms as well as looked after his education. We hear of "the little harness that the Earl of Warwick made for the King ere he went over the sea, garnished with gold."

It was sad that Bedford left England for the last time in these circumstances. He must have realised the ultimate hopelessness of the position in France he was pledged to maintain. The keystone of the Troyes settlement was the English claim it recognised to the French throne. The English could have had a perfectly good peace at any time, but for that. The French offers were generous: an increase of territory in Guienne, and possibly elsewhere, provided they were held from the French Crown, a large indemnity, a marriage-alliance. But Bedford would never give way on the fundamental point of the Treaty of Troyes, nor would the English Council. It may not be sufficiently realised that they could not, that they dared not. They would have been giving away the rights of their king. When he came of age they might have been held responsible with their lives for such a treason; even if the King himself did not exact the penalty, they would always have been open to the fatal charge at the hands of any opponents, at any turn in the political game. No one could take the responsibility, except the King himself. Here was one of the dire consequences of a royal minority.

In this impasse Philip of Burgundy, who had given up his earlier hope of dismembering France, decided to come to terms. At a meeting at Nevers in 1435 the terms essentially were worked out. What was not yet worked out was how his face was to be saved. For he had sworn a solemn oath to maintain the Troyes settlement, and there now ensued a warfare of political tracts— as inane as usual—as to his ethical obligations, the pros and cons, pro-Burgundian, pro-French, anti-one or the other, calling on the law of Nature, the law of God and other such useful concepts. For Burgundy there was a choice of ways out of his dilemma: a general peace-conference and, if that failed, a resort to the papacy, which could usually be relied on to absolve from inconvenient oaths, or obligations which had lost their force.

At this juncture Bedford died, in the castle at Rouen, on 15 September 1435. His long labours were at an end; he must have known that all had been ultimately in vain. Though he had not possessed his formidable brother's genius nor enjoyed his irresistible prestige, he had done his best to uphold his achievement. Clear-sighted and prudent, brave, patient and enduring, he had firm judgment, was a moderate man and never seems to have made a mistake that we can point to. In his administration of conquered France he was anxious to content the people at large; in Paris he was popular enough; he was particularly attentive to the necessity of knitting Normandy to England by mutual interest and good rule. It was not his fault if the exigencies of war ruined his hopes. He was a good man; his whole character was expressed in his motto, *A vous entière.*

Not the least of the ill consequences of his death was that it left the dreadful Humphrey now heir-presumptive to the throne.

Burgundy achieved his object in bringing about the peace-conference at Arras in July 1435 under the mediation of the papacy. The English sent a strong delegation under the Archbishop of York. Beaufort went, too, as an ambassador holding a watching brief; it seems that it was his part to try and salvage the Anglo-Burgundian alliance. "Both his country's and his own position were at stake: if the negotiations failed and Burgundy made a pact with France, part of the onus for failure would be laid to his account; far more important was the potential loss of the English conquest."[17] But the Duke of Burgundy had made up his mind to return to his place in the French royal house and look elsewhere for expansion. Faced with this extreme danger the English delegation was still not able to yield the claim to the French throne in order to reach a permanent settlement with France. All they could offer was a truce until Henry VI came of age, when he could settle for himself.

That was really the end of the matter. Philip drew his own conclusions, and most of the time of the papal mediators was taken up in saving his face for him. "In this they acted . . . as representatives of the highest ecclesiastical powers, who had commanded him to make peace with France, having declared that his oaths to the English were no longer binding." Of course these ecclesiastics were able to cite a lot of learned lawyers and casuists in support.

The total failure of the conference from the English point of view, its complete success from the Franco-Burgundian, had both immediate and far-reaching consequences in England. It led to an explosion of anger at Burgundy's desertion. Beaufort also drew his own conclusions: he realised that England must somehow be extricated from the fatal entanglement of Troyes and that peace needed to be worked for. On Bedford's death the main pillar of the Lancastrian house, the only one with any grasp of statesmanship, Beaufort inevitably became the leader of the peace-party, though without either the full authority or the unanimity of the country to enforce it. The whole issue became fatally caught up in the sinister dialectic of faction fighting and party struggle, and in the event all was lost. As happened in the 1760's and 1770's, which led to the loss of America, and again in the 1930's, which ended in the country itself being nearly lost.

In the 1430's even the mild Henry VI reacted sharply to Burgundy's desertion. He wept.

CHAPTER VI

Richard of York and Margaret of Anjou

At the time of the turning-point of Arras, Richard of York, born in 1411, was twenty-four. He was by far the richest magnate in the country. Ten years before he had succeeded to the vast inheritance of his uncle March—lands in most English counties, though with their main concentration on the Welsh Border, looking to the splendid castle of Ludlow on the Teme. In addition he succeeded to March's earldom of Ulster, with a dominant position in the English Pale, the lordships of Clare, Trim and Connaught. In time to come Ireland would provide a useful, friendly base. Richard was the son of the Earl of Cambridge executed for treason on the eve of the Agincourt expedition. Despite his father's attainder he succeeded to the entailed lands of the earldom. On his uncle's death at Agincourt he succeeded to the dukedom of York.

Such an agglomeration of territory practically equalled the palatinate of Lancaster—one begins to think ominously of Henry of Bolingbroke in 1399. Nobody had forgotten that March was the heir presumptive of Richard II, representative of the senior line of descent from Edward III. And, for the first time in the Mortimer family, this boy had been given the name of Richard, as if to remind them.

It was probably in 1438 that York married Cecily Neville, thus marrying into a powerful and rising clan, energetic, pushing, very much on the way up. It was above all prolific. Cecily's father, Earl of Westmorland, had had by his first marriage two sons and seven daughters, all marrying into noble northern families; by his second wife he had fourteen children, nine sons and five daughters, for whom marriages had to be found. So the Neville blood began to suffuse the peerage—like the Villiers strain in the seventeenth century. This second wife, Cecily's mother, was Joan Beaufort, Gaunt's daughter.

There came to be a severe dispute within the Neville family, for the Beaufort countess managed to swing the bulk of the Neville inheritance to her children, away from the children of the first wife. Later on, we find the clan divided in its sympathies and support between the house of Lancaster and the house of York. The most powerful of the Nevilles, Warwick the Kingmaker, became so not through any inheritance of his own, but through marrying the heiress of Richard Beauchamp, Earl of Warwick, with immense estates in the Midlands. This marriage made the Kingmaker in turn the second richest magnate in the kingdom, and gave him the base from which to earn his nickname. If it was the agglomeration of wealth, power and influence behind York that enabled him to challenge the house of Lancaster, it was the alliance of York and Warwick that enabled them to topple it over.

York got his first great appointment in 1436 as Lieutenant in France, a few months after Bedford's death. He was without experience, and no one could replace Bedford anyway, the sole repository of Henry V's legacy and tradition. The consequences of Arras were already being brought home to the English; it was an unsatisfactory time for everybody, a time of confusion out of which new alignments would come, abroad and at home. In London there was fury at Burgundy's desertion of the alliance, popular demonstrations against the Flemings, the sense of frustration turning jingoistic feeling now against former allies. Humphrey of Gloucester was first and foremost to cash in on this, the wheel of fortune turning his way again for a time. Some indication of the explosion of popular anger can be gathered from the number of poems written in scorn of the Duke of Burgundy, the flyting of the Flemings, and so on.

> O thou Philip, founder of new falsehood,
>   Disturber of peace, captain of cowardice,
> Sower of discord, reproof of all knighthood!

Philip took his opportunity to try and capture Calais. He brought against it a large number of troops, but they were raw levies in a state of insubordination, and shortly they had to retire with contumely. There followed more poems in contempt of the Flemings:

For fear they turned back and hied fast:
My lord of Gloucester made them so aghast
With his coming. . . .

Gloucester did indeed reply with a joyous raid into Flanders, burning and wasting, and returning with a good deal of loot. It can be imagined that these exchanges did nothing to help to solve the fundamental problem of English dominion in France. And before the year was out Paris was lost: Charles VII—that strange, unhappy man, yet with the curious perspicacity and talent of his family—was back in his capital.

York could do nothing about it; it was said that he soon grew weary of his task. It seems that he was dissatisfied with the terms of his appointment, which was costing him too much. He asked to be relieved of his office, and the experienced old campaigner Richard Beauchamp, Earl of Warwick, was sent over in his place. Warwick died at Rouen in 1439, and for a whole year no one was despatched to succeed him, while the English dominion was slowly nibbled away. The delay was almost certainly due to the tug-of-war between Gloucester and the Beauforts, for it looked as if Duke Humphrey would be nominated, then he was replaced by the Cardinal's nephew, Somerset. In the end York was again appointed, on better terms drafted by himself; but he did not go over until 1441.

Negotiations for peace had been going on under Beaufort's auspices since 1439, but with the worsening of the military position with every year that passed the terms became harder. The French were adamant that any territory occupied by the English should owe fealty to the French Crown. Beaufort's strength in the Council and the country was never strong enough to yield on this, against Gloucester and the "patriotic" party. York was now coming into politics under the aegis of Humphrey of Gloucester and taking his line—in time to come he would succeed to Humphrey's position against the embattled, but more pacific, Beauforts. The failure of the negotiations corroborated the Cardinal's view that peace must be made with France, even at the cost of larger concessions, and sealed by a marriage-alliance.

Hence York did not go over to Rouen until 1441, when, with old fighting Talbot, he relieved Pontoise. This was only a temporary relief, for in September it fell finally. Meanwhile the French

were increasing their pressure on Gascony, Charles VII leading
a large army against Bordeaux. The Council in England evidently
had no confidence in York, though they did not dare to recall
him. Instead, they sent over a larger force under Somerset, virtually to supersede him, under the injurious commission that he
was to be "the shield to his said cousin of York . . . he shall be
betwixt him and the adversary."[1] They added insult to injury by
asking York to "take patience and forbear him for a time" for the
£20,000 due to him, which had gone into equipping Somerset's
expedition. To crown all, Somerset accomplished no more than
York had done and returned to England to die in 1445. Henceforth, however, the Beauforts had an enemy in Richard of York.

York came to the front as Gloucester was forced to retreat. In
1441 Gloucester's position was much damaged by the discovery
of his Duchess's dabblings in sorcery—no doubt the orthodox
Beauforts conveniently brought them to light. Henry VI was unmarried, and Eleanor's husband was heir to the throne. The silly
woman got some priests to find out by the black arts "to what
estate in life she should come"—and this had the dangerous implication, in those credulous days, of compassing the death of
the King by witchcraft.[2] She had long used the sorceries of the
Witch of Eye in Suffolk—it was said that it was through her
potions that she had won Humphrey's love. The Duchess, brought
to book, could not deny the evidences of her diabolical traffic.
She was sentenced to several days of penance, walking barefoot
through London with a heavy taper, and then imprisoned for
life. Her companions were either burnt or hanged. A thrill ran
through London, which found its expression, as usual in those
days, in verse:

> All women that in this world are wrought,
>   By me they may ensample take:
> For I that was brought up of nought
>   A prince me chose to be his make [mate]. . . .
>
> I was so high upon the wheel,
>   My own estate I could not know;
> The Gospel accordeth thereto full well:
>   Who will be high, he shall be low.
>   Who may the wheel of fortune trow? . . .[3]

Or another poem with its glance at Humphrey:

> Thy lady was so proud and high of heart
> That she herself thought peerless of estate,
> And yet higher fain she would have start,
> But suddenly she fell, as was her fate.[4]

It all helped to settle Humphrey's hash as a politician.

With Humphrey checkmated and the Cardinal retiring, a new generation was coming to the fore. The leadership of the peace-party was seized by William de la Pole, Earl of Suffolk, grandson of Richard II's friend, who had been proscribed by the Appellants and died abroad. William's father had thrown in his lot with the victorious Lancastrians and died at Harfleur, the eldest son was killed at Agincourt. Succeeding his brother as earl, Suffolk married Alice Chaucer, grand-daughter of the poet, whose splendid tomb we see in her chantry chapel at Ewelme, with the wheels of her Rouet mother, sister of Catherine Swinford. Thus Suffolk was closely connected by marriage with the Beauforts; he became the active, impetuous leader of their peace-party.

Suffolk had spent seventeen years fighting in France, so he knew the situation there well. He was convinced that there was nothing for it but peace; though in his objective he was right, this was not the best frame of mind in which to obtain the best terms. On his return to England he had been given the custody of Henry V's chief prisoner, Charles of Orléans—on his death-bed Henry was said to have given instructions that Orléans should never be released except as a gage of permanent peace. Now in 1440 Orléans was released—greatly to Gloucester's indignation, who wrote a formal protest against it—simply to help to supplicate for peace. How had times changed!

Orléans did his best, though on his failure he did not return to keep his parole—unlike blind King John, Edward III's great prisoner at Crécy. The English Council were now, at long last, willing to give up the claim to the French throne, in return for territorial concessions. Then a marriage-alliance could seal the matter. What they had perhaps not appreciated was that "the claim and the territories were in point of fact interdependent, and in the end Suffolk was forced into being the agent by whom both were lost."[5] He was an able man, but he was not a wise one;

he was capable of asserting leadership in Council, for he knew what he wanted and was determined on it. He wanted peace, but he was brash, ambitious and self-seeking; he was convinced that peace had to be pushed through, but, a soldier rather than a diplomat, he may not have appreciated fully that to be too keen meant a weaker bargaining position.

Intimately tied up with the peace-negotiations was the question of a French bride for Henry, who had attained his majority in 1442. The clever, slippery Charles VII would not commit himself or offer one of his own family. But he was willing to agree to a lesser French princess, the young Margaret of Anjou, for whom no match had yet materialised. She was a younger daughter of René of Anjou, titular King of Naples—"le bon roi René" of Provençal tradition and of Alphonse Daudet. René's numerous titles were merely titular, he had little in the way of actual possessions and no dowry to offer with his daughter. To become Queen of England was a brilliant prospect, whoever the king, and no difficulty was made at Tours when Suffolk came over in 1443 to negotiate the match. To reward him for his services he was granted the wardship of Somerset's daughter and heiress, the Lady Margaret Beaufort—that luckier girl.

When Suffolk returned, having achieved a penniless French bride for the King of England, he was rewarded with a marquisate for his pains—giving him an envied precedence over his former fellows, the earls. Margaret's dowry was to have been a favourable peace with France; that was found much more difficult to obtain. All that was obtained with her was a prolongation of the truce. This was not merely unsatisfactory but of the utmost danger: the marriage should have come at the end to ratify a firm peace when obtained. The conclusion of the marriage was held up for over a year, and, when Suffolk went back in 1445 to claim the bride, he was kept waiting ignominiously for a couple of months before Charles VII and René were ready to attend the ceremony. This may well have opened Suffolk's eyes to the potential dangers, but by now he was hopelessly committed. It seems that the later charge against him that he was inveigled into promising to surrender the English positions and claims in Maine and Anjou is untrue; that the charge was made shows how completely he had identified himself with the fatal match and would be held responsible for it. For "he and the English Council which he represented had been put in a weak position by accepting Margaret while leaving the major question unsettled. Hoping optimistically to end the war, Henry had incurred liabilities that passed their imaginations."[6] It still passes our imagination how they could have done it.

Popular opinion later held that all Henry VI's troubles went back to his marriage with Margaret of Anjou, and, though this was an exaggeration, there was a great deal in it. He would have done better never to marry at all.

When Margaret arrived in England she was only a girl of fifteen. But she was well grown, spirited and precocious, "inheriting fully the virile qualities of her mother and grandmother, and also, as events soon showed, both the ability and the savagery which belonged to nearly all the members of the younger house of Anjou. She was well brought up, and inherited something of her father's literary tastes. She was a 'devout pilgrim to the shrine of Boccaccio,' delighting in her youth in romances of chivalry."[7] Little can she have imagined when she landed in England that her life would exceed these romances in adventure and tragedy, while finding little enough chivalry by the way. "Talbot, Earl of Shrewsbury, presented her with a gorgeously illuminated volume of French romances that 'after she had learnt English she might not forget her mother-tongue.' "

There was no danger of that. It was understandable that she should have French sympathies, but they were none the less injurious both to herself and to her husband's cause. For she had a passionate, one-sided nature, totally incapable of seeing any other side, and from the first she put herself in the wrong by making herself an advocate of French interests in the country of which she was queen. When her father urged the surrender of the English possessions in Maine to his brother Charles of Anjou, she replied: "in this matter we will do your pleasure as much as lies in our power, as we have always done already."[8] With such a weak husband as Henry this was fatal: she got him to pledge himself in writing to the surrender of Le Mans. This caused no end of trouble. It was enough to make even Gloucester right: *either* continue the war effectively *or* make peace. It shortly would appear

9

that to make a better fighting effort would have been a better way to peace. The English state, virtually without a head, caught in this dilemma could not make up its mind.

We may sympathise with a poor woman married to such a weak husband—and indeed his sexual inadequacy must have added exacerbation to the strain of her situation, with a woman of her temperament. When her son, Prince Edward, was born after eight years of barren wedlock, it released the flood-gates of passion. She fought like a tigress for him and his rights. But, indeed, it would have been better for him, for her and for Henry, if the child had never been born. When he came into the world Henry was sunk in melancholy madness and could recognise nothing. Henry was almost as chaste as Edward the Confessor, and when he recovered said that it must have been conceived by the Holy Spirit. No wonder the Yorkists put it about that the child was spurious, or that it was Edmund Beaufort's, the Duke of Somerset.

In her situation Margaret had to run the gauntlet of such scurrilities. In these earlier years Suffolk was thought to be too much attached to her. He seems to have had a romantic feeling for the lonely girl in her new surroundings and to have written her platonic poems in the manner of *l'amour courtois*. For now that there was a queen once more in England there was a revival of the Court, such as there had hardly been since the extravagant days of Richard II. It produced similar consequences in the formation of a Court-party, based on the royal household. The intimate friends of Margaret—as both Suffolk and his Duchess were, along with the Beaufort Somersets—became the Lancastrian party, later on held together and driven forward in spite of all disasters by her indomitable courage and drive. On the other hand, it would not have incurred such disasters if it had not been for her implacable, fighting spirit. Like those other French women in politics, Mary Stuart and Henrietta Maria, Margaret of Anjou was an inveterate partisan. She came to breathe the fire and slaughter of partisanship. "A stranger to the customs and interests of her adopted country, she never learned to play the part of a mediator, or to raise the Crown above the fierce faction fight that constantly raged round Henry's Court. In identifying her husband completely with the one faction, she almost forced the rival party into opposition to the King and to the dynasty."[9]

Suffolk had escorted Margaret to England in the spring of 1445; she landed at Portsmouth, feeling not very well, and was married to Henry quietly at Titchfield Abbey by Bishop Ayscough of Salisbury. The day was 23 April, St. George's Day—not a very appropriate patron, one would have thought, for such a match. She made her state-entry into London on 28 May, and was crowned in Westminster Abbey on 30 May. The expenses of her escort—over fifty ships to convey her, her household and attendant grandees—and of the lavish festivities to greet England's queen were something prodigious. She was followed by an embassy demanding the surrender of Maine. She got to work on the easy-going Henry, who made the promise. It can be imagined how palatable this was to the patriotic Gloucester, with whom we may for once sympathise. But Suffolk, supported by the Queen and the Beauforts, was supreme, in complete possession of power for the next few years—and would be called to account in the end.

Margaret managed to turn her husband's mind against his uncle, and by 1447 Suffolk had Gloucester isolated. Parliament was called at Bury St. Edmund's, in Suffolk country, where Gloucester could be overawed and brought to book. Apparently Suffolk intended to mount a case against him, to get him out of the way for the benefit of appeasement, and Gloucester was arrested. The shock brought on another, and final, seizure—he was suffering from "palsy" and had had previous strokes. But nothing would please people but to believe that the popular Duke had been made away with by Suffolk and Margaret.

A few weeks later Gloucester's old enemy, Cardinal Beaufort, died at Winchester, clear-headed to the last, arranging his affairs and his moneys on his death-bed. He left a legacy of some £2000 to his great-nephew, the King, who needed it; but Henry, with his usual unselfishness, refused it—his great-uncle had always been kind to him, he said, he did not need such a reminder. This was in some contrast to Margaret, who, the very day after Gloucester's death, had seized what she could of his possessions to add to her jointure.

With these deaths in 1447 we observe the fearful wastage of the time in those most exposed personages at the top of society, more open to its stresses and strains, the burdens to be carried, the risks to be taken. We should add the qualification "male personages," for the females survived. Shortly the wastage was to be doubled and trebled by the Wars of the Roses: the nobility would be heavy with the widows of dukes, earls and barons killed, executed or murdered. This would have a further effect in the multiple marriages of the widows: they would be doubly marriageable on account of their widows' thirds, the marriage jointures, from the previous husbands they had enjoyed. The effect of this again was to restrict the number of progeny, since some proportion of these widows would be beyond child-bearing. Take the Lady Margaret Beaufort as a prime example. Her first husband died when she was only a girl of thirteen, leaving her pregnant with the child who became Henry VII. She married twice more, Henry Stafford and then the Earl of Derby; but there were no more children.

This ties in with the social phenomenon observed by our historian—"a tendency to be remarked in the fifteenth-century baronage: the absorption of the smaller units by the larger, corresponding perhaps with the economic tendency of the rich to get richer but fewer."[10] We shall observe them shortly, absorbing each other, gorging and disgorging like reptiles, eating each other up. The aim, of course—understandable enough and even praiseworthy in itself—was "to conserve and add to, by every available means, the family patrimony." Less praiseworthy was "the way in which material considerations entirely outweighed the happiness or misery of the children united." Life was really a question of *sauve qui peut* for people at the top.

Take the royal family in itself, most exposed of all. Out of all Henry IV's likely brood of four adult sons—Henry V, Clarence, Bedford, Gloucester—there remained only the weakling sprig of a grandchild, Henry VI. Even of the one-time numerous Beauforts there would shortly be only females left, the whole claim of the house of Lancaster coming to rest on the shoulders of Margaret Beaufort, in this year 1447 now four years old. As against this deterioration of the Lancastrian stock we shall have now to set the numerous progeny of Richard of York by Cecily Neville—thirteen children of whom seven, four sons and three daughters, reached adult life. Then we shall observe the strains of high politics, the insatiable pursuit of power, wreaking havoc on the Yorkist royal stock, with killings, executions and murders. In any case, the

Yorkists were more prolific than the Lancastrians, particularly through the fertile Neville strain. The founder of the grand Neville fortunes "had succeeded through his enormous family of children in creating a dynastic network to include many of the noble houses of England."[11]

Perhaps, in addition to the political and economic factors influencing the outcome of this savage struggle for survival, we should make some allowance for eugenic considerations.

Events were moving to the first great crisis of the reign. York had been recalled from his Lieutenancy in France on a pretext; there ensued a power-struggle between him and Suffolk over the renewal of his office. In the end, after two years in which affairs in France had no direction, in 1448 Edmund Beaufort was given York's job, with his late brother's dukedom of Somerset to honour him in it. It was enough for York to be superseded by his rival, but the medicine was embittered by his being appointed Lieutenant of Ireland to keep him out of the way. For a year and a half he delayed going over; when he did he was received with goodwill, as the heir of the Mortimers, and Ireland became a base from which later to operate upon English affairs, for decades faithful to the house of York.

In the same year Suffolk's dangerous ascendancy, supported by Margaret, was signalised by his being raised to a dukedom, with precedence over all but the royal dukes. Nevertheless, the ground quaked under his feet: he certainly felt the tremors of the earthquake that would shortly engulf him. Again and again he procured indemnity from Council or Parliament for his policy of appeasement, in case the whole thing toppled over. His administration at home was no less unpopular; money was short, the Exchequer could not meet the demands on it or send adequate supplies to France. At the same time being in power, as usual, gave the best chance of engrossing what pickings there were going. Margaret, who had always been poor, helped herself and grew greedy; Suffolk helped himself to desirable grants and lordships. So did those horrid extortioners Lord Scales and Lord Say, the latter of whom built up a virulent hatred of himself in Kent which he and his son-in-law pilled and polled. They all came by sticky ends. Something of the atmosphere of this time of extortion and insecurity, with people's nerves on edge, can be seen in the contemporary ballad "Money, Money!"

> Above all thing, thou art a king
> And rulest the world over all:
> Who lacketh thee, all joy, pardie,
> Will soon then from him fall.
>
> In king's Court, where money doth rout,
> It maketh the gallants to jet [strut],
> And for to wear gorgeous their gear,
> Their caps a-wry to set. . . .[12]

Then the blow fell, after a time of confused counsels, refusal to recognise the realities of the situation, unpreparedness to meet the emergency that was clearly at hand, faction-fighting at home while the fundamental exigencies of the state had been played fast and loose with for the past decade—it all came home, as with us in our time in 1940.

The French had been waiting for an excuse to renew hostilities on favourable terms. One cannot blame them. They were provided with one by the failure to hand over places in Maine as promised. The subtle Charles VII shored himself up on both sides, by an alliance with both Burgundy and Brittany, before he attacked the English dominion in Normandy. In the course of the long struggle that had been his life, this strange, unattractive, intelligent man never made the mistake of overconfidence. He had built up a national militia; the antiquated feudal armies that had been defeated at Crécy and Poitiers, Agincourt and Verneuil, were transformed. The old English ascendancy in archery was more than countered by the development of artillery. It was the English who were now out of date in the technique of warfare.

With his two allies and three armies, Charles was able to assail Normandy, in 1449, on three sides. In quick succession Verneuil, Pont de l'Arche, Lisieux, Mantes fell. Charles VII took the field for the attack on central Normandy; the Vexin and east Normandy were overrun by the Burgundians; the Bretons invaded the Cotentin. The capital was disaffected and there was no defending it: in October, Rouen capitulated. On Christmas Day Harfleur, which stood a siege, was bombarded by Charles's artillery into submission.

Extraordinary as it seems, "the renewal of hostilities appears to have been no more anticipated by the home government than by Somerset."[13] It happens from time to time in the history of nations that their leaders are befooled by their own humbug.

That winter, too late and too slow, the last relief was sent over to Normandy: some four hundred lances and two thousand archers under Sir Thomas Kyriell—evidently no nobleman was willing to risk his reputation on a forlorn hope. The men were kept waiting about on the south coast and grew undisciplined; when Bishop Moleyns, who was closely associated with Suffolk's foreign policy, went down to Portsmouth to pay wages, he was murdered by the sailors as "the traitor who had sold Normandy." Here was a danger-signal for Suffolk in London.

In Normandy the French did not let up for the winter any more than Henry V had done. In the early months of the year Harfleur, Honfleur and Fresnay were lost. In April, Kyriell's defeat at the battle of Formigny sealed the fate of Normandy: he himself was taken prisoner, most of his men were slaughtered in position. "No such reverse had befallen the English since the days of Baugé" (1421)—i.e., in thirty years.[14] Perhaps it is the less surprising that they had become complacent. However, "the last relief sent by England to Normandy was thus disposed of." There followed the loss of Bayeux, Avranches and, after a siege, Caen. The siege of Cherbourg was a stiffer business, but it was eventually reduced after continuous firing from a battery of well-placed guns—the new arm which the French had developed. In August the news had reached London: James Gresham added a postscript to his letter to his master, John Paston, in Norfolk: "All this tofore was written on the Monday next after Our Lady Day. And this same Wednesday was it told that Cherbourg is gone, and we have not now a foot of land in Normandy."[15]

The hurricane of losses reminds one of nothing so much as 1940, which brought down the complacent Chamberlain. Suffolk had been nothing like so complacent, indeed he had sued out indemnity after indemnity fearing miscarriage. But he had to pay the reckoning all the same for his monopoly of power: since he had engrossed the advantages, social and financial, advanced his own interests while neglecting the country's, he would have to pay the penalty. A storm of petitions blew up against him from the Commons, and he was sent to the Tower—in part a measure of protection against the enraged people. Something of the hatred they felt for this talented, ambitious, unpopular man can be gathered from the verses that circulated at his fall:

> Now is the fox driven to hole!
> Hoo to him, hoo, hoo!
> For an he creep out,
> He will you all undo.[16]

They were determined that he should not creep out.

The charges of treason against him were quite unconvincing, though it is not beyond the bounds of possibility that he might have thought of marrying his son to Lady Margaret Beaufort, "presuming and pretending her to be next inheritable to the Crown."[17] (In two generations to come, strange to say, the York-ist claim to the throne would come to Suffolk's grandsons.) More immediately to the point were the charges against his administration: "he hath purchased many great possessions by maintenance and done great outrageous extortions." Maintenance meant the upholding of one's retainers or followers in their causes, right or wrong, sustaining them in their suits at law, in return for support, political, military or financial—a very characteristic phenomenon of the age of Bastard Feudalism in which we are moving, and without which the Wars of the Roses would hardly have been possible.

Suffolk defended himself with conviction, but there was no chance of his escaping the penalty for treason, if left to the Lords or Commons. So Henry exercised his prerogative to save his life, by banishing him for five years. At the end of April, after writing a touching farewell to his son, the Duke set sail from Ipswich. In the Channel his little ship was intercepted by a squadron lying in wait for him, led by a large ship of the royal navy, the *Nicholas of the Tower*. The Duke was ordered on board, and greeted with cries of "Welcome, traitor!" He was given time to shrive himself, in accordance with the superstition of the time, then put into a little boat, where an Irishman hacked off his head on the gunwale with half a dozen stokes. The body was then thrown on to the sands at Dover, whence it was taken by Henry's orders to be buried in the family church at Wingfield, where the tomb with its effigy can still be seen.

No one knows who the miscreants were, but every indication points to the perpetrators of the deed being connected with York. It can be imagined how the passionately resentful Margaret would feel about the shameful murder of her friend. But what are we to think of the deterioration of government and public order, when one of the King's own ships was used for the frustration of the King's sentence upon a fallen minister and his public murder on the high seas?

In England there was jubilation. The murder was celebrated in a poem of striking virtuosity, in which all the leading figures of Suffolk's party are called on by name to celebrate his obsequies, with antiphons in Latin from the Offices for the Dead.[18]

> Who shall execute his exequies with a solemnity?
>> Bishops and lords, as great reason is,
> Monks, canons, priests and other clergy
>> Pray for this duke's soul that it may come to bliss,
>> And let never such another come after this!
>> His interfectors blessed may they be,
>> And grant them for their deed to reign with angels,
>> And for Jack Nape's soul, *Placebo* and *Dirige*. . . .
>
> John Say redeth [counsels], *Manus tuae fecerunt me.*
> "*Libera me,*" singeth Trevelyan, "war [guard] the rear;
> That they do no more so, *requiescant in pace.*"
> Thus prays all England far and near.
> Where is Somerset? Why appears he not here
>> To sing *Dies irae et miseriae?*
> God grant England all in fere [together]
>> For these traitors to sing *Placebo* and *Dirige*.

Suffolk's death was followed by further acts of mob-violence, while government was paralysed. Bishop Ayscough, who had married Henry and Margaret and was a courtier rather than a diocesan, was caught in the country, dragged from the altar at Edington where he was saying Mass and done to death on a hill overlooking Westbury in Wiltshire. At the same moment Jack Cade led his rising in Kent, and once more the Kentishmen marched on London. It was a different affair from the Peasants' Revolt of Richard's reign; for the rebels now were men of substance, yeomen and middle-class folk, whose ire had been aroused by the extortions of household and government officials, particularly the hated Treasurer, Lord Say, and his son-in-law, Crowmer, sheriff of Kent.

Jack Cade also seems to have been an Irishman, and to begin with he used the name of Mortimer—these straws in the wind also point to York, who was thought at the time to be inculpated in the movement. The complaints of the rebels were mainly against the extortions and corruption of Court officials, the alienation of Crown lands to them, the interference with the course of justice (Margaret was constantly interfering in suits on her own or her servants' behalf), though the loss of Normandy by "treason" was also alleged.

> God be our guide,
> And then shall we speed.
> Whosoever say nay,
> False for their money ruleth!
> Truth for his tales spoileth! [robs]
> God send us a fair day!
> Away traitors, away![19]

When the rebels encamped on Blackheath, the King and his lords rode in arms through the City to meet them; but a detachment under two Staffords fell into an ambush and was cut up with the loss of its leaders. This disrupted the King's following, who, inclined to sympathise with the Kentishmen, turned to demanding the heads of Lord Say and his crew. Henry ordered Say and his son-in-law to the Tower, and, washing his hands of the affair, retreated to Kenilworth—very different conduct from King Richard's as a boy in 1381.

The rebels entered London. Lord Say was surrendered by his colleague, Lord Scales (his turn would come later), was given a mock-trial at the Guildhall and beheaded in Cheapside. His son-in-law and some others were executed without any form of trial. The citizens of London now had had enough of disorder and themselves took their defence in hand. There was a battle on London Bridge, after which the rebels retreated. Jack Cade took refuge in the fastnesses of the Weald, but was run to earth by the new sheriff, Alexander Iden (or Eden). Cade resisted and was mortally wounded; he died in the cart on the way to London, where his head was set up on London Bridge. There were further movements under their "captains" in Kent and Sussex, while in Wiltshire the whole county rallied behind the murderers of Bishop Ayscough and the King was forced to pardon them.

On top of these events, with which he may have had some underhand connection, the Duke of York landed from Ireland and gathered a large body of troops with which to march on London. The government reacted by recalling Somerset from Calais and making him Constable of England. It was a direct confrontation of Yorkists versus Lancastrians—the situation from which the Wars of the Roses sprang. The country was indeed on the verge of civil war; the lords were arming their retainers to make their way to the Parliament summoned. Attempts were made to intercept York on his way—these he evaded or there would have been a clash. The party-struggle was transferred to Parliament, where in January 1451 the demand was put forward for the removal of the Court favourites, held responsible for the loss of Normandy and the disturbances at home. It is noticeable that all these were either friends of Margaret or her officials, Somerset, the Duchess of Suffolk, Bishop Booth, her Chancellor, and others. Henry tried to conciliate matters, while the situation went from bad to worse abroad.

The intensity of the party-struggle in England—by its usual sinister dialectic—aided the country's enemies abroad. Charles VII was enabled now to push on with the conquest of Gascony, and appointed Dunois Lieutenant-General for the purpose. In this year 1451 both Bordeaux and Bayonne capitulated. But the French régime was unpopular, the English—who left the Bordelais much to themselves—popular. Besides that, there was the mutual interest of the wine trade: England was Gascony's chief market. Years later Charles VII, who had no illusions, admitted that Gascony "has been English for three hundred years and that the people of the region are at heart completely inclined towards the English party."[20] They now appealed for English assistance to drive out the French, and in 1452 a force was scraped together and sent out under the veteran Talbot.

Talbot was welcomed by Bordeaux and other Gascon towns as
a deliverer. Charles VII, reluctantly as usual, was forced to take
the field with a large army to deal with him. Talbot, like the
antique hero of an earlier age that he was, was killed on his white
palfrey by a cannon-ball while making a direct charge straight at
the French batteries and earthworks. "With John Talbot, the hero
of four-and-thirty years of warfare, perished the last hope of the
English dominion in France."[21] A recent historian of the age
remarks on "the scant recognition which the efforts of John Talbot
received from his English contemporaries: the French were more
generous in their praise."[22] The Elizabethans, too, we may add.
Talbot's personality, chivalrous and loyal, living a lifetime on
fields of battle not knowing what fear was, entered into French
legend. He is *"le roi Talabot,"* his war *"la guerre du roi Talabot."*

His death marked effectively the end of the Hundred Years'
War. The remnants of his expeditionary force had to find their
own way back, to take their part in the warfare now transferred
to English soil. English denizens were allowed to sail home; the
faithful Gascons were deserted, left to make the best terms they
could. Charles VII, who had come out so fortunate in the end
after such ignominious beginnings, presided over the reintegration
of France, first among medieval kingdoms, holding an unquestion-
able primacy in medieval civilisation.

For England, the person really responsible for these disasters,
it is ironic to think, was the hero-king, Henry V. It is also one
of the ironies of history that if his father had not displaced Richard II on the throne, the second half of the Hundred Years' War
might never have come about.

And what was there to show for it all?

Since the English state, distracted by party spirit, would never
make concessions in time, or bargain from strength instead of from
weakness, it was left with nothing but the empty title to the French
Crown, which successive sovereigns enjoyed through the centuries
until it was finally given up by George III at the Peace of Paris
in 1763.

CHAPTER VII

The Wars of the Roses

If we are pedants we should not call them the Wars of the Roses. It is not contemporary nomenclature, and it seems that, though the white rose was used among other Yorkist emblems, the red rose of Lancaster did not appear till later. The apposition of the white rose and the red, and their union in the Tudor line, was very much a Tudor theme.

> "I love the rose both red and white."
> "Is that your pure perfect appetite?"
> "To hear talk of them is my delight!"
> "Joyed may we be,
> Our prince to see,
> And roses three!"[1]

This is from a song written the year after Bosworth, to celebrate the birth of Prince Arthur in 1486, first child of Henry VII and Elizabeth of York, a sprig of both houses.

Since the theme goes back such a long way, and the name "Wars of the Roses" has been sanctified by long usage, perhaps it might be permitted? It would indeed be rather pedantic to forgo it here and now. What's in a name? That which we call a rose by any other name would smell as sweet.

Far more important than pedantry is to get the character of the war right. It was, in its most obvious sense, a party-conflict between the houses of Lancaster and York for the possession of the Crown. "The prize at stake was, after all, the greatest earthly prize within the reach of any of them—the Crown of England with all the wealth, power, and influence that went with it."[2] But it was much more than this. As our most recent historian of the age sees well, "in every instance a change in the succession raised the problem of the local balance of power; and to think of the dynastic struggle as fought out simply between the supporters of Somerset and the Queen on the one hand, and an opposition with the traditions of Mortimer, Clare, Salisbury and the great baronial consolidations of the fourteenth century on the other, is to neglect its organic nature."[3]

Again, in different areas of the country, in almost every county, "it was not the cause of York or Lancaster so much as the local situation and the attitude of local personalities that governed allegiance to the magnates or prompted . . . the transfer of loyalty on the part of the retainer."[4] It was the breakdown of government at the centre that gave these local and regional struggles for power, the family feuds and personal hatreds, their chance. In little Cornwall it becomes Bodrugan against Edgcumbe; in larger Devon, Courtenay against Bonville. At the beginning, when York marched on London in 1452 to demand a change of government, he was accompanied by the Earl of Devon, head of the Courtenay family. But when York aimed further at the Crown itself, the Courtenays remained true to their allegiance, a consistently Lancastrian family; in consequence the Bonvilles were Yorkists. Over the immense North the breakdown of government at the centre gave its opportunity for the grand feud between Nevilles and Percies; in South Wales, between Jasper Tudor, Earl of Pembroke, and the Herberts, who were granted his earldom when the Yorkists won.

The truth is, however, that the Yorkists were a minority party. At the beginning "from the lords as a whole the Duke got little support. To them a Yorkist succession implied the predominance of Neville, Mowbray, de Vere and their dependants, the consolidation of important power-groups in central and southern England."[5] There were other areas where Yorkist sympathies were dominant, or became so: in York itself, in Kent and, above all, London which had the greatest interest in order and good government, if only for commercial reasons, though not only those. The sympathies of the country in general, noticeably of the Church, which was more representative than any other institution, the guardian of public decency and tradition as Parliament was of constitutional law and custom, were on the whole with the constituted royal house. The country gentry were in general loyal to their king, and Henry, whose incompetence as a ruler let loose the

flood, remained personally popular. Indeed, the very meekness of
his character, his unselfishness and genuine desire to please everybody, staved off the conflict longer than might have been expected.

The prize was too great to resist. Whoever got control of government at the centre was able to reward his supporters with lands
and lordships, profitable grants and offices. The grasping Treasurer, Lord Say, came to a bad end all those years ago; yet we
have his representatives with us still. Office offered the open door
to influence and wealth. "It was an essential feature of the life of
the upper ranks of lay society in later medieval England that the
road to success lay in the service of the Crown."[6] Take the case
of John Trevelyan, a household official of the second rank who
is regularly inveighed against in the poems directed at Henry's entourage:

> The Cornish chough oft with his train [deceit]
> Hath made our eagle [the king] blind.

Trevelyan had come a long way from that bare and windy spot
of the name high above the banks of the river Fowey; but once he
was entrenched in the royal household he could marry an heiress,
come by the desirable estate of Nettlecombe in Somerset and never
look back. That immensely distinguished clan, who have contributed so much to English public life and letters, all go back to
that simple fact. Though it is half a millennium since John Trevelyan
served in Henry VI's household, the Trevelyans are with us still.

We do not have to waste much time over theory, legitimist or
otherwise, in the matter. "It seems probable that, if only Henry
VI had been able to rule with even average competence, the Yorkist claim, no matter what degree of theoretical validity it might be
deemed to have, would never have been advanced at all. . . .
The many magnates, the gentry, and their men, who fought and
risked their lives and all they possessed during the civil wars, did
not sacrifice themselves for the sake of uncertain theoretical principles. They chose their sides for the sake of family connections
and interests, on the principle of 'good lordship,' perhaps for the
sake of simple 'good fellowship,' and even, once blood had been
drawn, on the immemorial, aboriginal principles of the feud."[7]
When the eminent Lancastrian lawyer and constitutional theorist

Sir John Fortescue wrote a book against the Yorkist claim through female descent, the Yorkist Edward IV, having won, pardoned him on condition of writing a book to answer to his own book. It was a punishment to fit the crime. So much for political and constitutional theorising!

On the other hand, once the central issue of the succession was thrown open to the arbitrament of war, the upshot became a matter of chance. The Lancastrian house would never have lost the throne if it had not been for the debility of Henry VI. Even then, it would probably not have been overthrown but for the chance of the military ability of the young Edward IV. When the Yorkist house was well in the saddle, after a quarter of a century of successful rule, it would not have lost out to the unknown Henry Tudor if Richard III had not murdered his brother's children and turned the country against him.

"The royal power must, therefore, be set and judged against this background of engagement and allegiance"[8]—and, we can add, of interest and opinion, of custom and sentiment, even, in the end, of people's feeling for the decencies of life.

It was, then, no mere dynastic quarrel that we have under observation, but an organic struggle, out of which modern England was born.

York had come over from Ireland to attack Somerset's administration and oust him. But he himself had lost ground through his suspected connection with Cade's rising. His charges against Somerset were mainly concerned with the negligence that had lost Normandy. For a time York himself was held in custody, then there was a pacification. In 1452 and 1453 the King and Queen made progresses through the country hoping to pacify people, after the disasters abroad, and to keep some semblance of order. We derive a vivid picture of the way things were breaking up, the consequences in the localities, from the Paston letters at this time.

Here is the Earl of Oxford writing to the Duke of Norfolk in the late summer of 1450: "Forasmuch as I am informed that certain noble knights and squires of this county dispose themselves to be with your lordship in hasty time at Framlingham, there to have communings with your good lordship for the sad [sober] rule and governance of this county, which standeth right . . .

indisposed, God amend it. . . ."⁹ In October a servant of John Paston's writes the news from London: "Sir, an it please, I was in my lord of York's house and I heard much thing, more than my master writeth unto you of; I heard much thing in Fleet Street. But, sir, my lord was with the King, and he visaged so the matter that all the King's household was and is afeared right sore. And my said lord hath put a bill to the King and desired much thing, which is much after the Commons' desire." This brings us very close to the sense of events, for York had a good deal of sympathy among the Commons with his complaints of bad government and his campaign for reform. His difficulties were with the Lords, who distrusted him and what his campaign might further portend.

In April 1452 the Duke of Norfolk—the last Mowbray duke, a supporter of York's—descended on his county to inquire into the complaints against Lord Scales's retainers, "saying that we would abide but a short time here, and after our departing he would have the rule and governance as he hath had aforetime. 'We let you wit [know] that next the King our sovereign lord, by his good grace and license, we will have the principal rule and governance through all this shire, of which we bear our name, whilst that we be living, as far as reason and law requireth, whosoever will grudge or say the contrary.'"¹⁰ Next year, on St. George's Day, John Paston complained to the sheriff that he had been man-handled in Norwich Cathedral by one of the Duke's retainers. Charles Nowell and "five of his fellowship set upon me and one of my servants . . . he smiting at me, whilst one of his fellows held mine arms at my back. . . . Which was to me strange case, thinking in my conceit [opinion] that I was my lord's man and his homager ere Charles knew his lordship, that my lord was my good lord, and that I had been with my lord at London within eight days before Lent, at which time he granted me his good lordship so largely that it must cause me ever to be his true servant to my power."

In such a passage the generalisations of the historian are brought home vividly: in those times of danger it was essential to recommend oneself to someone more powerful for protection. The only safe place was to be in a monastery, to be some sort of churchman; even so we have seen that even bishops were not immune from murder. In spite of its obvious risks the system of retaining was on the other hand "a steadying influence in a society where old institutional loyalties were breaking down."[11] England was coming out of the cocoon of age-long medieval feudalism; this uncomfortable period of the fifteenth century has come to be described as that of Bastard Feudalism. Out of the break-up of the old society a freer and more flexible modern society was emerging, its customary obligations and routines flexed by the pervasive influences of money.

In April 1453 the Queen descended upon Norwich with her ladies. Margaret Paston wrote to "her right worshipful husband" with the tidings.

The Queen came into this town on Tuesday last past after noon, and abode here till it was Thursday, three after noon. And she sent after my cousin Elizabeth Clere to come to her; and she durst not disobey her commandment, and came to her. [John Paston as Norfolk's man would be a Yorkist.] And when she came in the Queen's presence, the Queen made right much of her and desired her to have an husband, the which ye shall know of hereafter. But as for that, he is never nearer than he was before. The Queen was right well pleased with her answer and reporteth of her in the best wise, and saith, by her troth she saw no gentlewoman since she came into Norfolk that she liked better than she doth her. . . . I pray you that ye will do your cost on me against Whitsuntide that I may have something for my neck. When the Queen was here I borrowed my cousin Elizabeth Clere's device [evidently a brooch or jewel], for I durst not for shame go with my beads among so many fresh gentlewomen as here were at that time.[12]

It is pleasant to come upon these feminine amenities among all the masculine scufflings for power and place and profit, the lawsuits and man-handlings and murders. This gives us as good a close-up of Margaret as we could hope for—she and Henry were progressing about the country showing themselves and organising sympathy in the power-struggle being waged. It was all too much for the King's frail health; in August he was struck down by complete prostration, mental and physical, apparently the result of a sudden start or fright. He lay in numb, dejected melancholy, having completely lost reason and memory, and could neither walk nor stand. For a time the government—in which the able Cardinal

Kemp was the leading official—tried to conceal the gravity of the King's condition, for fear of a York regency. Somerset had lost influence and respect with the final loss of Gascony. Then, on St. Edward's Day, 13 October, the Queen gave birth to a son.

Henry was at Windsor, sunk in listlessness, apathetic, unaware, when his son was brought to him at New Year's tide, 1454. A news-letter of the time tells us the story.

> At the Prince's coming to Windsor the Duke of Buckingham took him in his arms and presented him to the King in godly wise, beseeching the King to bless him. And the King gave no manner of answer. Nevertheless the Duke abode still with the Prince by the King. And when he could no manner of answer have, the Queen came in and took the Prince in her arms and presented him in like form as the Duke had done, desiring that he should bless it. But all their labour was in vain, for they departed thence without any answer or countenance, saving only that once he looked on the Prince and cast down his eyes again, without any more.[13]

The same news-letter tells us that all the lords were arming their servants, beginning with the Chancellor, Cardinal Kemp. The Earl of Wiltshire and Lord Bonville had caused it to be publicly cried at Taunton that every man willing to serve them should have 6d. a day. The Duke of Exeter and Lord Egremont, a Percy, had had a meeting at Doncaster and sworn a compact. The Duke of Somerset's harbinger had taken up all the lodgings that could be had near the Tower—evidently for his following; the Duke had been sent to the Tower in November, as a concession to the opposition. "Item, the Duke of Buckingham hath done to be made 2,000 bends with knots [his family emblem], to what intent men may construe as their wits will give them." The household officials, Tresham and Trevelyan, had petitioned the Lords for a garrison for Windsor to safeguard the King and Prince.

What was Margaret to do at a juncture like this, in a foreign country, with all her friends falling round her, the King an imbecile?

She was a woman of an undaunted, royal courage; her spirit never failed her in the successive crises that constituted her life henceforward. She had grasped the essential weakness of York's

position with the Lords—that they did not trust him and suspected his intentions. This same January the Queen put forward
a demand that the regency should be placed in her hands, with
all the leading appointments in Church and State—that she should
exercise the powers of the Crown. But York was on his way to
London with his son Edward, Earl of March, the Earls of Salisbury
and Warwick and all their following. Along with York came—no
doubt uncommitted to him—the two Tudor earls, Richmond and
Pembroke, half-brothers of the King.

In March, Cardinal Kemp died; government was crumbling.
York could not be excluded any longer: immediately after, he
was made Protector and constituted his own government. He
made his Neville brother-in-law, Salisbury, Chancellor. He did not
make many changes: he came into power in a spirit of compromise, with the good resolution to reform administration and to
that end to keep the parties together so far as possible. In this
spirit he nominated Thomas Bourchier, who had connections in
both parties, to succeed Kemp as Archbishop of Canterbury. For
the next thirty years "true to his character as the nominee of a
compromise, he continued throughout a long career to serve whichever party was in the ascendant with praiseworthy impartiality."[14]
He crowned both Yorkist kings, Edward IV and Richard III; he
lived long enough to perform the same service for the Lancastrian
Henry VII.

York did not have the opportunity to prove himself in government, let alone reform it, for at Christmas 1454 King Henry recovered his wits. It was a national calamity that he ever did:
what hope of reform and unity there was vanished. Edmund Clere
at once wrote John Paston the news.

> Blessed be God, the King is well amended and hath been since
> Christmas Day; and on St. John's Day commanded his almoner to
> ride to Canterbury with his offering, and commanded the secre-
> tary to offer at St. Edward's [the shrine at Westminster]. And
> on the Monday afternoon the Queen came to him and brought
> my lord prince with her. And then he asked what the Prince's
> name was, and the Queen told him Edward; and then he held up
> his hands and thanked God thereof. And he said he never knew
> till that time, nor wist not what was said to him, nor wist not
> where he had been whilst he hath been sick till now. And he

asked who was godfathers, and the Queen told him and he was
well apayed [content].

And she told him that the Cardinal was dead, and he said
he knew never thereof till that time; and he said one of the wisest
lords in this land was dead. And my lord of Winchester [Bishop
Waynflete] and my lord of St. John's [prior of the Order of
Jerusalem] were with him on the morrow after Twelfth Day,
and he spoke to them as well as ever he did. And when they came
out they wept for joy.

And he saith he is in charity with all the world, and so he
would all the lords were. . . .[15]

Alas, Henry's return to his senses put that hope out of court.
York's Protectorate lapsed; Somerset was released and given
York's strategic post as captain of Calais, from which to interfere
in force in English politics. Salisbury ceased to be Chancellor;
Wiltshire was made Treasurer, Exeter set free. The Lancastrian
partisans were back. York went to the North to collect forces to
defend himself against those being brought against him. On 22
May the two little armies came into collision at St. Albans. The
King's forces were holding the town; York's, a good deal larger,
were to the east outside. The conflict was held up all the morning while messages went to and fro, York demanding the surrender of Somerset and others as traitors. This demand could not
be met; the King replied with a command to "void the field and
not be so hardy to make any resistance against me in mine own
realm."[16] To which the Duke, advised by the lords of *his* council,
replied that "the King, our sovereign lord, will not be reformed
at our beseeching nor prayer, nor will not understand the intent
that we be come hither and assembled for."

With that the attack was launched upon the town, which was
broken into at three places, the King's position cut in two,
while Warwick attacked in flank. The intervention of the young
Neville Earl of Warwick decided the matter, and, whether justifi-
ably or not, he got the credit of the action. He certainly had the
energy that goes with a man's good opinion of himself: the first
appearance on the scene of the man who would become known
as the Kingmaker. Henry stood meekly by his banner until he
was surrounded; grazed in the neck by an arrow, he was taken
into a tanner's cottage for attention. The engagement lasted less

than an hour, and it seems that only some six score men were killed. But among them were leading Lancastrian personages: Somerset himself (his son was wounded), the Earl of Northumberland, Lord Clifford, and the son and heir of the Duke of Buckingham. It has been observed that the civil wars which this battle initiated were marked by a rather new feature in medieval warfare—the severity of the losses among the leaders and men of rank, the increasing savagery as the struggle took on the character of a blood-feud. Lancastrians and Yorkists came to hate each other with a bitter hatred.

After the battle the victors waited on the King, knelt before him and renewed their allegiance, which Henry, with his usual meekness, accepted. Nevertheless, a dividing line was reached with this skirmish: henceforth the issue of power would be settled by overt force, i.e., war. This first battle of St. Albans can be regarded as the opening of the Wars of the Roses.

The King rode back with the victors to London, treated with every mark of respect, while the City turned out to greet him. York took over Somerset's military post as Constable of England; no less important the new man, Warwick, ablest of the Nevilles, got the key-post of Calais. With all these excitements Henry fell ill again at the end of the year, though not so completely as before—he was able, poor man, to transact a little business. York was made Protector again, though he had to use the persistency of the Commons in Parliament as a lever against the reluctant Lords. Unfortunately Henry recovered, and at the end of February 1456 came personally to Parliament to relieve the Protector of his office in proper form.

These events left York confronting the Queen henceforth as the leader and the moving spirit of her party. The paradox of the situation is that the Lancastrian party would hardly have kept going but for her fighting spirit; on the other hand, but for her it would not have been reduced to being a party. The house of Lancaster was the constituted authority in the state; everyone recognised that hitherto, including York, in spite of his having broken his oath in taking up arms against the King. In a sense we can say that Margaret drove him to it: hers was the spirit of pure partisanship, not what that of a queen should have been. Henry would have been content to have York undertake the burden of government for him. Early in 1456 a servant of Sir John Fastolf's reported to him: "the King, as it was told me by a great man, would have him [York] chief and principal councillor, and so to be called his chief councillor and Lieutenant as long as it should like the King."[17] On the other hand stood Margaret: "the Queen is a great and strong-laboured woman, for she spareth no pain to sue her things to an intent and conclusion to her power."

That autumn she got her way, having removed Henry from London and York's influence, into the Midlands where she was building up her party, with the Court based on Kenilworth. Once more she got York's ministers out and replaced them with Lancastrians and her own churchmen, like Bishop Booth. She wished to have York and Warwick arrested and impeached, but here she was frustrated. York left the Court "in right good conceit with the King, but not in great conceit with the Queen."[18]

In these years before the decisive struggle in 1459–61 "the government of England was conducted not from London but from the provinces. . . . The Crown was to abandon the attempt to govern the country."[19] The parties were building up their strength, watching each other, waiting for each other's moves. A phrase from a letter of the time describes the situation concisely: "my lord of York is at Sandal still [his castle in Yorkshire] and waiteth on the Queen, and she upon him."[20] By this time they hated each other: York had an unforgivable record in Margaret's eyes, and she would wreak a terrible revenge upon him.

Each was looking for support abroad. York was seeking the alliance of Burgundy, and using Calais under Warwick as a base for negotiations. Margaret was looking for support both to Scotland and to her long-lived uncle Charles VII, who had survived everything. In 1457 Charles sent a squadron under Brézé—now Seneschal of Normandy since its recovery—from the Loire into the Channel, where the Normans and Bretons thoroughly sacked Sandwich. On their way home they paid their respects at Plymouth, where they burned the quarter by Sutton Pool—it is to this day known as Britonside. Landing at Fowey they burned and pillaged, and attacked Place, the fortified house above the harbour where they were successfully repulsed from the high walls by the Mistress Treffry of the day. One way and another the French were getting their own back—but these events did not enhance the popularity of Henry's French queen. The country was falling apart, even as France had done under Henry's grandfather.

A last effort was made to keep things together in 1458, through the mediation of Archbishop Bourchier. The lords were gathering in London for a grand Council, to deal among other things with the dispute between Nevilles and Percies which had led to open fighting in the North. The streets of London were swarming with armed retainers; the mayor and citizens with difficulty managed to keep what order there was. People were spoiling for a fight, the militant energies of the fighting class having been denied the outlet they had enjoyed in France for so long. At the last moment there was a reconciliation: complicated awards were worked out with the object of healing the blood-feud begun at St. Albans, and York apologised for the unconstitutionality of his action. Ordinary folk rejoiced at the hope of peace: "the news whereof made all men so glad as that all sorts of men everywhere gave by mutual congratulation apparent testimony of rejoicing without measure."[21]

There followed an extraordinary scene in London, a "love-day" procession to St. Paul's on Lady Day, in which the poor king marched with the crown on his head; before him walked hand in hand those pairs of enemies, Somerset and Salisbury, Exeter and Warwick; after him came the grand enemies Richard of York and Queen Margaret, also hand in hand. The event was celebrated by a poem as usual:

> At Paul's in London with great renown
> > On Our Lady Day in Lent this peace was wrought;
> The king, the queen, with lords many a one,
> > To worship that Virgin as they ought
> Went a procession and spared right nought,
> > In sight of all the commonalty,
> In token that love was in heart and thought.
> > Rejoice, England, in concord and unity.[22]

It was all a hollow farce. Warwick returned to Calais, which he was organising as an independent base of operations. Margaret tried to oust him in favour of the young Duke of Somerset, but failed. Exeter had lost respect by his failure to intercept Brézé and keep command of the Channel, by virtue of his office as captain of the sea. Meanwhile Warwick was exercising it and winning popularity by his exploits in the Straits of Dover. The Lancastrians had no luck. In May, Warwick attacked a large fleet of twenty-eight Spanish armed merchantmen with his small squadron and carried off a prize. He followed this up by summoning the salt fleet bound for Lübeck to strike their flag to the English claiming sovereignty in the Straits, and on their refusal took them into Calais. Returning to England for Parliament that autumn he had a narrow escape from a broil between one of his men and one of the royal guard: the Earl had to leap into a barge on the Thames, make his way to the Tower and thence back to Calais.

Next spring he did better in a running fight with five big Genoese and Spanish carracks, three of which he captured after two days' hard fighting. These exploits, whether justifiable or not, roused the country's spirits frustrated by unredeemed defeat and political distraction. They appealed also to the acute anti-foreign sentiment exacerbated by the sense of treacherous desertion no less than humiliation. And along the Channel coast that had suffered recent depredations Warwick built up popularity and a following, particularly in disaffected Kent, that was of strategic importance in the war about to break out: it opened the road to London for the Yorkists.

In the spring of 1459 Margaret was in Cheshire, Richard II's old recruiting ground, distributing her son's badge of the Swan as Richard had his of the White Hart. In the summer York and Salisbury sent Warwick word that the moment had come for him to bring over his picked men from Calais. Warwick's father, Salisbury, marched from Yorkshire to join York in his Ludlow stronghold. Margaret sent her Cheshire men to intercept Salisbury, which they did at Blore Heath near Market Drayton: they were badly cut up by the Yorkists, their leader, Lord Audley, killed and Salisbury was able to join York at Ludlow, as was Warwick also. Now the King, with a much larger army, marched on Ludlow. Just outside the town at Ludford Bridge the royal army bore down on the Yorkists, who had not yet collected any other support than the Nevilles. The Calais contingent, professional soldiers, would not fight against their king, and after dark defected to the royal standard.

This left the Yorkists utterly exposed and in utmost danger: there was nothing for it but to fly and await a better day. This exposes once more how much of a minority party the Yorkists were—and this, in a way, makes Margaret right to fight on as she did all the way to the end, though nothing could excuse her alienation of York in the first place. The Yorkists broke camp at once. The Duke fled with his younger son to his base in Ireland, where he was warmly welcomed and gathered support. The elder son, Edward, Earl of March—that title by which all the trouble came, made his way with Warwick and Salisbury into Devonshire, whence Sir John Dynham shipped them across Channel and so back to Calais. A hastily summoned Parliament at Coventry attainted them all; their offices were distributed among faithful Lancastrians, while all the remaining lords were made to swear oaths to Prince Edward as well as to the King and to promise support and protection to his wife and son.

It only serves to illuminate the spreading sense of insecurity, the state of nerves they were all living in. For the government had failed to deal with the Yorkist leaders and now had to expect the invasion they were organising from abroad. In January, Dynham led a very successful raid on Sandwich: he captured Lord Rivers and his wife (Bedford's widow) and his son Sir Anthony Woodville, and took most of the ships in harbour back to Calais. Thence Warwick sailed for Ireland, to plan their measures with York. One upshot was the effective manifesto they put out against the misgovernment of the land, the incompetence of ministers and their oppressive instruments. Point was lent to this by Exeter allowing Warwick to slip by him in the Channel on his way back to Calais. Yorkist propaganda was beginning to tell, not the less so for having a good case.

At the end of June young March, with Warwick, Salisbury and their following, landed at Sandwich; in their company was a loquacious, enthusiastic Italian of a papal legate who wholeheartedly lent himself to Yorkist purposes. Marching on London, Warwick persuaded the City authorities to take his side; the Lancastrian lords took refuge in the Tower, while Yorkist heads were taken down from London Bridge for burial. Warwick next addressed himself to the authorities of the Church in convocation and, winning them provisionally over, set off with a bevy of bishops in his train to find the King at Northampton. Buckingham taunted the ecclesiastics with their time-serving and pointed out, what was indeed obvious, that there could now be no peace with Warwick. The battle that ensued was a brief one: it took place in the low-lying meadows between Northampton and Delapré Abbey to the south. The King's army had taken up a defensive position within entrenchments, which were now flooded by heavy rain, while the guns on which it relied were rendered useless. Once more Lancastrian ill-luck held. Once more after a short engagement there was a notable slaughter of Lancastrian leaders: the Duke of Buckingham, the Earl of Shrewsbury, the Percy Earl of Egremont, Lord Beaumont, and there were heavy casualties in the royal army.

Once more, as after St. Albans, the Yorkist lords sought out the King to assure him of their loyalty and their desire for good government. Henry was brought to London in all respect, and lodged in the bishop's palace. The lords in the Tower now surrendered, but the unpopular Scales, attempting to take sanctuary at Westminster, was recognised by Thames watermen and killed. The news of the day was expressed in verse; a ballad set up on the gates of Canterbury describes the situation at this time:

> Send home, most gracious lord Jesu most benign,
> Send home thy true blood unto his proper vein,
> Richard, Duke of York. . . .[23]

Though respectful in its treatment of Henry, the implication was clear enough. York was of the true royal blood; perhaps Prince Edward was not; nothing was said of the Queen, a foreigner. The poem implies what would probably be the solution of the dilemma most agreeable to the country at large: Henry as king to call home York as regent to govern the realm.

The Yorkists were now in a position to summon Parliament to settle the government of the country. York left Ireland in September and advanced in great state this time to claim the throne. Hitherto he had borne only the arms of York; now he blazoned the royal arms of England, asserting his legitimate descent through Lionel of Clarence, the senior brother of the Lancastrian Gaunt. When Parliament met at Westminster, York advanced to the empty throne and laid hand upon it as if to occupy it. He received no encouragement from the assembly—in complete contrast to what had happened in 1399. In this awkward situation, with York standing beside the throne, Archbishop Bourchier came forward to ask tactfully if he would like to see the King. York made his famous reply, with its claim to the throne: "I know of no person in this realm the which oweth not to wait on me, rather than I on him."

This did him no good with the assembly, which must have noted the contrast with the conduct of the King, always courteous and considerate to everyone—impossible to conceive of the royal Henry behaving with discourtesy. However, York retired to take possession of the King's own apartments, leaving the Queen's to Henry—she had taken refuge in North Wales. York proceeded to lay claim to the throne on the ground of hereditary right alone, and submitted it in constitutional manner to the Lords. The Lords traversed it on grounds of their repeated oaths of allegiance to the existing royal house, its recognition again and again by Parliament in its acts and laws. There was no doubt about the matter: the Lords, representative as they were of both State and Church, did not want York as king. And this in spite of the dispersal and destruction wrought among Lancastrian partisans, the large number of them dead or absent. It is an impressive tribute to the strength of the dynasty after all: people felt that this was the constitutional royal house. The extraordinary thing is that York should have miscalculated so badly. As we shall shortly see, he was a rash man. The Yorkists were apt to be.

Nevertheless they held the power. A compromise was arrived at which probably represented the general wish of the nation, if it could have been elicited. Henry was to retain the Crown for life; York and his heirs were to succeed him. The principality of Wales was assigned to York and his sons for their support; meanwhile he was to exercise the government as Protector. Henry was left in the bishop's palace in the City; York took over possession at Westminster.

The Queen was still at large: it was not to be supposed that she would assent and yield up the rights of her son without a fight for them. After the battle of Northampton she had escaped into Cheshire: the extraordinary *épopée* of her wartime adventures begins. Near Malpas she and her son fell into the hands of a band of armed men. They seized her baggage and then began to quarrel over the booty. Margaret's intuition told her to appeal to the decency of a youth among the band, whose appearance betokened that he was superior to the rest. She was not wrong: he took them up on his horse, and in the confusion got them away into the forest for refuge. There, Margaret, who was a great reader of romances, conjured up brigands behind every tree; and at length, as she afterwards recounted in exile, one appeared *"hideux et horrible en l'aspect."*[24] Trusting to instinct again—with her always more powerful than reason—she placed her boy in his hands, with "Save the son of your king!" The man responded to her appeal and saw them through safely to Harlech. Thence she made her way to Denbigh, where Jasper Tudor and Exeter joined her.

The Lancastrians were gathering their forces in the North: Percies, Dacres, Cliffords and the northern Nevilles who had been done out of their rights by the more successful southern branch—Salisbury, with his numerous brood of children headed by the fortunate Warwick, richest of the lot through his wife. The young Duke of Somerset and the Earl of Devon went north to join them, where the Lancastrians were pillaging Yorkist estates. York immediately marched north to deal with the situation. Optimistic and overconfident as he and his family all were, he took too small a force with him. He reached his own castle at Sandal, but found himself cut off by superior forces and sent for his son March to come to his aid. Before they could reach him he imprudently accepted the challenge the Lancastrians made. They presented themselves in battle array to the north of the castle, between Sandal and Wakefield. York rushed with his force downhill from the main gate to the south, where he had to wheel round the base of the hill to get at the enemy, and was conveniently caught in flank, "like a fish in a net, or a deer in a buckstall."[25] Here he fell, fighting at the head of his men—not very wisely for a Protector and Heir to the realm.

His younger son Rutland was escaping along the road to Wake-field, when a few yards from the bridge he was overtaken by Clifford and stabbed. "By God's blood, thy father slew mine, and so will I do thee." There was the blood-feud, open and un-ashamed. Among the slain were young Lord Harington, Sir Thomas Harington and his son Sir John—we see the way in which families were being decimated; Lord Bourchier's son, a Hastings, a Parr and Salisbury's second son, Sir Thomas Neville. In the night Salisbury himself was captured and beheaded. The heads of these leading Yorkists were then sent round to decorate the chief towns in Yorkshire, that of the Duke being sent to York where it was stuck on the walls crowned with a crown of paper and straw.

It is interesting that the Tudor chronicler Edward Hall, whose account of the engagement remains our chief authority, was de-scended from David Hall, who fell in it. Another member of the family may have been present and handed down his account.

This event precipitated the decisive actions of the next few months, and they came thick and fast.

In the first place, York's death left Margaret face to face with Warwick and young Edward of March, both abler men. Margaret herself crossed the frontier into Scotland to secure an alliance with Mary of Guelders, which she achieved at the price of sur-rendering Berwick to the Scots. The arrangement was confirmed by a large assembly of Lancastrian lords at York, the northern capital. This fetched the approval of the ally of the Scots, Charles VII, who thereupon opened the Channel harbours to the Lancas-trian enemies of the Yorkists controlling London. One sees how civil war plays fast and loose with the interests of a country.

With this trump card Margaret was enabled to make her fa-mous march south, with a large army of Northerners, with the aim of treating the Yorkists in London as they had done the Lancas-trians in the Tower.

In Wales, as a result of her efforts abroad, Jasper Tudor, Earl of Pembroke, and the Earl of Wiltshire landed with a mixed force of French, Bretons and Irish to raise Wales for the Lancastrians. This gave Edward of March the opportunity to show his quality. He was only nineteen, and was on his way to reinforce Warwick in

London before he was caught by Margaret's northern army. With the speed that was characteristic of him Edward turned back at once, overtook the earls and destroyed their force at the battle of Mortimer's Cross near Wigmore. That morning a curious natural phenomenon had alarmed his men—they had the credulity of medievals—when three suns were seen reflected in the firmament. A medieval commander had to be ready for this kind of thing, and he at once turned it into a good omen. "Be of good comfort and dread not. This is a good sign, for these three signs betoken the Father, the Son, and the Holy Ghost. And therefore let us have a good heart, and in the name of Almighty God go we against our enemies."[26] The chronicler adds, that he then "made his prayers and thanked God; and anon freshly and manly he took the field upon his enemies and put them to flight."

He chased them as far as Hereford, but the slippery Jasper got away—as he always did, until he finally won with his nephew upon the field of Bosworth. But his father, old Owen Tudor—husband of Catherine of Valois, ancestor of the lucky Tudors, was caught and beheaded in the market-place. And his head was "set upon the highest grice [step] of the market cross; and a mad woman combed his hair and washed away the blood off his face, and she got candles and set about him burning, more than a hundred." At the last as at the first Owen had a way with women. He cherished the belief that he would never be beheaded until he saw the axe and the block; and even "when he was in his doublet he trusted on pardon and grace till the collar of his red velvet doublet was ripped off." He had been so lucky in life. At the end he remembered his luck and his Queen: "that head shall lie on the stock that was wont to lie on Queen Catherine's lap."

Meanwhile Margaret was marching south with her considerable array of Lancastrian notables and her large army of wild Northerners, looting and living off town and country on their route along the Great North Road: Grantham, Stamford, Peterborough, Huntingdon. All suffered their visitation, "as they had been paynims, or Saracens and no Christian men," wrote the horrified chronicler of Croyland Abbey, crowded with folk who had taken refuge there out of the way in the Fens.[27] The report of the Northerners' outrageous doings helped to rally the South against their lawful

Queen and lend support to the Yorkists at this juncture. What people felt can be gathered from Clement Paston's letter to his brother:

> In this country every man is well willing to go with my lords here; and I hope God shall help them, for the people in the North rob and steal and be appointed to pill all this country and give away men's goods and livelihoods in all the south country, and that will ask a mischief. My lords that be here have as much as they may do to keep down all this country, more than four or five shires; for they would be upon the men in the North, for it is for the weal of all the South.[28]

In the break-up of the country that letter speaks for the south-eastern counties, the most advanced, the richest and most progressive areas, against the backward and rude North. Here is another factor to remember in the complexities released when there is confusion and chaos at the head of a society. The South-East, in despair of good government, is in process of moving over to the Yorkists, willing to give them a try.

Margaret was drawing near more rapidly than Warwick expected, and in fact she effected a surprise. The Yorkists expected to intercept her along the northern route into St. Albans; but at Dunstable she crossed over to Watling Street and approached from the north-west. This effectively turned Warwick's flank and prepared positions at the eastern end of the town. The Lancastrians by-passed the town to the north, thus dividing Warwick's army in two, and came out on Barnet heath where the main struggle took place. Once more, as at Ludford Bridge, a contingent of the Yorkist troops had difficulties of conscience in fighting against the royalist cause and passed over to the Queen's side in the course of the battle. This completed the Yorkist rout. The St. Albans chronicler attributed the defeat of Warwick's men to their lack of endurance, and this to the fact that they were Southerners having to contend with Northerners. Warwick managed to escape with his body of men and make, not for London, but for the Cotswolds to join up with the victorious Edward of March, already a better soldier, marching from the west.

Warwick had brought the King with him to the field of battle; it is reported that while the battle raged Henry laughed and sang

1. Richard II.

2. Richard II yields the crown to Bolingbroke.

3. Henry Bolingbroke leads Richard II to London, 1399.

4. Henry IV: from the tomb in Canterbury Cathedral.

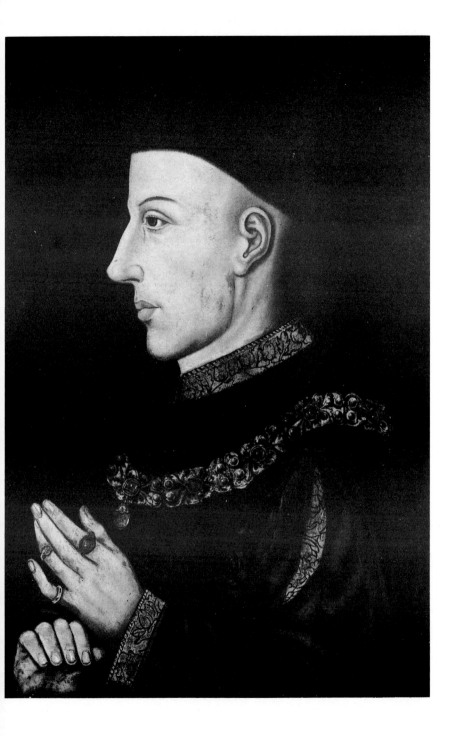

5. Henry V.

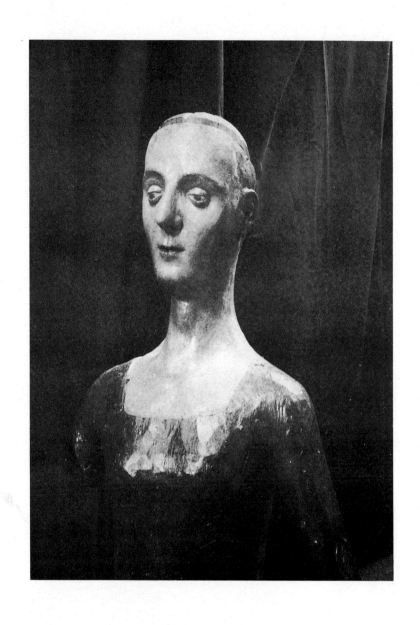

6. Queen Catherine: funeral effigy.

7. The Child-King Henry VI.

8. Margaret of Anjou.

9. Henry VI.

10. Edward IV.

11. Elizabeth Woodville, wife of Edward IV.

12. Richard III.

13. Lady Margaret Beaufort.

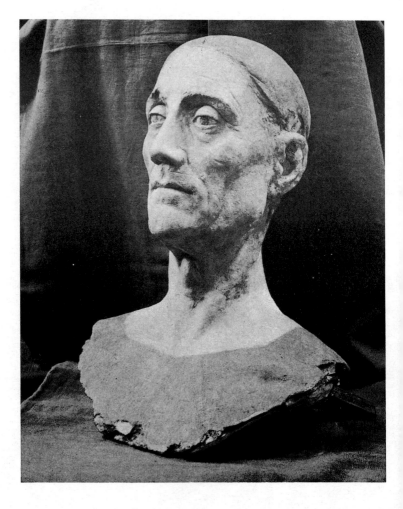

14. Henry VII: funeral effigy based on a death mask from Westminster Abbey.

15. Elizabeth of York, wife of Henry VII.

16. Henry VII: bust by Pietro Torrigiani.

under a tree. (Perhaps, from an ultimate point of view, it was a more sensible activity than the other.) In the confusion of War-wick's retreat it was impossible to take the King with him, and this most valuable piece on the chessboard fell into his wife's hands. Henry was brought to Lord Clifford's tent, where he embraced wife and son once more. Clever Dr. Morton was present, the Prince of Wales's Chancellor, who produced a book of orisons, and Henry blessed his son and knighted him. The Prince's badge, the ostrich feathers of the Princes of Wales, had been borne by the royal army that day, and now the boy knighted some thirty of his victorious following. The first person was the doughty soldier, Andrew Trollope, who said: "my lord, I have not de-served it, for I slew but fifteen men. I stood still in one place [he had hurt his foot] and they came unto me. But they bode still with me," he added modestly.[29]

There followed only three executions: of those who had had charge of the King during the battle, Lord Bonville, Sir Thomas Kyriell and the banner-bearer. Lord Montagu would have been beheaded, if retaliation had not been threatened against Somerset's brother in Yorkist hands. The little Prince of Wales, a boy of eight, was made to preside over the court-martial that sentenced these men and then, with his mother, to witness their executions. He was being "blooded."

The game was apparently in Margaret's hands: it is thought that if she had entered London now, with the King, the royal house would have been reinstated. But the City had the worst impression of the Northerners, and remained barred and bolted behind its walls till terms of no pillaging were exacted. A deputation of ladies was sent out, the dowager Duchesses of Buckingham and Bedford (mother, by Lord Rivers, of Elizabeth Woodville), to fix up terms. But the citizens were not having Margaret and her Northern-ers in at any price: they took matters into their own hands, over the heads of the civic authorities, and opened their gates to March and Warwick instead on 27 February 1461. For Margaret there was nothing for it but to retire with her Northerners, looting and living off the country as they went—but with the King now in her possession—to the northern capital.

The fate of the kingdom was in suspense. With the King now out of their hands the Yorkists had to make a momentous decision. They could not go on with the constitutional formula by which Richard of York ruled in Henry's name; Richard was dead and Parliament was not in session. There was nothing for it but to make his son Edward king. He was made king by acclamation—as we have seen, that was an element in the rite, as it had been from the time of that other king by conquest, William the Conqueror. On 1 March his soldiers acclaimed Edward as king, on 4 March the citizens of London in St. Paul's. Thence he was enthroned in Westminster Hall, and went in procession to the Abbey, where St. Edward's sceptre was placed in his hands. Finally he was acclaimed again, and the lords present knelt and did homage to him as king by hereditary right.

It was not a coronation: for that Edward would have to fight.

There was no time to lose: Margaret had King Henry and a large army with her, with the undoubted balance of the nobility; she had the open door to Scotland at her back, the alliance with France and communications with France and Brittany through Jasper Tudor's Pembroke. On paper she ought to have won. The Yorkists were a minority party; but they had London and the South-East with them, and the extraordinary chance of Edward's exceptional military ability. It was now to be put to the test.

In the latter half of March he was moving his forces north for the decisive battle, joining up with Warwick and Fauconberg's contingents. He could not afford to wait for Norfolk's, though the East Anglians would at length have their chance against the Northerners. Edward caught up with the much bigger Lancastrian army at Towton, stationed in a strong position on a little plateau beside the road from Ferrybridge to York. Behind the Lancastrian position was the valley of the Cock beck, a narrow but deep stream in spate. The Lancastrian army may have been some ten thousand strong, the Yorkist considerably less; the numbers were greater than had ever been seen before on a field of battle in England. Since it was Palm Sunday Henry wanted a truce that the feast might be kept religiously. No one wanted to listen to his mild voice. The battle was fought with grim determination on both sides, in ghastly weather for "all the season it snew."

The Lancastrians had the advantage of position; the Yorkists had to fight their way inch by inch up the slopes. Then the house of Lancaster had its usual stroke of ill-luck: a snowstorm from the south-east blinded them and impeded their bow-shots. It became a desperate hand-to-hand struggle on the plateau, and the Yorkists were being worn down by sheer weight of numbers, when the arrival of the Norfolk men up the road from Ferrybridge turned the left flank of the Lancastrians. It not only decided the struggle but turned defeat into a rout, for the Lancastrians were now driven back down into the Cock valley where hundreds were drowned in the swollen stream. There was a terrible slaughter in this late unexpected reverse, and many of the best Lancastrian leaders were killed: yet another Percy Earl of Northumberland dying for the house the Percies had placed on the throne; the Lords Dacre of Gillesland, Neville, Clifford, Wells, Willoughby, de Mauley and famous Sir Andrew Trollope, who had led the van with Northumberland. The Earl of Wiltshire was subsequently captured and beheaded; so too with the Earl of Devon.

For the house of Lancaster, Towton really decided the issue. But we must not forget that the decision was made not by the country, but by force.

Margaret managed to escape into Scotland, however, to carry on the struggle, carrying Henry and Prince Edward with her; they were accompanied by Somerset, Exeter, Hungerford, de Roos and Chief Justice Fortescue. If only Edward had been able to seal the door into Scotland he might have rounded up this remnant of the Lancastrian leadership. But beyond Newcastle he could not go, and the loss of Berwick closed off Scotland. This meant that Margaret's intrigues could still keep the Lancastrian cause going from these bases, in spite of smashing defeat.

Edward returned to make a triumphal entry into York as king, his first act being to remove the heads of his father, his brother and his uncle from the gates of the city and to bury them with their bodies at Pontefract. He celebrated Easter with great pomp and splendour—already a marked contrast with the humble Henry —in the northern capital, and then took the road south for his coronation.

CHAPTER VIII

Edward IV: The Yorkist Experiment

There could be no greater contrast than that between King Henry VI, a holy and humble man of heart, no good as a ruler, and the young man who took his place at the age of nineteen. Edward IV was not only the handsomest prince, but if anything the handsomest man of his time—so the historian Commines described him after seeing him face to face. He stood head and shoulders above other men, nearly six feet four inches—which gave an even more striking impression then, when medieval people were on the average shorter than we are today. He was broad-chested and well-knit, brown-haired and with a pleasant expression. He was very engaging. As Miss Scofield demurely says, one of his most endearing characteristics was his active desire to give pleasure, which, where the women were concerned, he was well equipped to give. When he was leaving the Netherlands after his exile in 1471 he walked along the road to Flushing instead of going by boat as planned, simply to give the country folk the pleasure of seeing a procession. When enjoying himself at Windsor he invited the mayor and aldermen of London, "for none other errand but to have them hunt and be merry with him."[1] In the first flush of his youth when he was still slender, he must have been irresistible. So at any rate the women found: he became a tremendous womaniser. Where the sainted Henry was surrounded by churchmen—and the Church was really with him—Edward had numerous mistresses, and made many explorations among the wives of his London citizens. He was easy-going and very familiar. It did not detract from his popularity.

Sir Thomas More, who knew people who had known Edward well, describes his personality vividly for us.

He was a goodly personage and very princely to behold, of heart courageous, politic in counsel, in adversity nothing abashed, in prosperity rather joyful than proud, in peace just and merciful, in war sharp and fierce, in the field bold and hardy, and nevertheless no farther than wisdom would, adventurous. . . . He was of visage lovely, of body mighty, strong and clean made. Howbeit in his latter days, with over-liberal diet, somewhat corpulent and burly, and nevertheless not uncomely, he was of youth greatly given to fleshly wantonness. . . . This fault not greatly grieved the people. . . .[2]

Edward's popularity was as much of a weapon as the other weapons he carried. He was indeed a natural leader of men: without his exceptional military, and in the end political, ability—for he learned from experience—the Yorkists would never have won. What people wanted from them was what the rightful king was incapable of giving them—good government. So Yorkist rule was in the nature of an experiment: it would have to prove itself by its success. After two decades of successful rule on Edward's part it can be said to have justified itself.

It is impossible here to give a detailed account of Edward's crowded reign. And indeed that is not my purpose in this book, but, as far as possible, to make the long duel between the house of Lancaster and the house of York, and its outcome, intelligible. Edward's reign, as a whole, falls neatly into two decades. In the first, 1461–70, he is engaged in consolidating his position with the aid of his overmighty subject, Warwick the Kingmaker, who felt that Edward owed his kingdom to him and the support of the Nevilles; in suppressing remnants of Lancastrian resistance about the country; lastly in a duel with Warwick for supreme power and the direction of the country's policy. In the second decade, 1471–83—after being driven from the country for a time by Warwick and the pathetic, shadowy Re-adeption of Henry VI— Edward emerges unquestioned master over both Warwick, the treacherous Clarence (Edward's own brother) and the Lancastrians, to rule the country as he saw fit, and to do it very well.

There followed his early death—he was only forty when he died—leaving his heir, Edward V, only a boy. There were all the dangers of a minority again. The kingship was seized by the boy's uncle, Richard III, and both Edward's boys made away with—or the Lancastrians, in the person of Henry Tudor, might never have come back. The story of the dynastic struggle does not cease to be extraordinary, full of sudden turns and unexpected changes and chances; indeed, it becomes more sinister and lurid, until customary and constituted ways return with the last sprig of the Lancastrians. Even so, Henry Tudor would not have won if Richard III had not defeated himself: the strange battle of Bosworth, decisive as it was, was not so much a victory as a betrayal of Richard by his own side. That is what has to be accounted for.

In this later period, the prelude to Bosworth, we see the Yorkists eat each other up—or they would never have had to yield to the Welsh Pretender, last hope of his house, abroad. Edward IV was easy-going enough; but he was not made like Henry VI, whom he put to death. One day when King Henry was riding into London through Cripplegate, he saw a ghastly-looking object on a stake over the gate, and was told it was the quarter of a traitor executed for treason against himself. "Take it down at once," he said. "I would not have a Christian body so treated on my account for anything."[3] Edward IV, on the other hand, had his brother Clarence put to death in the Tower; it may have been dire necessity, but it was done. The third brother, Richard, then had Edward's two boys murdered in the Tower. Nobody had any doubt at the time who was responsible for it. It is not too much to say that the family of York was a family stained with blood.

From his triumph on the field of Towton, Edward rode slowly south through May and June to his coronation. He visited various areas—Lancashire and Cheshire, faithful to the Lancastrian cause, to overawe them with his presence. Thence he came down Watling Street to Stony Stratford, where he stayed a couple of days, to be overawed in turn by another presence. Something must have happened there, for Grafton nearby in the forest was the residence of the Lancastrian Lord Rivers, father of Elizabeth Woodville. Her mother, his second wife, was that beautiful Jacquetta of Luxemburg whom the great Duke of Bedford had married, shortly before his death. Elizabeth had inherited her mother's beauty and had been recently widowed, her husband Sir John Grey having been killed at the second battle of St. Albans, fighting for Margaret. Hitherto they had been faithful Lancastrians. Suddenly, from Stony Stratford, Lord Rivers was pardoned, and in a month's time his son, another Lord Scales, received his pardon too. The spinster

heart of Miss Scofield leaped at the explanation: "who can doubt
that a pair of bright eyes which Edward IV had just seen, probably
for the first time . . . had pleaded for a father's pardon?"[4]
Evidently the seed had not fallen on stony soil. Right up to the
early years of this century an ancient oak was to be seen in the
forest, which folk called the King's Oak and venerated as Edward
and Elizabeth's trysting-place; hence Grafton came by its name,
Grafton Regis.

Edward went on to be crowned in the Abbey by Archbishop
Bourchier at the end of June. Money was short, as it continued
to be with such outlay on the wars; the cash for the festivities
was raised by the obliging archbishop exacting a tenth from the
convocation of Canterbury. Edward had sent at once for his two
young brothers, George and Richard, whom their mother—Cecily,
Duchess of York—had hurried across to the Netherlands on Margaret's near approach to London the previous year. These boys
were now created Dukes of Clarence and Gloucester, royal titles,
and there was a large elevation of Yorkists to the peerage, where
the Lancastrians were still in a majority. When the Yorkist
Parliament met in November the Lancastrian kings were declared
"intruders," Edward IV the true heir and representative of Richard
II, and there followed a large-scale attainder of Lancastrian peers
and supporters, including such personages as Chief Justice Fortescue and Dr. Morton. Edward himself, always gallant to the ladies,
produced a roll of exemptions for the dowager Duchesses of Bedford (Elizabeth Woodville's mother), Somerset, Norfolk, Suffolk
and Buckingham, and for that royal person waiting in the wings,
Margaret Beaufort, Countess of Richmond, mother of the little
Henry Tudor.

Edward was by nature conciliatory and even too ready to make
friends; though he made mistakes this way, it was politic of him
in the long run. It was much less in keeping with Warwick's
nature, who played a dominating rôle in these early years and
certainly underrated the independence and strength of Edward's
character. The magnificent Warwick behaved more like a Grand
Vizier; Edward owed his throne to the Nevilles—who were everywhere—and he was certainly made to feel it. A young man for a
ruler, he was learning: he behaved himself with restraint and
circumspection, except in affairs of the heart. Thus he managed
to work in harness with the dominating Warwick. Even so, it took

FRANCE 1430

The Anglo-Burgundian territories are grouped thus:

A. i. The Duchy of Normandy.

    ii. The *Pais de Conquête*: The lands which Henry V had conquered between the Norman frontier and Paris, corresponding to the ancient Vexin, English and Norman.

   iii. The Maine border.

B.   The territories which accepted Henry VI as the result of the Treaty of Troyes: the Île de France, the Chartrain, Champagne, Picardy.

C.   The Burgundian fiefs which Philip of Burgundy held of Henry VI as King of France: Burgundy (Duchy of), Artois, French Flanders, along with County of Burgundy.

D.   Brittany during the time when Duke John recognized Henry's claim.

The early governorships were:

Lower Normandy, the Earl of Suffolk; Champagne and Brie, the Earl of Salisbury; Alençon, expanded into Maine, 1425, Sir John Fastolf. The Duke of Bedford, was Count of Maine, and as such had headquarters at Le Mans.

Demesne of Charles VII.

Boundary (fluctuating) of Lancastrian France.

(Based, with acknowledgement, on the map of the late Professor James Tait in R. L. Poole, *A Historical Atlas of Modern Europe*, Plate 56)

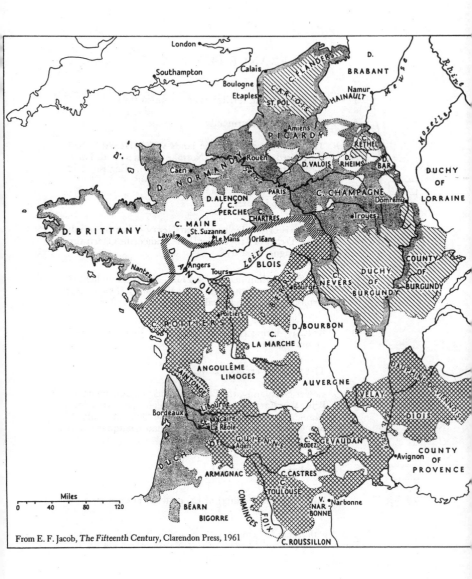

From E. F. Jacob, *The Fifteenth Century*, Clarendon Press, 1961

them three and a half years to subdue the remains of Lancastrian resistance.

In South Wales, Edward's faithful supporters the Herberts made a clearance and Jasper Tudor's castle of Pembroke was surrendered to them. With the castle was captured Jasper's nephew, little Henry Tudor, a boy of four, who was taken into the Herberts' household to be brought up. Jasper's castle and earldom were taken from him and given to Herbert, who becomes the (Yorkist) Earl of Pembroke: very confusing. The little boy's royal patrimony and the title of Richmond were confiscated to Edward's brothers in turn. Years afterwards Henry Tudor told Commines bitterly that from the age of five he was either a prisoner or a fugitive— such was his impression of the life he had lived.

Lancastrian resistance was much stronger on the Scottish Border, where Margaret was in alliance with the Scots and the Percies held Northumberland for Henry. In 1461 they besieged Carlisle; War- wick's brother Montagu raised the siege, while Warwick repelled further raids along the Border. Next year, Charles VII having at last died and been succeeded by an even more slippery customer, Louis XI, Margaret left Scotland, landing in remote Brittany on Good Friday 1462, to reach terms with him for an attack on England. Mean as could be, the mistake he made was in

Giving too little, and asking too much.

He insisted on Calais being mortgaged to him—one can imagine the unpatriotic impression in England, after the surrender of Ber- wick; and then he sent far too small an armament, though under the doughty Brézé, to Scotland with Margaret. There she picked up Henry, and made for the Northumbrian coast, where she gar- risoned the strongholds of Alnwick, Dunstanburgh and Bamburgh. The approach of Warwick with an army forced Margaret to put out to sea. She had her usual ill-luck: a storm dispersed her ships, many of her Frenchmen were taken on Holy Island, she herself escaped in a small fishing boat in heavy seas to Berwick.

With his large forces Warwick was able to reduce the Northum- brian strongholds. But the moment he turned his back and went south, they were surrendered to the Lancastrians again—which showed plainly enough where Northumbrian sympathies were. In the summer of 1463 Margaret decided to seek better support on the Continent. Parting from Henry, "never again to meet on earth,"

she left Bamburgh with her son, the Prince of Wales, under
Brézé's conduct.[5] Landing at Sluys she found herself in the territory of her Burgundian adversary and threw herself on his generosity. The indomitable woman landed "in a destitute condition,"
depending on Brézé for her daily bread. "In Northumberland, a
herring a day had been her ration." What a *renversement* since
the day, only a few years before, when Margaret Paston had seen
the Queen at Norwich attended by her fine, "fresh gentlewomen"!

Nevertheless, since Louis was engaged in betraying her—as,
sooner or later, he betrayed everyone—she insisted on an interview
with Philip of Burgundy to find out where she stood. Disguised
as a simple peasant-woman she drove in a common four-horse
wain—not without risk of capture by the English at St. Omer—
to extract some money from Philip and to be forwarded to Louis.
Meanwhile Louis had agreed on a truce with Edward IV, which
meant that Margaret would be immobilised and kept as a gage in
France, until the next turn in the political kaleidoscope, when she
and her son could be let out once more to serve Louis' purpose
in distracting England.

In England, Edward was in great jollity, pursuing his courtship
with Elizabeth Woodville, with whom he was undoubtedly enamoured; unfortunately for him the way to her charms was only
through marriage. He had brought back the young Duke of Somerset with him from the North, and was doing everything to win
him over. When Parliament met Somerset was restored in "name,
state, style, honour and dignity." He even recovered the lands he
had lost by his attainder, while Edward gave him considerable
sums of money. (The Duke of Exeter was in the Netherlands beg-
ging his bread.) The two young men hunted together, Edward
arranged tournaments for his new-found friend; they often shared
a bed; after all they were two unmarried young men together.

Nevertheless, at the end of the year, Somerset stole away to
share King Henry's poverty in Bamburgh, and shortly to die for
him. He was a Beaufort: he could not do otherwise.

For nine months, extraordinary as it seems, from the autumn
of 1463 to May 1464, Henry reigned over his little shire around
Alnwick from his stronghold on the great rock at Bamburgh,
looking out over those sombre basalt cliffs and the cold northern
sea—the ancient capital of Northumbria. Somerset's arrival with

his men was the signal for renewed risings in the North, in the wild Pennines where Skipton Castle was seized, in South Lancashire and Cheshire, while Jasper was at work in Wales. Three times Warwick thought that he had subdued the North; but he hadn't. His brother Montagu was sent to crush the last embers of resistance. At a skirmish in Percy country near Morpeth a Percy was killed; then at Hexham the last little Lancastrian force was crushed. Somerset was captured and beheaded at once; then Lords Hungerford and de Roos, and several knights. At York, in Edward's presence fourteen of Henry's personal attendants were executed; lastly, the captain of Bamborough, Sir Ralph Grey, of the Northumbrian family to become so famous in later English history.

One sees how tenacious Lancastrian devotion was to their rightful king, and the Yorkist determination to root it out, making successive murderous inroads into the Lancastrian peerage and gentry. "Yet these judicial executions made any reconciliation of parties more difficult than ever."[6]

Henry had not been in these last actions, but at Bywell Castle in the valley of the upper Tyne, whence he was spirited away by his faithful adherents and lost to view. Some of his personal belongings were found, including his "bycocket," or red coroneted cap—which was venerated by the faithful after his martyrdom. Touching it was thought a sure cure for headache—one perceives the mad logic of folklore beliefs. King Henry's Lament refers to this period when he was wandering in the hills and dales of this remote Pennine country; perhaps, for once, we will quote it in the original fifteenth-century spelling as an example, somewhat rebarbative as it is:*

> Sum tyme I rodde in clothe of gold so red,
>   Thorow-oute ynglond in many a town;
> Alas, I dare nowth schewe now my hede—
>   Thys word ys turnyd clene uppe so down! . . .

> Of the bledde ryall I am kom;
>   Kynge herry of Monmowthe me beforn,
> He was my fadir and I his sone,
>   And of qwen kateryn was I born.

> Many a man for me hath be slayn. . . .[7]

* And also to show that there is no point in pedantically retaining it.

During these months men did not know whether Henry was alive or dead. He was moved about from hiding places near Appleby in the Lake Country, then Furness, across to Bolton in the Pennines, lastly to Clitheroe, among faithful Tunstalls, Tempests and Talbots. Some relics of the King were preserved at Bolton right up to the dispersals and decline of our time—a boot and glove, the latter of diminutive size, a small hand incapable of rule. The King's whereabouts were at last betrayed by a monk, and he was taken by a Harington, who got the Tunstall estates for his services. Henry had a valet in attendance, and two learned chaplains, one of them formerly Dean of Windsor. Brought to London, Henry was escorted by Warwick through the city to guard against any manifestations of sympathy: no pretence of respect this time, his feet were bound to the stirrups by leather thongs. He was taken to the Tower, where he disappears from view for the next five years.

Meanwhile Edward had accomplished his secret marriage. On 30 April he rode over to Stony Stratford as if to hunt in the forest. Very early next day—the romantic heart of Miss Scofield leaps to think it was "May Day morning, just the time for romance"—Edward married the luscious widow, *"pour sa beauté et par amourette,"* who was five years his senior and already the mother of two sons.[8] The only witnesses were the bride's mother Jacquetta, two gentlewomen, the priest and a youth "to help the priest sing." Nothing of this was known to Edward's lofty and superb mentor, Warwick: Edward, always affable and wishing to avoid displeasure, would have to face the music later.

Warwick was deep in negotiations with Louis XI for a French alliance, to be sealed by a marriage of Edward to Louis' sister-in-law. Of course there were great advantages: it would end the house of Lancaster's chief hope of foreign support in France and (with it, as always) Scotland, and thus give security to the new dynasty, still very insecure. Warwick was a man of one idea, and this very much his own idea. What Louis wanted was to inveigle England into his war with Burgundy, which meant quarrelling with her chief market in the Netherlands. Indeed the commercial link with the Netherlands was a dominant strand in England's foreign policy during all this period, from Edward III's Burgundian alliance onwards. Edward IV, who had a far more flexible mind, appreciated this and was determined to keep on good terms with Burgundy. It was curious that Warwick should not have appreciated the strength of English hostility to France, and the unpopularity of another French marriage, with the warning of Margaret of Anjou before his eyes. Lost in his idea of his own grandeur, the Neville Kingmaker was out of touch with what common people thought—or perhaps he did not care.

The showdown came at a meeting of the Council at Reading in September, when final instructions were to be drawn for Warwick's grand embassy to France to conclude the marriage. Edward was driven to confess that he was already married and to whom—a Lancastrian widow with children of her own. There was a deep popular prejudice against a king marrying a widow, i.e., someone not a virgin—another touch of anthropological interest in this medieval period so full of it. There was consternation: the announcement caused "great displeasure to many great lords, and especially to the larger part of all his Council."[9] The house of York would pay bitterly for Edward's marriage later. For the present all behaved well: Elizabeth was escorted by Clarence and Warwick into the abbey church and there honoured as queen. Edward, already well-nigh smothered by Nevilles, had taken an independent step and shown that he had a mind of his own; he attempted to mollify Warwick by making his brother Archbishop of York, yet another Neville in high place, entrenched in the North.

Edward was anxious to have his questionable wife properly esteemed and prepared a grand coronation for her, on Whit Sunday 1465. In order to bring home to everybody that his wife's ancestry, if only on the mother's side, was as good as his own, a brilliant suite was bidden over under her kinsman Jacques of Luxemburg, head of the house of St. Pol. The royal manors of Greenwich and Sheen were granted to the late widow, now queen—it is difficult to understand a handsome young man being so enamoured, as people found it even then. Something had to be done to bring up to scratch her by no means exalted relations on her father's side: the Woodvilles were a new family, of considerable talent, but of no extraction. However, the new Queen was already on the look-out for them. She had managed to catch the heir to the ancient Arundel earldom for one of her sisters. Two other sisters were married to the heirs of the Earls of Essex and Kent. Then the Duke of Buckingham, who was a royal ward still in his minority, was married off to Catherine Woodville—and, immensely aristocratic and of royal blood, he hated her and the Woodvilles ever after. (This led to terrible consequences after Edward's death, in the minority of *his* son.) The ancient dowager Duchess of Norfolk, getting on for four score, found herself marrying John Woodville, a lad of twenty. The lady was aunt to Warwick, to whom the marriage was "a sore trial"—one would have thought it was more so to the bridegroom; everyone was shocked at this match, but a Woodville would enjoy, if not the wife, at any rate her property. Mary Woodville was married to the heir of Lord Herbert, Edward's closest friend. For her son, Thomas Grey, the Queen bought from the impoverished Duchess of Exeter, for four thousand marks, the daughter and heiress of the exiled Duke, who had been promised to Warwick's nephew. (Well, people said, weren't the Woodville's Lancastrians anyway?) Lastly, there was the father. The faithful Mountjoy was removed from the office of Treasurer to make way for Lord Rivers, now made an earl.

The new Queen's family were in clover. And naturally people, particularly the Nevilles, were furious.

On Edward's part it was not all besottedness on a female who was out to make the most of the chance a little thing had brought her. There was an element of calculation in it: Edward was building up a personal party wholly devoted to himself. The no less numerous Nevilles were too much with him and around him and on top of him. But the Woodvilles were not rooted in the country as the Nevilles were: they brought no accession of power to the dynasty. They did, however, have the sense to support Edward's personal policy of friendship with Burgundy. In the end they paid a terrible price for their elevation, as the house of York proceeded to eat each other up. This the Lancastrian house, less passionate and more respectable, did not do.

What brought about the fatal breach between Warwick and Edward was not the marriage nor the Queen's regrettable relations but, as usual, the struggle for power. Human beings will do anything for supreme power at all times and in all places. Warwick was determined to force the French alliance on Edward at all costs —it became the touchstone of the older man's power and influence over the younger who was king. Warwick was also tempted by a pastmaster at tempting mortals on their weaker side, Louis XI, who offered him the principality of Holland if he would displace Edward. There was another string to Warwick's bow: he would marry one of his daughters (his heirs, for he had no son) to Edward's next brother, Clarence. For all Edward's attentions his Queen had not yet produced a son, merely daughters—Elizabeth in 1466, Mary in 1467, Cecily in 1469. Clarence was a willing tool. Tall and good-looking he was not without charm; he was eloquent and plausible, restless, intriguing, treacherous. It seems that he could not bear to be the second person to anybody. Instead of helping his brother to root the Yorkist dynasty in the realm he turned out to be another Humphrey of Gloucester, only worse. Nevertheless he was next brother to Edward: perhaps through marrying him to his daughter Warwick could seat the Nevilles on the throne itself.

With these aims, and with these tools, Warwick proceeded to undo all the good work he had done for the house of York, uprooted Edward for a time, put Henry VI back on the throne, brought Margaret and her son back to England, to the death of both father and boy, as well as his own.

For some time Warwick had been acutely dissatisfied and marked his dissatisfaction by remaining away from Court in the North. Meanwhile Edward brought his policy of friendship with the Netherlands to good point by marrying his sister Margaret to Charles the Bold, Duke of Burgundy. This proved a good investment for the house of York. It may have decided Warwick to come into the open against his former protégé, the King. Warwick had been exhibiting signs of disloyalty for some time, and Edward had recruited to himself a personal body-guard. Rumours were put about that Edward was a bastard—he had been born abroad —and that Clarence, who had been born in Dublin in 1449, was the legitimate heir of York. This tale, which was raised at the time of Edward's unpopular marriage, was put to more malign use later by the third brother, Richard. What a lot they were, to be sure!

In June 1469 Warwick with his elder daughter Isobel and his brother, the Archbishop, converged on Sandwich; so also Clarence. So also his mother, Cecily Duchess of York, much to their surprise. She must have got wind of the conspiracy and have done her best to stop the rift within her family. In vain: in July, Warwick crossed to Calais, where his archiepiscopal brother married Isobel to Clarence. It was an act of state in direct defiance of the King, and upon its heels Warwick and his son-in-law returned in force and advanced upon London, putting out the usual proclamations against misgovernment, in this case directed against the King's evil advisers the Woodvilles. This coincided with a rising instigated by the Nevilles in Yorkshire.

Edward was completely taken aback by open war from this quarter: his overconfidence betrayed him, he was away from his capital which he had left undefended. He was now caught between two stools. At Edgecot his friends the Herberts were crushed by the Northerners and both of them beheaded. Earl Rivers and his son Sir John Woodville were taken in the West Country and executed. It fell to Edward, with his great friend Lord Hastings and his brother Gloucester, to be captured by the Archbishop— for a soldier that must have been the unkindest cut of all. However, Edward put the best face on the situation, was genial to Warwick and Clarence and agreed to their demands. The situation was very much like that of 1460 over again, with Warwick playing the part of Richard of York. But Edward was no Henry VI, and Warwick found that he could not control the country in his own person without the King.

Edward had been rusticated to the Neville fortress of Middleham in the far North, and then allowed on parole to go south to Pontefract. There was no demand whatever for Clarence in any quarter; nor did Warwick, who had taken his measure, make any move in his favour. On the contrary, we find Lincolnshire early next year shouting for King Henry. Meanwhile Edward had been conducted back to London by the Neville archbishop—more of a Neville than an archbishop—and one would have supposed that Warwick would have been satisfied with what he had achieved: the elimination of the Woodvilles. Not so: what he wanted was to re-establish the dominion he had exercised over his protégé in the first years of his reign and to have the direction of the country's policy. He had by this time a perfect fixation on the French alliance: with more than a tinge of megalomania he was determined to force it not only on Edward but on a recalcitrant country. To this end he stirred up local rebellions to confuse government, under cover of which to forward his plot. When these risings were successfully repressed, it was found that Warwick and Clarence had been behind them. Summoned to London to be called to account, they fled across the Channel to take refuge not in Calais, which refused to admit them, but in the dominions of Louis XI.

Warwick had at last come to his fatal turning-point. He could not rule England through Edward, nor could he through Clarence, who was a non-starter. Perhaps if he were to come to terms with Margaret of Anjou and restore Henry, he would rule at last in England? This at any rate was the plan that Warwick and Louis excogitated between them. Thus the greatest servant of the house of York passed over to the enemy.

Louis would aid the restoration with a fleet, men and money; in return Warwick promised to make England an ally of France for war on Burgundy. Since Clarence was no good for his purposes Warwick would marry his other daughter Anne to Prince Edward, Henry and Margaret's son. Here the great difficulty would be Margaret, even to bring her to meet Warwick, yet nothing could be done without her.

Since her return from her adventures in England in 1463 Margaret had been living with her son and a small suite of faithful attendants at St. Mihiel in Bar, a small duchy of her father's, on the Marne in north-eastern France. She was living on a pension allowed her by the impecunious René. Her chief attendant was the distinguished lawyer Chief Justice Fortescue, who was engaged in instructing the Prince for the rule over the country he would never exercise. For him Fortescue wrote his book, *De Laudibus Legum Angliae*. Fortescue wrote, "we be all in great poverty, but yet the Queen sustaineth us in meat and drink, so as we be not in extreme necessity. Her highness may do not more to us than she doth."[10] It was touching the way the judge warmed the cockles of his heart in the bitterness of exile with the thought of the superiority of English laws. He threw himself with enthusiasm into supporting Warwick's scheme, grasping at what was the best hope of a Lancastrian restoration, and drawing up a programme for it to pursue.

Margaret was overborne by the pressure put on her from one side and the other: at this juncture one feels sorry for her. She doubted the sincerity of her great enemy, who had publicly declared her son a bastard. She did not wish to be put on the throne of England again under his aegis. She did not want her son to marry Warwick's daughter. Yet his defection from the house of York was the best chance for the Lancastrians in two decades. Warwick wisely left the task of persuading her to Louis XI, the most persuasive, and the most treacherous, of men.

In the end they all met at Angers—Louis and René, Margaret, Warwick and Fortescue—and at the end of July 1470 terms were worked out. Warwick went down on his knees before the Queen and asked pardon for all the wrongs and injuries he had done her in the past. He was kept there a quarter of an hour, and then pardoned; he thereupon did homage and fealty, swearing to be a faithful subject of the King, Queen and Prince unto death. He was. In the end Margaret consented to the marriage of her son with his daughter, and they were married. She did what she could to protect him and herself: her precious only son was not to go over to England with Warwick, but to wait until he had secured the government and made the country safe for him. By one of the ironies of history her caution, in this instance, played her false. The event was too pitiful.

The parties swore on the relics of the True Cross in the cathedral at Angers to be faithful to Henry VI, and shortly after Warwick sailed.

Once more Edward IV allowed himself to be caught out by overconfidence, and a genial contempt for Warwick's military capacity. Edward was far away in the North when Warwick landed in Devon—the West Country was Lancastrian in sentiment—and won the race to London. Indeed Edward unaccountably delayed, and on his way south was very nearly surprised by the defection of the Marquis Montagu, Warwick's brother, with his body of troops. Edward managed to escape by boat across the Wash to King's Lynn, with only Gloucester, his crony Lord

Hastings and the new Lord Rivers, and thence fled to the safety of the Netherlands.

In London, Edward's queen was expecting another child; dismayed, she fled in the night into sanctuary at Westminster with her three daughters. There her first son, Edward, was born, with the abbot and prior for godfathers, under no favourable omen. Henry VI was brought out from his long imprisonment in the Tower, where his keepers had provided better for his spiritual than his physical needs: he was "not worshipfully arrayed as a prince and not so cleanly kept as should seem such a prince."[11] Once more poor Henry was led in procession to St. Paul's, crown on his head, Warwick carrying his train, the faithful Lancastrian, Oxford, bearing the sword of state. Once more Henry took up life in his apartments at Westminster, from which the Kingmaker had ejected him ten years before, where "daily much people and in great number" came to partake of his hospitality. He had indeed never ceased to be beloved by his people: how could anyone hate such a man?

> As scripture saith, blessèd they be
> That merciful be in word and deed,
> For they shall find of Christ so free
> Mercy also in time of need. . . .[12]

Alas, no mercy came his way in the hour of need.

A pleasant consequence of Henry's Re-adeption, this unexpected reversal of things—though the chronicler Warkworth tells us that Henry was welcomed back by "the more part of people"—was the one and only visit that it enabled young Henry Tudor, now a boy of fourteen, to pay London and the Court, to be welcomed by his uncle the King. Jasper, who had been surreptitiously back in Wales in 1468, never betrayed by his own people, had got young Henry from Lady Herbert, made a widow by her own Yorkist leaders—Warwick and Clarence had had her husband beheaded after Edgecot. Naturally the Tudor chroniclers said that Henry prophesied great things for the boy—that was common form. Naturally, too, Jasper must have hoped for the restoration of the boy's royal earldom of Richmond; but that had been given to Clarence: it was impossible for Warwick to take it from him.

Warwick was already having difficulty enough with Clarence,

who, incapable of filling the first place, was unwilling to fill the second. Besides, Warwick had not reversed his life's work in order to share power with anyone. What then had Clarence gained by his treason to his brother? Parliament, assembled in November 1470, entailed the succession upon Henry's male heirs, and failing them upon Clarence and his; but this was to be no further forward than he had been under Edward. Here was an immediate source of danger to the new régime. However, it pleased people by one act of popular justice: the horrid Yorkist Tiptoft, Earl of Worcester, who had introduced a new mode of death from abroad —impalement on a stake—met his deserts at the hand of his former friends. He was a cultivated, talented, Italianate type, fond of books and culture, much under the new Renaissance influence coming from Italy. Yet at the last he showed himself a true medieval: he asked the executioner to give him not one blow but three, in honour of the Trinity.

Now that Warwick was the sole ruler he wished to be he found himself under constant pressure from Louis to deliver the goods he had promised: to bring England into the French alignment against the Netherlands, to declare war against Burgundy until all its territories were conquered. This was clean contrary to English interests, and especially to the commercial interests of London, so bound up with the Netherlands. On foreign policy Warwick's régime, like so many, foundered; but it was in any case riven by its inner contradictions, Clarence against Warwick, Lancastrians who would not accept their old enemy's leadership but were waiting for Margaret and Prince Edward to come.

The Yorkist Edward was back before them. His friendship with the Netherlands had stood him in good stead, and with their support he made his come-back, landing at Ravenspur, the now vanished port at the mouth of the Humber where Henry of Bolingbroke had landed in 1399. "It must be admitted that Edward's kingdom manifested no enthusiasm when it learned that he had returned."[13] The important port of Kingston-on-Hull refused to receive him. Like Bolingbroke Edward gave out that he was returning only to claim his rightful dukedom of York. His proclamations he put out in the name of King Henry VI, and this sufficiently ingratiated him with the northern capital for him to be admitted. "Always ready to do the daring thing," he left his forces outside, "and wearing the ostrich feather badge of the Prince of Wales and cheering for King Henry and his son, he entered York with only sixteen or seventeen men." Here is an indication of the way people in general felt in the country: the house of Lancaster was the royal house, even in York from which its rival took its title.

Arrived in the Midlands, Edward proclaimed himself king, while attempting to bring Warwick to terms. But Warwick had irretrievably committed himself: there was no turning back now. Not so with Clarence, who was willing, indeed anxious, to perjure himself once more. He came up from the west with his troops, and met his brother at Banbury. There he was well received; Clarence addressed Edward's men in his best manner, Edward promised Clarence's men his "grace and good love." With a couple of days' start on Warwick, Edward entered London; King Henry fell into his possession. Henry had been left by Warwick at the bishop's palace by St. Paul's in the City. Archbishop Neville brought him forth, now a man of fifty, frail and failing. Edward gave the King his hand with cold civility, but Henry diffidently offered to embrace him: "my cousin of York, you are very welcome. I know that in your hands my life will not be in danger."[14] Edward seemed touched and assured him that he had nothing to fear; nonetheless he was sent to the Tower, along with a number of bishops, usually Lancastrian in sympathy. At the same time Warwick was betrayed by Louis' choosing this moment to make a truce with Burgundy. Meanwhile the bulk of Lancastrian support was waiting for its own leaders. With his world falling apart Warwick had come face to face at last with Edward IV.

The battle of Barnet was fought on Easter Day 1471, in a fog which much influenced the outcome. (The people, with their usual prescience, thought that it had been raised by Friar Bungay.) Of the royal forces the Lancastrian Exeter commanded the left wing, Oxford (an able soldier) the right; Warwick's brother Montagu held the centre, astride the St. Albans–Barnet road in this familiarly fought-over country, Warwick had the reserve with the guns, useless in the fog. In the poor light Gloucester outflanked Exeter, while Oxford at the other end of the line outflanked Hastings and his men got out of touch with the main battle which was fought out stubbornly in the centre between Edward and Montagu, who was killed. When the Lancastrian Oxford managed to get his men back into the action, they mistakenly in the fog fell upon Montagu's division. The cry of treachery went up; Warwick's reserves were insufficient to hold the line from breaking, he was overborne by numbers and in the crack-up killed. Edward had the bodies of the two grand Nevilles, his cousins, sent to be exposed naked—in case there was any doubt—in St. Paul's, where they lay in their coffins at the foot of the image of Our Lady of Grace.

That same day Queen Margaret with her son and his wife, Warwick's daughter, landed at Weymouth. Too late. The stars in their courses fought against the house of Lancaster.

If only Margaret had come earlier she would have brought an accession of strength to Warwick that should have tipped the balance. But she had not been able to overcome her misgivings, and Warwick had fought without the aid of Somerset, or Devon, or Jasper Tudor, without the presence of the Prince. In the end it was Louis who propelled her to her fate, the last act of her tragic story, and decided that she must sail at once. Even so, when she embarked on 24 March, storms in the Channel drove her back to port again and again before she could make the English coast.

At Cerne Abbey in Dorset, Margaret was met by Somerset and the Earl of Devon with the news of Barnet. But they persuaded her that they could raise a larger army than Edward's from the faithful West Country, and shortly recruits began to come in in good number from Devon and Cornwall, Somerset, Dorset and Wiltshire. It was decided to march up the western side of England, in order to link up with Jasper Tudor, and make for loyal Lancashire and Cheshire. But Edward, reassembling and refreshing his troops after Barnet, was yet, with his well-known speed and concentration, too quick for them. For some little time people did not know which way things would go. "The world, I assure you, is right queasy," wrote Sir John Paston to his mother. "God hath showed himself marvellously like him that made all and can undo again when him list; and I can think that by all likelihood shall show himself as marvellous again, and that in short time."[15] Translated into the language of common sense, this looks forward to a Yorkist victory.

Once more Edward's speed and concentration made havoc of

the Lancastrians. Near Bristol, Margaret turned aside, to be welcomed by the third town in the kingdom and given desirable reinforcements—including the town's Recorder, subsequently killed—
and some guns. This enabled Edward to catch up with her before
she could get across the Severn. At Tewkesbury the Lancastrians
turned at bay, just beyond the abbey in enclosed country with
hedges and ditches that gave some defence. Margaret and her
ladies had barely time to seek refuge in a nearby monastery.
Gloucester commanded Edward's van and began the onslaught next
day. Somerset and Sir Hugh Courtenay "broke the field"—just as
Oxford's men had done at Barnet—and took Edward by surprise, until they in turn were caught in flank by a well-concealed
contingent of lances posted in a wood nearby as a reserve. This
freed Edward to deliver the *coup de grace* at the Prince of Wales's
position in the centre. His men broke; the Prince himself was
overtaken and killed, though he cried for succour, it is said, to
Clarence, his brother-in-law, who had sworn fealty to him in
France.

There was another noble killing of Lancastrians in this battle,
and still more after it: besides the Prince, there were Somerset's
brother, Lord John Beaufort, the Earl of Devon, Lord Wenlock,
and the Queen's staunch friends Sir Robert Wittingham and Sir
Edmund Hampden, of that name to become so famous later.
In the fury of the pursuit Edward entered the abbey, where many
of the leading Lancastrians had taken refuge, sword in hand so
that the church was polluted and had to be cleansed of the stain.
Nevertheless, on the Monday these men were dragged out to be
tried summarily by court-martial under Gloucester and beheaded:
the Duke of Somerset, Sir Hugh Courtenay—another member of
that Devon family being torn to pieces for its loyalty to the royal
house, the prior of the military order of St. John's, and among
other well-known families an Audley, a Tresham, a Clifton. Henry
VI's son was buried, as befitted a prince, in the choir of the abbey;
the rest about the church, where their memorials are now, or in
the churchyard.

In this terrible time of confusion, when all was in suspense and
no one knew where to look for government, London was in grave
danger from the Kentishmen under the lead of the Bastard of
Fauconberg. This brave fighting captain was an illegitimate

sprig of the Nevilles, and had been placed by Warwick in command of the ships in the Channel to intercept any help coming to
Edward. One sees what a close thing it was, if only these dis-
parate movements could have been co-ordinated. Now, too late,
the Bastard led his Kentishmen—he got a great deal of support
from Canterbury—against London. The citizens repelled his onslaught on London Bridge, though he burned the new Southwark
gate and damaged the suburb. He next got round the City on the
north to attack Aldgate and Bishopsgate, where the citizens defended themselves vigorously. It was only on the approach of
Edward's army that he withdrew, and was pursued to Sandwich
where Edward captured his ships. Edward appreciated a good
fighting captain who could be made use of and pardoned the
Bastard to serve under Gloucester on the Scottish Border. Fauconberg's family loyalties were too strong, however; attempting to
escape, he was captured and Gloucester had him beheaded at
Middleham. Canterbury had already received its punishment: its
liberties and franchises taken away, many citizens arrested, a number hanged.

On his way thither Edward had passed through London, arriving on 21 May for a second reception by his capital after a victory
within the month. It showed that he had had to fight for it, and also
that he owed his triumph to force, in which his own military ability
was a decisive element. He brought with him, to grace his triumph,
Queen Margaret riding in a chariot; her spirit broken at last by
the death of her son, she had sent a message from her monastic
retreat that she was "at his commandment." What was the point of
fighting on any more? All that the country wanted now was a
return to order, firm government.

On the very night of Edward's entry into London, Henry VI
was put to death by his order; Richard of Gloucester was at the
Tower to execute it, as we know. It was a matter of urgency, for
Edward and Richard were to press on immediately into Kent after
Fauconberg. From that point of view it might be regarded as done
in the heat of war, in the midst of these critical events. It was also,
of course, politics: so long as Henry's son was alive it was im-
politic to kill the father; now the Yorkists could make a clean
sweep. The contemporary chronicler Warkworth tells us that
Henry "was put to death the 21st day of May, on a Tuesday

night, betwixt 11 and 12 of the clock, being then at the Tower the Duke of Gloucester, brother to King Edward, and many others."[16] Such also was the opinion in the City, as we know from *The Great Chronicle of London* on Henry's death: "of whose death the common fame then went that the Duke of Gloucester was not all guiltless."[17] Commines, who was in a position to hear, wrote that, if what he was told was true, Gloucester "killed poor King Henry with his own hand, or else caused him to be killed in his presence in some place apart."[18] Such was "the general belief at the time," says Edward's chaste biographer, Miss Scofield, "official explanations notwithstanding." Of course it was put out that "of pure displeasure and melancholy he died." Nobody believed that.

Next day, when Richard of Gloucester had ridden on to Kent, Henry's body was brought dead through London. London had no doubt how the sainted king—whose incapacity as a ruler had caused all these troubles—came by his death: when his body was exposed at St. Paul's, it "bled on the pavement" and again at Blackfriars. It was then taken up the Thames to be buried at Chertsey, though later Richard as king had Henry reburied among the kings at Windsor: an act of reparation, it did not do Richard any good.

Henry was immediately venerated by people as a saint and martyr: they offered up their prayers to him.

> A prince thou wert meek and benign,
> > Patient in adversity
> Wherefore thou hast a crown condign [worthy]
> > In bliss of all felicity,
> > Where joy hath perpetuity:
> > > In the which bliss the king of grace
> > > Hath granted thee a joyful place.[19]

In the centuries since, the cult of Henry VI has never been entirely extinguished, and even in this century efforts have been renewed at Rome to have him canonised and raised to the altars as a saint. But perhaps it may be uncertain whether he performed any miracles.

Chief Justice Fortescue received his pardon from Edward in triumph, and like a man of sense accepted the condition of turning his pen as well as his coat. To this we owe his famous book, *The Governance of England,* with its diagnosis of the ills from which Lancastrian government had suffered—the poverty of the Crown as against the wealth of its overmighty subjects, the great houses. Hence it is that the wise Chief Justice died comfortably in his bed—and can still be seen in his scarlet robes as a judge upon his fine tomb in the family church at Ebrington in Gloucestershire, not far from the dread field of Tewkesbury.

The uncatchable Jasper had slipped away once more from faithful Wales, this time taking his young nephew, last hope of the Lancastrians, with him. With him went the future.

CHAPTER IX

Yorkist Rule

In 1471 Edward IV was a man of twenty-nine and might have looked forward with confidence to many years of rule, to seeing his sons grow up to maturity and thus settling the house of York upon the throne for good. After all, Henry of Lancaster had taken the throne not his own in 1399 and settled his house upon it for three generations. But there was a fundamental difference between the Revolution of 1399 and the events of 1461 renewed in 1471. In 1399 Henry of Lancaster had been called to assume the Crown by the will of the nation, so far as it could be elicited, certainly by the bulk of the magnates, the Church, the Lords and Commons in Parliament. The plain fact about the Yorkist dynasty was that Edward IV had captured the Crown by force in 1461, lost it to a combination of his own party supporters with the Lancastrians and recaptured it by force and luck in 1471.

However, he had won it fairly by his own exertions, by his victories in the field, his own military ability, and might well look forward to a life of more ease and less struggle—to ruling successfully without having to exert himself so much. This was roughly what came about. His faithful biographer, Miss Scofield, observes a certain deterioration of character in this second half of his reign: he becomes more and more interested in money, more thrifty and avaricious. This only means that he is becoming a better ruler: he has tumbled to the fact that finance is the key to all successful government. The fact that the financial debility of the Crown was the essence of its weakness was being enforced in the famous book that Fortescue was writing in these very years. Everybody must have known it, but Edward acted on it and corrected it. Hence he became a very successful ruler: the country got from him the efficient government, and even an attentive reform in administration, that Edward's father had promised. We can say that with the son the Yorkist experiment thoroughly succeeded.

Some people may have been somewhat misled by the other side to Edward's nature. Physically he became increasingly luxurious and self-indulgent; he had always been—with his physique how could he not be?—a womaniser and he did not cease to be, though Sir Thomas More tells us that he became less so. Edward would say that he "had three concubines which in diverse properties diversely excelled, one the merriest, the other the wiliest, the third the holiest, harlot in the realm."[1] Evidently Edward had a sense of humour. Lord Hastings was his boon companion in these pleasures, and that meant that there was no love lost between him and the Woodvilles; this became politically important at a later juncture. Edward could make his charm for women pay, as with the Suffolk widow, of whom he was asking a benevolence of £10, a considerable sum in those days; he kissed her so agreeably that she made it £20 on the spot. Even Louis XI may have been taken in: he was of the opinion that Edward "strongly loved ease and pleasure," and so he did. But in 1475 Edward underwent the labour of the Great Expedition, assembling the largest army the English had yet taken to France; and though Edward was willing to be bought off, it was an immense price that Louis had to pay. Commines said of Edward, *"nul autre chose il n'-avait eu en pensée qu'aux dames, et trop plus que de raison, et aux chasses, et à beau traiter sa personne."*[2] Commines was wrong; Edward did not allow his pleasures to come in the way of business. It is true that he got fat, but with his height and the magnificence of his dress he could carry it off, and many fat men have been good men of business.

Edward was now in a position to carry forward his own private commercial ventures, which helped with other things to make him the richest and most sumptuous prince of his time. In these decades exports of cloth were much increasing: the fifteenth century saw the profitable change-over from exports of raw wool to manufactured cloth. In spite of the political upsets of the time there is visible evidence of the increasing wealth of the cloth-producing areas in the splendid fifteenth-century churches of East Anglia, of the Cotswolds, of Somerset and Devon. Even in remote and poor

Cornwall this, the second half of the century, was the age in which most of the parish churches were rebuilt on a larger scale. And there are besides the more specialised foundations of Oxford and Cambridge colleges, the splendid fanes of Henry VI's chapels at Eton and at King's College, Cambridge, of Edward IV's at Windsor. We are told by a contemporary chronicler that by amassing wealth Edward outdid all his predecessors in collecting gold and silver plate, tapestries, *objets d'art,* in costly building.

His main business, however, was government and, whatever people thought of his enjoying ease and sensuality, he gave this his unremitting attention. "The King himself became once again very much more the actual, and less the nominal, source of administrative action. The King personally took strong measures to suppress the more flagrant outbreaks of lawlessness and violence. He personally sought to remedy the financial maladies which had beset and brought low the preceding régime. . . . He revived the Chamber of the Household as a highly important finance office of receipt and expenditure."[3] The result of this was to make the administration of the Crown lands more direct and speedy, and more readily open to his own eye and surveyance. This brought officials of the royal Household directly into contact with county administration and local justice. Avery Cornburgh, for example, yeoman of the Crown and Chamber, squire of the body, was—though not a native of Cornwall—the most important official in its administration.

Then, too, Edward "became better endowed in landed estate than any of his recent predecessors. He brought to the Crown the vast possessions of the duchy of York (including the inheritance of Mortimer); he confiscated the duchy of Lancaster, which he at once made into a 'corporation sole,' separate and distinct from other Crown lands but annexed to the Crown in perpetuity (as it still is today). He was strong enough to resume by act of Parliament large areas of Crown lands which had been formerly alienated; he was destined also to receive numerous large windfalls in the shape of forfeited lands from attainted rebels, whether of Lancastrians, or later of Nevilles, or later still of his attainted brother George of Clarence." In addition, he had the grant of the customs, he got a ransom of fifty thousand crowns for Margaret of Anjou; from his French expedition he inveigled out of Louis

XI an immediate payment of seventy-five thousand crowns and twenty-five thousand crowns every Easter and Michaelmas as long as he lived. In the end Edward was rolling in gold—a pretty good index of the success of his reign.

No crowned head could achieve this and at the same time wallow in self-indulgent ease and security. And from the first— naturally in view of the circumstances of Edward's return—his worst worries came from within the bosom of his own family. There was the constant problem of what to do with Clarence. If Clarence had not played traitor Edward would not have been driven from the throne. Edward had received him back kindly and allowed him to resume his office as Lieutenant of Ireland. The third brother, Richard of Gloucester, had remained loyal all through and Edward was to reward him richly. Gloucester was again made Constable of England—Warwick's grand office—and Admiral. Gloucester was also looking out for himself and meant to marry Warwick's second daughter, Anne, co-heiress with her sister, Clarence's wife, to the vast inheritance of their mother.

Clarence intended to have the lot. Actually these huge estates belonged by right to Warwick's widow, the Beauchamp heiress, and from the sanctuary at Beaulieu she put in her protest against her inheritance being granted away over her head. Nobody paid any attention to that; in the summer after Barnet and Tewkesbury all the North Country estates were granted to Gloucester, and Clarence was furious. It then appeared that Anne Neville had no wish to marry the unattractive Richard—Clarence, though unreliable, was at least tall and good-looking; Gloucester, the penultimate child in the large York brood, was short, lean and thin-faced, with one shoulder higher than the other, secretive, an introvert with none of the expansive charm of his brothers. (Even Clarence must have had something about him: he was the favourite with his sister Margaret, Duchess of Burgundy.) Rather than marry Richard, Anne allowed herself to be concealed as a kitchen maid in the house of one of Clarence's dependents. It did not take Richard long to discover her whereabouts and place her respectably in sanctuary while he pleaded his case for her before king and Council. After all, he had earned the right to such a bride—or, rather, to the half of the immense inheritance that went with her.

Edward richly rewarded Richard's loyalty throughout the crisis of 1469–71. Already Warden of the West Marches towards Scotland, Richard was given authority over the Earl of Northumberland as Warden of the Middle and East Marches. For the rest of the reign he was in effect viceroy in the North, the government of which he exercised from his favourite Middleham Castle in beautiful Wensleydale—a Neville stronghold, by the way. It was a soldierly task to rule the wild Borders, and Richard, essentially a soldier, ruled it efficiently and well. He thus won the confidence of the North, in particular the gratitude of the city of York, grateful for good government after years of disorder. Nor did this exhaust Edward's generosity to the brother he could rely on: Richard was given the lucrative stewardship of all the duchy of Lancaster lands in the North, and an immense grant of lands forfeited by the Earl of Oxford and other Lancastrians.

All this added to Clarence's jealousy and anger, who was lucky to be left with the Lieutenancy of Ireland and his wife's half of the Warwick inheritance. Edward did his best to mediate between the brothers, and got Clarence to accept his brother as a prospective brother-in-law, though they "shall part no livelihood." Richard surrendered to brother George the office of Great Chamberlain of England and agreed to his having the earldoms of Warwick and Salisbury, in right of having married the elder sister. Richard was now free to marry the younger sister and carried her off to her own Middleham, where in 1473 their only child, another Edward, was born.

Clarence did not cease to be discontented and a source of trouble. The insidious Louix XI is said to have promised to aid him in another attempt on his brother's throne—the ultimate prize that seduced them all (except poor Henry VI, who was born to it and could well have done without it)—by releasing Oxford and his de Vere brothers for a descent on the English coast. After hovering about the coast all that summer, keeping Edward on the alert as well as anxious about his brother's loyalty, Oxford captured St. Michael's Mount in October, where the Cornish welcomed him with "right good cheer." It was a matter of months before the Mount surrendered, in February 1474—the leading Cornish York-

13

ist, Henry Bodrugan, had conducted an ineffectual siege, was quite
unrepresentative of the county in which he played an unrespect-
able, predatory rôle.[4] The defenders of the Mount surrendered
to the offer of pardon; Oxford was sent to Hammes Castle, where
he remained prisoner for several years but ultimately made good
his escape to take the lead in the Lancastrian command at Bosworth.

The ill-will between Clarence and Gloucester continued to
make news and add to a sense of insecurity. Sir John Paston wrote
at this time that the great men about the King had sent "for their
harness . . . the Duke of Clarence maketh him big in that he
can, showing as he would but deal with the Duke of Gloucester.
But the King intendeth . . . to be as big as they both and to be
a stifler atween them."[5] Paston then added, what was in people's minds, that "under this there should be some other thing
intended and some treason conspired; so what shall fall can I not
say." The dowager Countess of Warwick was now in Gloucester's
custody, and "to purchase peace between the King's brothers
Parliament now sanctioned unblushingly the partition of her estates
. . . 'in like manner and form as if the said countess were now
actually dead.' "[6] As a historian one accepts a good deal of what
transpires in the human struggle for survival, but these creatures
remind one of nothing so much as gilded reptiles gorging on each
other.

Edward had successfully married his sister to Charles the Bold,
Duke of Burgundy, and in 1474 he betrothed his little daughter
Cecily to the heir of Scotland. The house of York was beginning
to graft itself on to the ruling houses in Northern Europe, though
it had as yet nothing to show compared with the alliances of the
royal house of Lancaster. Nevertheless these were both effective
blows against Louis XI, and now that England was once more
strong something of what he had earned for his interventions in
English affairs was coming home to him. In 1475 the Burgundian
alliance for war against France was reconstituted—it was just
forty years since the fateful Treaty of Arras, when Burgundy had
deserted: Charles promised to take part with an army until Edward had obtained his right and title to the Crown of France—
that old and trampled theme. And Charles consented to Edward
being crowned at Rheims—as Henry VI had never been.

Now that the country was strong again English pride might be assuaged for the long humiliations it had endured under Henry VI. Parliament voted a large grant to renew the war with France, and Edward assembled the largest and best-equipped army yet to leave the country. When he crossed the Channel, Duke Charles met him with none of the promised forces—the Burgundians were otherwise engaged, pillaging in far-away Lorraine. In disgust Edward came to his fateful decision to open negotiations with Louis, who was only too relieved to pay the price of buying Edward off. As to the decision in itself Clarence was with Edward; it appears that Richard, like the military type he was, a man of fixed ideas, was in favour of fighting.

Edward and Louis met on 29 August 1475 on a bridge constructed over the river at Picquigny, the ever-mistrustful Louis having Commines dressed up to impersonate him as a measure of precaution—bridges had been so unhealthy for French royal persons since the murder on the bridge at Montereau. The chivalric Commines was of the opinion that Edward made a great mistake by the advantageous peace he concluded, that the disgrace of being bought off outweighed the honour of all the nine victories the King had to his credit. We are not of this opinion. As to military honour Edward's victories speak for themselves; he had never been defeated in battle. For the rest, it was much more sensible to make the utmost financial use of his advantage over Louis than to involve England once more in an endless French war in pursuit of a medieval dream. Commines remained a medieval in his judgment; Edward showed himself a modern-minded man.

He came back from this triumph of common sense to face more troubles raised by Clarence. With his ever-unsatisfied itch for first place Clarence wanted to take advantage of his wife's death to marry Mary, the heiress of Burgundy. This would give him a principality from which to make trouble and get his own back on his enemies. Louis XI, with his itch for mischief-making, did not fail to pass on to Edward what Clarence promised he would do in England once he was in possession of the Netherlands. Clarence had not forgotten the exemplification of the great seal, which he kept in secret, dating from Henry VI's Re-adeption, making him the next heir to the kingdom after Henry and his son. It was undoubtedly Clarence who originated the base but baseless rumours of Edward's bastardy, which Richard was to make such use of later.

It looks as if Clarence suffered from genuine persecution-mania. He took to absenting himself from Court, fearing he would be poisoned there. He pursued to the death innocent servants whom he charged with poisoning his wife and infant son. Another member of his household, Thomas Burdet of Arrow—of the family to which Holinshed a century later was steward, was arrested and put to death, along with an Oxford clerk, on the ground of attempting to contrive the King's death by magic arts. This was a warning, but Clarence appealed to the Council over the King's head to assert their innocence, thus making an open scandal and calling the King's justice in question. He followed it up by instigating a rising in Cambridgeshire and Huntingdon. It was at last too much for Edward's patience; he had his brother sent to the Tower.

In the interval there took place an important state-marriage. Edward's second son, little Richard, Duke of York, who was born in 1473 and had now attained the mature age of four, was married to Anne Mowbray, aged six, in St. Stephen's Chapel at Westminster. This was in order to obtain the grand inheritance of the Mowbray Duke of Norfolk to support Edward's second son; Edward had already created the little Richard Duke of Norfolk in anticipation of it.

Next day Clarence was brought to book for his misdeeds by attainder in Parliament. Edward charged him with "more unnatural and loathly treason" than had been found at any time previously during the reign. Attainder of high treason meant death, but Edward could not make up his mind to give the word. No one pleaded for Clarence; he had no party and few friends; the Woodvilles pressed the case against him with his brother. At last the word was given and Clarence met his death in the Tower on 18 February 1478. There is no reason to doubt the story that he was drowned in a malmsey-butt. A contemporary French chronicler says that he was drowned *"en un bain, comme l'on disait."*[7]

Our most recent historian concludes that "death was perhaps too severe a medicine . . . Clarence was a nuisance rather than a great danger."[8] An ardent advocate of the Yorkists says sympathetically: "the record of Clarence's follies has survived; his winning charm can only be guessed at."⁹ It is certain that Edward came to regret his severity on his brother: he is said to have repined later, "O unhappy brother, for whose deliverance no man asked!" If he could have seen into the not distant future, only a few years ahead, and what would happen at the hands of his other brother, he would have had still more reason for bitterness of spirit. As Professor Chrimes sums up: "Edward IV might well have taught his brother a severe lesson, and stopped short of fratricide. But he did not; he was too powerful now for anyone to restrain him; he could not even restrain himself. He was to regret his action in his own lifetime. He forgot that, although 'stone dead hath no fellow,' there had once been four Yorkist brothers, then three, and now there were to be only two. The precedent of slaughter within the Yorkist family had been set, and its consequences might be far-reaching."¹⁰

Richard emerged in these last years of Edward's reign as the first servant of his brother and of the state. His services in the North were indeed indispensable. There was a reckoning to be made with Scotland, the "auld ally" of France and of Henry VI; opportunity was provided by the disputes between the feckless James III and his brother Albany, and occasion presented by raids in force over the English Border. In 1482 war was planned against Scotland at Fotheringhay Castle, the Yorkist stronghold in Northamptonshire, where Richard had been born thirty years before—and where Mary Queen of Scots was to perish a century or so later. Edward and Richard were there along with Albany, who accompanied Richard on the campaign. A large army was raised, no expense spared—these things were possible now under Edward's successful rule.

Richard's first objective was Berwick, the key to Scotland which Margaret had had to barter away twenty-one years before. The town surrendered, leaving the castle to withstand a siege, while Richard marched through the Lowlands, laying waste and ravaging, to Edinburgh which surrendered to him. He found no disposition on the part of the Scots to displace James III by the still more light-weight Albany, and withdrew to complete the reduction of Berwick. It seems that Edward was somewhat dissatisfied by no larger an achievement for so great an expenditure of money. But Richard achieved the essential—the unconditional surrender of Berwick, which commanded the road into Scotland, in Scottish hands for so long.

This achievement was rewarded in spectacular fashion in January 1483, when the wardenship of the West Marches was confirmed to Richard and his heirs for ever, along with the city and castle of Carlisle, all the Crown lands in Cumberland, and such lands as they might conquer across the Border. This was really to erect a palatinate for Richard and his heirs, like the palatinate of Durham, and would provide "a strong and unified defence force balancing the Percy defence on the other side."[11] It envisaged setting up Richard and his family in the North for good— an admirable arrangement. Moreover, Richard nourished his popularity in the North: at his suggestion Parliament exempted the four northern counties, with York and Kingston-upon-Hull, from the levy of a tenth and fifteenth in return for their contribution to the campaign. In other ways also Richard exerted himself to look after the interests of York, his northern capital, where his efficient rule was properly rewarded by personal popularity.

All should have been well with the Yorkist dynasty for years, if not for good, but that Edward fell suddenly and mortally ill, when still only forty, leaving his son a boy of twelve—born on All Souls' Day 1470 in sanctuary at Westminster—offering too easy a temptation for the fatal Yorkist propensity to eat each other up.

Edward was ill for only a matter of days. The contemporary French chronicler Basin says definitely that the illness was brought on by too hearty a dinner of fruits and vegetables on Good Friday, and the symptoms, the briefness of the illness, seem to indicate typhoid. On his death-bed Edward was worried above all by the necessity to compose the dissensions between his boon-companion, Lord Hastings, and the Queen and her brothers. Edward was so attached to Hastings that he had offered him a burial-place in St. George's Chapel at Windsor that they might be near each other even in death. Hastings was in regular attendance upon Edward as lord chamberlain, responsible for household arrangements; he had also been given the key-position as captain of Calais which Warwick had found so advantageous. This made him at loggerheads with Lord Rivers, who claimed that it had been promised to him.

Sir Thomas More, who learned much of what happened in these next years from people in a position to know at the time, some of them eyewitnesses of events, tells us that "King Edward in his life . . . albeit that this dissension between his friends somewhat irked him, yet in his good health he somewhat the less regarded it, because he thought, whatsoever business should fall between them, himself should always be able to rule both the parties."[12] That was a reasonable calculation, besides *divide et impera* has always been a part of kingly craft. But *now* . . . himself dying prematurely, with his sons not yet thirteen and ten respectively, "then he considering the youth of his children, albeit he nothing less mistrusted than that that happened," Edward called the leaders of the two parties to his bedside.

More tells us that the Queen bore a special grudge against Hastings "for the great favour the King bare him, and also for that she thought him secretly familiar with the King in wanton company." No doubt. Hastings and Dorset, the Queen's son by her first husband, "with divers others of both the parties" came into the presence, "the King, lifting up himself and underset with pillows," addressed his last energies to reconciling them for his children's sake. "And therewithal the King, no longer enduring to sit up, laid him down on his right side, his face towards them; and none was there present that could refrain from weeping." The lords comforted him with good words as well as they could, and in his presence forgave each other and joined hands together, "when, as it after appeared by their deeds, their hearts were far asunder."

And so, with all his victories, Edward went out of this world, 9 April 1483, not yet forty-one.

CHAPTER X

Richard III's Usurpation

It was natural, and in accordance with constitutional usage, that Richard of Gloucester should become Protector. There was the precedent of 1422 available, when Humphrey Duke of Gloucester became Protector for his infant nephew, Henry VI, though he did not have the tutelage, or personal guardianship, of the boy. It appears that by his later will Edward IV may have changed his mind about the guardianship of his sons, from the Queen surrounded by her Woodville relations, to his last surviving brother, of the royal blood. And Richard had always been loyal and reliable. It would be expected by the country that he should assume the position that was his by right during the minority of his brother's son. Moreover, as the contemporary observer Mancini, who was in England at the time, tells us, Richard enjoyed general esteem for the decency of his private life and his good government, as well as respect and even renown for his military record—the difficult tasks had been entrusted to him and he had performed them well.

In 1422, however, Humphrey had been recognised only as *primus inter pares;* he did not exercise the powers of the kingship, the Council ruled, as we have seen. It soon transpired that this was a precedent Richard did not intend to follow. There was another, more fateful precedent in the events of 1399. As the latest historian of the reign says, "obviously Richard was not unacquainted with history and precedent. He knew about Henry IV's usurpation, he had heard of his father's bid for the throne; he had been brought up in the Warwick household and knew the story of 1470; he had studied his brother and helped him to win Crown and kingdom. . . . On a longer historical view, the 'occupation' of England or the seizing of the Crown may be compared, in its day-to-day development, with an equally famous occupation with which this story began."[1]

Our story indeed comes full circle. The events of 1399 received an even more malign reverberation in 1483—"the only year since the Conquest," Professor Pollard points out in a succinct phrase, "in which there have been three English kings, including incidentally the whole Yorkist dynasty."[2]

Richard was in the North when his brother died; the young King Edward V was residing at Ludlow, as Prince of Wales, with his uncle Lord Rivers to look after him. In London the Council was divided between Hastings' party, which held that the Protector should govern, and the Queen's party, which stood for a governing Council of which the Protector should be merely the chief member. The Woodvilles knew what they might expect from power being concentrated in the hands of Clarence's brother, when they had been chiefly responsible for Clarence's destruction—which, some said, Richard would avenge. (In a sense, he did—in his own way.) Hastings, who was Richard's friend, alerted him as to the situation in London, and warned him to come up with a strong force to assert his right as against the Woodvilles, who meant to escort the young king to London with an overpowering force that would dominate the situation. Immediately after, the Duke of Buckingham—anxious to assert his precedence in the kingdom's affairs and to play a leading rôle, and despising the Woodville family into which he had been married against his will—sent a servant to Richard assuring him of his support and arranging to meet him on his way south. This was invaluable: Richard would never have been able to accomplish what he did without Buckingham's support.

Here was an alliance of Richard, Hastings, Buckingham, which represented the house of York and the magnates of the realm, against the Queen and the upstart Woodvilles. (All the intelligence, and ability of the Woodvilles, strange to say, never won them any popularity.) At this point Richard wrote to the Queen and to the Council, assuring them of his allegiance to his nephew, and demanding the position that was his by right and by his brother's will. The Woodvilles were in control of the Tower, of which Dorset was constable, of the fleet, of which Sir Edward Woodville was in command, of the young king, in the person of

Earl Rivers, and of Edward's accumulated treasure. The Queen's party intended to have her son crowned as early as 4 May, after which the powers of the Protector would lapse, and meanwhile to control the situation by the large force by which they would bring him to the capital. Hastings forced their hand by threatening to retire on Calais if the numbers were not considerably reduced; in the interest of amity the Queen agreed.

Two groups were now converging on London. Rivers was conducting the King along Watling Street and had reached Stony Stratford by 28 April. They were ahead of Richard, who arrived at Northampton the day after. Hearing of this, Rivers left the King and his forces at Stony Stratford and rode back the few miles to Northampton to pay his respects to Richard. Later in the day Buckingham arrived. They all supped amicably together at Richard's table and passed the evening convivially. That night the two Dukes laid their plans and at dawn Rivers was arrested, the road to Stony Stratford guarded to prevent the King and his escort getting wind of it. When the two Dukes caught up with him Richard knelt to him as king, then explained that his own life was in danger from conspiracy, that he had been obliged to arrest Lord Rivers and would have to remove others who were implicated from Edward's entourage. The young King, who had been well brought up and was well educated, replied with dignity that his ministers had been chosen for him by his father, and could therefore be only faithful and good. He could believe nothing evil of them, unless it could be proved.

The reply to this was to arrest before his face both his half-brother, Lord Richard Grey,[3] the Queen's son by her first husband, and faithful Sir Thomas Vaughan, the young King's chamberlain. Richard dismissed the royal escort to their homes and, with the King now in his power, conducted the whole party back to Northampton, whence Rivers, Grey and Vaughan were expedited to Yorkshire and ultimately to ominous Pontefract, where they were beheaded at the end of June, when the time was ripe. At Northampton the two Dukes "took again further counsel; and there they sent away from the King whom it pleased them, and set new servants about him such as liked better them than him. At which dealing he wept and was nothing content, but it booted not."[4] Richard wrote justifying his action to the Council, where Hastings could present his case and look after his interests.

In London the news added to the general sense of insecurity and alarmed the Queen into taking sanctuary at Westminster with the little Richard, Duke of York, her daughters, her son Dorset and her brother Lionel, Bishop of Salisbury. In London there was already current "a sinister rumour that the Duke had brought his nephew not under his care but into his power, so as to gain for himself the Crown."[5] Richard wrote to the mayor to reassure the citizens: no one had had such solicitude for King Edward and all his—and this was true enough. On 4 May the young King made his entry into London with the two Dukes, guarded the whole time by their troops, in case of any attempt, "since," Mancini says, "the Welsh could not bear to think that owing to their stupidity their Prince had been carried off." At the head of the procession trundled four wagon-loads of arms which had been supplied with Woodville devices, while criers informed the populace that these had been stored along the route to slay the Duke of Gloucester. Play-acting—for it was known well enough that they had been stored along the northern route for the war against the Scots. This increased the wonderment and insecurity. Edward V was conducted to the Tower and preparations advanced for his coronation.

At his first Council, Richard was confirmed as Protector, with the additional title of Defender of the realm. He was given power "to order and forbid in every matter like another king," and, unlike Humphrey, he was given the guardianship of the King's person. Things were evidently going to be very different from 1422. Before Edward IV's death the country was on the verge of war with France—this added to the sense of crisis and the willingness to concentrate power in the hands of Edward's soldierly brother. Archbishop Rotherham had given up the chancellorship; his place was taken, if unwillingly, by Bishop Russell. A friend of Richard's, a mere John Wood, was made Treasurer; Hastings kept his high offices, though unknown to himself he was being watched by Catesby, a fellow Leicestershireman of his, anxious to advance himself at Hastings' expense, sounding him how far he would go along with the Protector in his plans. Buckingham received a tremendous reward for his support: as Chief Justice and Chamberlain of both North and South Wales, Constable of all the royal castles in five western counties as well as in Wales, he took the place of the little Edward as prince there, virtually a viceroy of the West. But observe that this immense concentration of power was designedly removed from the capital: Buckingham's only power there personally depended on the Protector. It did not take Richard long to get the fleet away from Sir Edward Woodville, seducing them by an offer of pardon; this Woodville managed to get away with only two vessels to Henry Tudor, awaiting the outcome of it all in Brittany.

Before the middle of June the Protector was ready to strike. Like Bolingbroke in 1399 he had a very tight schedule, for the coronation of Edward V was fixed for Sunday, 22 June. But this was not going to be a constitutional revolution like 1399, with a candidate called to the throne by the magnates and the Church —really the will of the country as expressed through them; it was going to be a *coup d'état* of an Italianate kind—there was something Italianate about the Yorkists—like Renaissance Italy, contemporary Visconti or Sforza.

Very cleverly the Protector divided the Council. The regular administrative officers met at the Tower in proximity to the young King, who signed the official papers put before him—we have his signature on documents, along with Richard's and Buckingham's. Preparations for the coronation went forward here. Richard's own circle met at his house of Crosby Place in Bishopsgate Street, and here the effective plans were made. The shrewd and cautious Lord Stanley—husband of Henry Tudor's mother— told Hastings that he much mistrusted these two separate councils, "for while we talk of one matter in the one place, little wot we whereof they talk in the other place."[6] "My lord, on my life never doubt you," replied Hastings; he thought he had his own creature, Catesby, whom he had raised up and trusted with all his secrets, to inform him of what went on in the Protector's *conciliabula*. Little did he suspect that it was the other way round.

No doubt Richard would gladly have carried Hastings, who had long been his friend and associate, with him in his plans. He found out through Catesby that he could not; it seems that, doubtful at the turn of events, Hastings was ready for a *rapprochement* with the Woodvilles. And there was a useful go-between in Jane Shore, Edward IV's mistress, who had then been taken over

by the handsome Dorset, from whom Hastings had her—always
willing to do good offices—since Dorset was in sanctuary. Richard
—who had none of these impediments in his temperament, was
not interested in sex and seems to have disapproved of loose living
—was ready.[7]

On 10 June he wrote to the faithful city of York to send up as
many armed men as possible, "to aid and assist us against the
Queen, her blood-adherents and affinity, which have intended and
daily doth intend to murder and utterly destroy us and our cousin
the Duke of Buckingham and the old royal blood of this realm."[8]
No evidence whatever of any such conspiracy; but how well we
understand these things in our own disgraceful century, with the
similar excuses put forward for worse outrages in Nazi Germany
and Soviet Russia. Next day he wrote north to Lord Neville to
come up prepared to do him service. In the background to the
events of the next days we must hear the tramp of Richard's
Northerners marching south to the capital.

On Friday 13 June—unlucky day—there was a full meeting of
the Council at the Tower, to make final arrangements for the
coronation. The Protector arrived late, about nine o'clock, saluting
the councillors courteously, saying merely that he had overslept.
After chatting around for a while, he said to the Bishop of Ely—
the famous John Morton, from whom the young Thomas More
could have had it: "my lord, you have very good strawberries
at your garden in Holborn: I require you, let us have a mess of
them."[9] Morton sent his servant in all haste to fetch them; meanwhile the Protector prayed the lords to excuse him for a little
while. It was an hour before he came back, in a changed mood,
with a lowering countenance and biting his lips—a habit he had at
moments of tension—and burst out with a charge of conspiracy
against him on the part of the Queen's folk, aided and abetted
by some of the Council.

More play-acting—the Protector gave a prearranged signal,
banging his fist on the table; someone posted outside cried
"Treason," the chamber filled with armed men. Richard accused
Hastings of treason, and others of plotting against him. In the
scuffle of the arrests Stanley was struck, so that the blood ran about
his ears; he, Archbishop Rotherham and Bishop Morton were
taken away into confinement. Hastings was immediately taken out

to be beheaded on the Green beside the chapel: the Protector swore that he would not go to dinner until his head was off. However, he was not so inhuman as not to give him a few moments for a priest to shrive him. Hastings was then and there executed upon a long log of timber waiting upon the Green for repairs. The indictment against him had already been prepared for the benefit of public opinion. Justice had been done upon a traitor, and Richard made a hypocritical bid in the name of morality by charging Hastings with having set the young King a bad example by sleeping with Jane Shore only the night before. (It was exactly like Hitler's bid at the time of the blood-oath of 30 June 1934, when he claimed that he was Justiciar for the German people, and that his former friend Röhm had slept the night before his execution with one of his storm-troopers.)

This was not what mattered, a matter of private choice. What mattered was that Hastings had received no trial whatever: he had been put to death simply upon the Protector's order. This was the very definition of tyranny—the suspension of justice, execution without trial: the Protector was already, in the exact sense of the word, a tyrant. This was the turning-point: after that no one could feel safe, there was an element of terror in the government. First, the Woodvilles had been eliminated; then the independent element in the Council; those who remained were at Richard's service. Before the end of the month the order to kill Rivers, Grey and the aged Sir Thomas Vaughan was carried out by Ratcliffe, one of the inmost of Richard's agents, on his way south with his Northerners to ensure London before Richard's coronation. The respectable Archbishop Rotherham and the very able Bishop Morton were confined in separate castles in Wales, the latter in Buckingham's charge at Brecon—and that shortly bred important consequences.

It remained for the Protector to get his other nephew, little Richard, Duke of York, out of sanctuary and into his hands. This disagreeable task he laid upon the shoulders of pliable Archbishop Bourchier, whom we have already observed to be no Becket. The Queen regarded the request with the gravest mistrust, but was reassured by the Archbishop; the mother's instinct was appealed to by the need of her elder son for company in the Tower, where he was dejected and melancholy. (Well he might

be!) Clarence's son, the little Earl of Warwick, was already in the
Protector's household; he offered no danger to Richard's plans,
his blood was attainted by the attainder of his father. Edward's
coronation was postponed.

For the Protector to proceed with his plans it was necessary
to bastardise his brother King Edward's children, if not King
Edward himself. Richard proceeded to propagate the story of
Edward's pre-contract with Lady Elizabeth Butler, to invalidate
his marriage with Elizabeth Woodville. He also put about Clarence's old story that Edward himself was illegitimate—with its
aspersions on their mother's honour which Cecily, Duchess of York,
deeply resented. (But what a brood she had given birth to!) On
22 June, which was to have been the little Edward's coronation
day, the Protector, Buckingham and their supporters gave their
official presence to the disgraceful sermon preached by Dr. Shaw,
the mayor's brother, at St. Paul's Cross, declaiming the story of the
pre-contract, the illegitimacy of Edward's children and the conclusion that Richard was the sole true representative of the house
of York and should be entitled king.* In other parts of the City
preachers were instructed to go further—the pulpits were the
broadcasting stations of the day—and preach that Edward IV had
been illegitimate too. To Buckingham was allotted the chivalrous
task of addressing the mayor and citizens at the Guildhall on
these themes; eloquent as he was, he needed a good deal of erroneous history to shore up his arguments.

As in 1399 speed was the essence of the proceedings. Propaganda, no new phenomenon, had prepared the public mind for
what followed that week. Parliament had been postponed, but the
lords had been summoned to London, though carefully instructed
to leave their armed retinues behind. Richard's armed Northerners were now arriving at the climax of events—evidence of how
well planned these movements were, if with a soldierly rather than
a civilian mind. On 25 June a petition was presented to an
assembly of lords and commons asking the Protector, on the
ground that Edward's marriage (which had never been popular)

* Sir Thomas More tells us, p. 59, that "Dr. Shaw by his sermon lost his
honesty and soon after his life, for very shame of the world into which
he durst never after come abroad." True it is that Shaw died next year,
cf. Gairdner, *Richard the Third*, 80.

was not a true marriage, to assume the Crown. In the atmosphere of doubt that had been created, and in the very real crisis of affairs at home and abroad—to which the rule of a boy not yet thirteen was hardly appropriate—it was not surprising that the assembly gave their assent. After all, Richard—though not yet a fully known quantity—was known to be a more than competent soldier and an efficient ruler.

Next day there was a large concourse of citizens at Baynard's Castle, where Buckingham took charge of the proceedings and presented the petition to the Protector to assume the kingship. With a great deal of feigned reluctance—more play-acting—Richard in the end consented. He then rode to Westminster Hall and usurped the throne, taking the king's seat in King's Bench—as his father had offered to do in 1460—and in the presence of all the judges adjured them, in the regular form at the beginning of a reign, to execute justice according to the laws of the realm. This was the date, 26 June 1483, from which he decided that the official acts of his reign should begin. He thereupon was dramatically reconciled—for the benefit of a public not all of whom were taken in—to an old antagonist of his house, Sir John Fogge. We can say that Richard III *was* a melodramatic actor.

The preparations for the coronation of young Edward V on 22 June were now available for Richard III's on 6 July, "by which time large forces from the North had arrived and no counter-coup was possible."[10] The ceremony, to make up for any dubiety there might be about it, was of exceptional splendour and marked by exceptional rewards. John Howard was created Duke of Norfolk, his son Earl of Surrey. The ceremony was ordered by Buckingham, but his Woodville wife was not present. The new Queen's train was borne by Lord Stanley's wife, the Lady Margaret Beaufort, Henry Tudor's mother. Archbishop Bourchier anointed and crowned king and queen; Buckingham and Norfolk presented them to St. Edward and stood on either side of them at the shrine.

What must have been the thoughts of the actors in this sacred scene?

And what, meanwhile, of the Princes in the Tower?

The traditional story, as it has come down to us, is perfectly plain and clear. And it is significant that everything that has come

14

to light in our time is completely consistent with it, bears it out, confirms it. Strange as it may seem after so long a lapse of time, a good deal has come to light in our day. There is, first, the discovery and publication of Mancini's account of Richard's usurpation of the throne, *De Occupatione Regni Anglie;** Mancini was in England at the time, and though he left for France immediately after Richard's coronation he expresses the fears that were already entertained, not unnaturally, for the safety of Edward's children. From France, Mancini kept in touch with events in England, and learned of Dr. Argentine, the Strasbourg doctor who was in attendance on the young King, of his expectation of death. There has been a detailed, precise and independent examination, by Mr. Lawrence Tanner and Professor William Wright of the Royal College of Surgeons, of the bones of the two boys of about thirteen and ten discovered in 1674 when the staircase in the King's lodgings at the Tower was demolished—exactly where Sir Thomas More says they were buried by their murderers, "at the stair foot, meetly deep in the ground under a great heap of stones."[11] *The Great Chronicle of London* has at last been published, and that gives us a pretty good idea in general of what the citizens thought at the time and shortly after.

Then there is Sir Thomas More's famous account of Richard's usurpation, which has at last been critically studied in our time so that we can appreciate as never before its precise and unique value. On the one hand, we now realise that it is an unfinished, unrevised, uncorrected first draft, certainly not intended for publication in its present state. Hence the errors of detail, the lapses of memory, the gaps left in the text to be filled in later. On the other hand, Professor A. F. Pollard, first of early Tudor scholars in our time, has pointed out, with the usual penetration of his able mind, wherein the unique value of More's *History* resided. It is that More was in a position to learn about these events from a considerable number of people "who had participated in public affairs while Richard reigned and were not only alive when More was writing, but were his friends, acquaintances, or neighbours."[12] But of course.

It should not be necessary to say as much, except that there

---

* Brought to light by my former pupil, Mr. C. A. J. Armstrong, in 1936.

are crackpots about; they proliferate in this field as about Shakespeare: people who do not qualify to hold an opinion, much less
express one.

After Richard had got both his nephews into his possession in
the Tower they were never seen outside of it again. *The Great
Chronicle of London* tells us that "during this year the children
of King Edward were seen shooting and playing in the garden of
the Tower by sundry times."[13] Mancini tells us that "after Hastings was removed, all the attendants who had waited upon the
King were debarred access to him. He and his brother were withdrawn into the inner apartments of the Tower proper, till at last
they ceased to appear altogether. A Strasbourg doctor [this was
Dr. Argentine], the last of his attendants whose services the King
enjoyed, reported that the young King, like a victim prepared for
sacrifice, sought remission of his sins by daily confession and
penance, because he believed that death was facing him."[14]
Mancini, during his mission in England, was in a position to meet
people near the centre of affairs: "I have seen many men burst
forth into tears and lamentations when mention was made of him
after his removal from men's sight; and already there was a suspicion that he had been done away with." And Mancini pays a
tribute to the young King's education and attainments, in particular "his special knowledge of literature, which enabled him to
discourse elegantly, to understand fully, and to declaim most ex-
cellently from any work whether in verse or prose that came into
his hands, unless it were from among the more abstruse authors."
That is a convincing touch for a boy of thirteen, and Mancini
adds a word as to his dignity and charm of countenance.

Common sense tells us that the order for the murder of the
Princes would not be given until after the coronation in July,
when London had emptied of its grandees and Richard himself
was away on tour through the country. And this is precisely
what Sir Thomas More had heard from those in a position to
hear at the time. "I shall rehearse you the dolorous end of those
babes, not after every way that I have heard, but after that way
that I have so heard, by such men and by such means, as
methinketh it were hard but it should be true."[15] We see how
careful More is, if we did not already know what a conscientious
and scrupulously truthful man he was.

More tells us that it was after the coronation while on his progress to Gloucester that Richard had time to reflect on the danger to himself of allowing his brother's boys to live. He sent a confidential servant, John Green, to Sir Robert Brackenbury, constable of the Tower, with a letter of credence to him to put them to death. Brackenbury "plainly answered that he would never put them to death to die therefore." Green came back to Richard with this answer at Warwick—and we know that Richard was at Warwick for a week from 8 August.[16] At Warwick the job was taken over by Sir James Tyrrell: "the man had an high heart and sore longed upward, not rising yet so fast as he had hoped, being hindered and kept under by the means of Sir Richard Ratcliffe and Sir William Catesby." Here was a motive; when Richard found Tyrrell willing, he sent him off at once with a letter to Brackenbury "by which he was commanded to deliver Sir James all the keys of the Tower for one night, to the end he might there accomplish the King's pleasure in such thing as he had given him commandment."

More tells us that the two ruffians who committed the deed were Miles Forest, "one of the four that kept them," i.e., attended upon the boys, "a fellow fleshed in murder before time. To him he joined one John Dighton, his own horsekeeper, a big, broad, square, strong knave." These two smothered the boys under the feather-bed and pillows, and then "laid their bodies naked out upon the bed and fetched Sir James to see them. Which, upon the sight of them, caused those murderers to bury them at the stair foot." When the bodies were discovered in 1674 they were tumbled in one above the other, face to face, Edward on his back, Richard lying face downwards on him. More adds that when Tyrrell brought the King the news Richard expressed his intention of removing the bodies from so vile a corner and burying them elsewhere, "because they were a king's sons." That, too, is a convincing touch; we know that Richard had Henry VI honourably reburied at Windsor. He made that reparation to the murdered king; he could not touch the subject of his nephews' bodies in the two years of life and rule that remained to him. It was a couple of months, October to be precise, before the rumour of what had happened in the Tower began to spread; the stench of the deed stank to high heaven and in the end overwhelmed him.

For in all the evil deeds of this period, the killings on the field of battle or in peacetime, the executions with or without trial, the murders, fifteenth-century people in general drew the line at killing women or children—in that unlike our own more disgraceful century—and these Princes were Richard's own brother's children.

Various suspicious rewards appear in the documents of that year. It may not be possible to pin down John Green—it is a common name—but a Warwickshire John Green received a general pardon from the Crown of all offences on 20 September.[17] We find Forest as keeper of the wardrobe at Barnard Castle—that Neville stronghold. Sir Thomas More tells us that "at St. Martin's," i.e., in the sanctuary of St. Martin-le-Grand, he "piecemeal rotted away." And, true enough, he died shortly after this deed. Bracken-bury received a number of important grants within the year; Tyrrell was made, very appropriately, Master of the King's Henchmen, as well as Master of the Horse.[18]

Richard's progress that summer was exceptionally lavish of largesse—we can all understand why: he was purchasing favour and support. Contemporary observers noticed that he impoverished the resources of the Crown by the extravagance of his grants. Needs must. At Reading he delivered Hastings' widow from all the consequences of his alleged treason, just as if it had never been—preserved his blood from attainder and his lands from forfeiture, and gave her the valuable wardship of his son and heir. At Woodstock he liberated a considerable area of land which his brother had arbitrarily annexed for his own pleasure to Wychwood forest. To Gloucester he gave a generous charter of liberties and immunities. He declined, as Edward would never have done, the offer of benevolences to defray the expenses of his progress, de-claring propitiatingly—the motive was too obvious—that he would rather have their hearts than their money. At Tewkesbury, re-visiting the scenes of the battle and the abbey where now lay Clarence not far from Henry VI's son, Edward Prince of Wales, Richard made a most munificent gift out of Clarence's estates.[19]

In Yorkshire, Richard met his son Edward at gloomy Ponte-fract—the boy was so sickly that he could not ride and had to be carried in a chariot to York for his grand investiture as Prince of Wales. At Sheriff Hutton, Richard established Clarence's son, Warwick, under the care of John, Earl of Lincoln, the son of Richard's sister, the Duchess of Suffolk. Behold Time's whirligigs and revenges: this John de la Pole was the grandson of that most Lancastrian Suffolk, who had been barbarously beheaded in the Channel for the love of Henry VI and Margaret of Anjou. Owing to the self-destruction of the Yorkist family, Richard would have to make him his heir. Pleased with his reception at York, Richard granted the city a remission of more than half the taxes they yearly paid to the Crown.

This was being too liberal, and shortly Richard would feel the pinch of his extravagant generosity. On the other hand, he was a competent ruler: there is no reason to doubt that he would have made him an able king, if he had not been the murderer of his nephews, one of them his king.

In the second half of September he had to turn his steps south, whence he heard ill news. He was never to know any security or even respite again.

The movement of revulsion from Richard was rooted precisely in anxiety about the fate of the Princes, and it began in London and the home counties where people had best reason to suspect what had happened. The Croyland chronicler tells us that people "began to murmur greatly, and to form meetings and confederacies . . . in order to deliver them [the Princes] from this captivity."[20] People did not know what had happened; murderers do not publish proofs of their deeds—so that it is fatuous to ask for direct proofs. People knew well enough what to expect from the man who had killed his friend Hastings without trial, who had had Rivers, Grey and Vaughan done to death, even if he had only supervised Henry VI's murder on his brother's orders. The rumour ran about London that Edward's daughters should escape from sanctuary and take refuge overseas, "in order that, if any fatal mishap should befall the said male children . . . the kingdom might still, in consequence of the safety of the daughters, some day fall again into the hands of the rightful heirs." The answer to this had been to place a strict watch upon the sanctuary at Westminster so that no one could go in or out without permission. It was a very emergency state of affairs: one cannot imagine things going on for long like this.

"At last it was determined by the people in the vicinity of
the city of London, throughout the counties of Kent, Essex, Sussex, Hampshire, Dorset, Devon, Somerset, Wiltshire and Berkshire,
as well as some others of the southern counties of the kingdom, to
avenge their grievances before-stated." It was natural enough that
in this first tremor, when people still hoped that the Princes might
be liberated and were unsure of their fate, the Woodvilles were
concerned. The Bishop of Salisbury slipped out of sanctuary at
Westminster to get to work in his diocese; he was joined there
by his nephew, the Marquis of Dorset. In Kent and Surrey, Sir
Richard Guildford took the lead; in Berkshire, Sir Richard Woodville was supported by the ancient Stonors; in Wiltshire there was
Sir John Cheney, who had been replaced by Tyrrell as Master of
the Horse. In Devon the leading family, the Courtenays—the
Bishop of Exeter, his kinsman Edward, with St. Leger and others
—came into the open.

Then, in September, the country was electrified by the news
that Richard's right-hand man in taking the crown, Buckingham
himself, had come out against Richard. What accounted for this
astonishing defection just at this moment? Moreover, the situation
was transformed; for Buckingham was not coming out for the
Princes, but for the Lancastrian claimant overseas, Henry Tudor.
How to account for this transformation?

The answer to both questions is simple, indeed obvious, as the
historian Gairdner clearly saw: the realisation that the Princes
were dead itself effected the transformation. There was no point
in going on with the movement to liberate them now.

Richard had had his last meeting with Buckingham, while on his
progress, at Gloucester. From here the King went on to Warwick, whence he gave his orders for the murders in the Tower.
Buckingham rode on to his castle at Brecon, where he had Bishop
Morton in his charge. The clever young Thomas More was brought
up a page in Morton's household as archbishop at Lambeth, and
is well able to tell us the kind of man he was. "The Bishop was a
man of great natural wit, very well learned and honourable in
behaviour, lacking no wise ways to win favour."[21] He had been a
faithful adherent of the royal house of Lancaster in adversity as
well as prosperity; he had gone into exile with Margaret of Anjou
and "never came home but to the field," i.e., of Tewkesbury. Yet

Edward IV pardoned him, held him in high respect for his devotion to the defeated cause and "from thenceforth treated him both in secret trust and very special favour." Such a man Richard had reason to fear, and, as we have seen, imprisoned him and drove him from the Council on the day of Hastings' public murder. More tells us in conclusion that Morton, "by the long and often alternate proof, as well of prosperity as of adverse fortune, had gotten by great experience the very mother and mistress of wisdom, a deep insight in politic worldly drifts."

Morton now got to work on Buckingham, and indeed there was plenty to work on. For Morton had the great advantage that he was not only a wise politician but he was a priest: he could appeal not only to Buckingham's ambition but to his conscience, not only to his jealousy and cupidity but to his remorse and his loyalty. A faithful adherent of the royal Henry as long as he lived, Morton was able to remind Buckingham that both his father and his grandfather had died for King Henry. Though the direct male line of Lancaster had been obliterated, Buckingham himself was descended in the female line from Edward III—and the great bulk of Edward III's descendants stood by the royal line of Lancaster. Its representative now, through the Lady Margaret Beaufort—whose second husband had been Buckingham's uncle, was Henry Tudor, Earl of Richmond, the alternative to the tyrant. (For Richard's rule, try as he might, was tyranny in the exact sense.) Would not the best thing for the country, the right solution to the long struggle between the houses, "with infinite benefit to the realm, by the conjunction of those two bloods in one whose several titles had long unquieted the land," be for the heir of Lancaster, Henry, to marry the heiress now of York, Edward IV's eldest daughter, Elizabeth, and thus achieve unity and peace?

Buckingham's letter of invitation to Henry was dispatched on 24 September 1483—it reminds one of nothing so much as that other letter, representative of both parties, sent in 1688 to William of Orange to come over and deliver England from the rule of a tyrant. The invitation to Henry came from both parties, Yorkists as well as Lancastrians. In the background was his mother, the Lady Margaret, keeping him informed as to the situation, raising money for him in London, in a position to influence the Stanleys. The date fixed for the rising was St. Luke's Day, 18 October; the

Duke informed Henry that his supporters would take up arms all over the South and West on that day, he himself would raise the standard in Wales, and this was the moment for Henry to make a descent upon the coast.

The men of Kent were so anxious to begin that they betrayed the movement by breaking out prematurely on 10 October. This alerted Richard, and the faithful Norfolk was able to prevent a junction between the rebels of Kent and Surrey, thrusting towards London, and those of East Anglia. Rebels against Richard raised their standard all along the South, in their county towns at Maidstone, Guildford, Newbury, Salisbury, Exeter, Bodmin. The news of Buckingham's defection took Richard by surprise; he wrote to his Chancellor in agony of spirit a bitter postscript to his official orders, a protest at "the malice of him that had best cause to be true, the Duke of Buckingham, the most untrue creature living . . . there never was falser traitor purveyed for . . ."[22] The angry phrases betray how much there had been between them. This was followed on 23 October by an extraordinary proclamation betraying Richard's state of mind. It was one more appeal to morality, inveighing against the immoralities of the rebels, and "the damnable maintenance of vices and sin, as they had done in times past, to the great displeasure of God, and evil example of all Christian people." The immoralities of Dorset were specified in particular, in dishonouring "sundry maids, widows, and wives"; immense prices were offered for the heads of the Duke, the Marquis or either of the two bishops.

At this moment the tyrant had a signal stroke of luck—his last: the weather came to his rescue. The West of England was deluged by a tremendous autumnal storm. The rivers became impassable; many people were drowned in the floods, serious damage was done to shipping, especially at Bristol. Buckingham had left it too late: he found himself cooped up in Wales, his forces, which could neither be fed nor supplied, melting away. In any case he was not popular in Wales: the Welsh would effectively rise only at the appearance of their own deliverer. Buckingham marched through the Forest of Dean hoping to cross the Severn to link up with the Courtenays in the West Country. Frustrated at the river he turned north-east, his followers deserting from hunger and despair, until he finally went into hiding in Shropshire and was

betrayed by one of his own retainers. (The man who had made
Richard king was evidently not popular.) Meanwhile Morton fled
in disguise to the fens of his own diocese, Ely, whence he escaped
to Flanders.

At Exeter, Henry was proclaimed king by the Bishop, Sir Walter
Courtenay of Powderham, and Edward Courtenay of Boconnoc,
now head of the main line after the decimation of the family in
the Lancastrian cause. With them were associated the representative leaders of Devon and Cornwall, Sir Robert Willoughby,
Arundells, Edgcumbes, Treffrys and ancient John Trevelyan. The
storm that ruined Buckingham in Wales—known for years after
as the Great Water or the Duke of Buckingham's—drove Henry's
little squadron of ships back into port in Brittany. When he could
put out again, it was too late: he arrived off Poole to find the ap-
proaches well guarded, and then moved westward to Plymouth.
He was invited ashore by men in arms, assured that they were
Buckingham's. The cautious Henry learned better, and slipped
away to fight another day. Stricken by the ill news the Courtenays
fell back on Cornwall, where Henry was proclaimed at Bodmin,
the county town.[23]

Richard was served well by luck in this year 1483, and only
too well by his own energy, speed and decision. He had posted
himself strategically at Leicester to intercept Buckingham, but on
the collapse of his movement Richard marched swiftly to Salisbury
to deal with the Woodvilles. They had already absconded, but
Buckingham was brought prisoner to him there. The Duke ear-
nestly besought an interview with Richard, who wisely refused, for
we learn from Buckingham's son years later that the father meant
to take the chance to stab the tyrant to the heart. (Something
powerful must have come between Richard and the man who had
made him king.) Buckingham was beheaded in the market-place
at Salisbury on All Souls' Day, and, what shocked the Croyland
chronicler more, it was a Sunday.

Richard marched swiftly on to Exeter, where he had his own
brother-in-law, Sir Thomas St. Leger, executed though large sums
were offered to spare his life. (St. Leger had married Richard's
sister, Anne, Duchess of Exeter.) Richard was determined to
make a signal example of him—though nothing did any good: the
country had turned against him. It is not too much to say that he

had turned its stomach. On his approach the Courtenays and others of the West Country gentry escaped across the Channel to Henry in Brittany. There Henry's supporters, Yorkists as well as Lancastrians, were gathering together for another day. In the cathedral at Rennes on Christmas Day Henry took a solemn oath to marry Elizabeth, heiress of the house of York, on coming to his kingdom, and thereupon all gave their allegiance and fealty to him as king.

It is ironical to think that if it had not been for the winds and waves of that tempestuous autumn Richard's rule might well have ended in the first six months of his usurpation. As it was he had nearly two more years of rule, of doubt and anguish, of inner torment, before he was called to his account. In January next year he was denounced before the bar of European opinion, by the prolocutor of the French States General, as the murderer of his brother's children. If only Richard could have produced them to stop people's mouths . . . But he never could, for the worst of all reasons: they were dead.

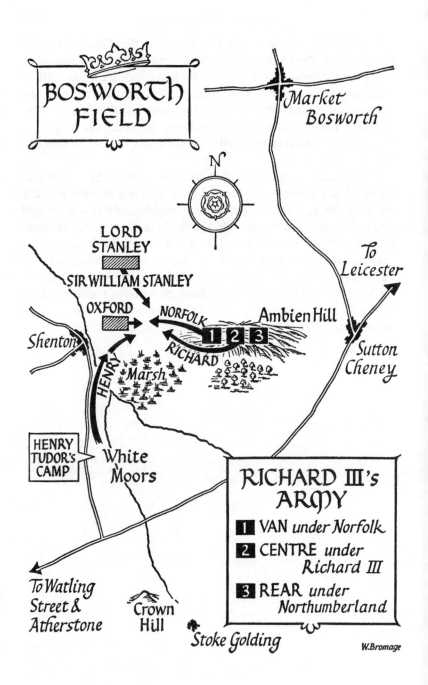

BOSWORTH FIELD

Market Bosworth

N

To Leicester

LORD STANLEY

SIR WILLIAM STANLEY

OXFORD

NORFOLK

Ambien Hill

Shenton

RICHARD

1 2 3

Sutton Cheney

HENRY

Marsh

HENRY TUDOR'S CAMP

White Moors

RICHARD III's ARMY

1 VAN under Norfolk

2 CENTRE under Richard III

3 REAR under Northumberland

To Watling Street & Atherstone

Crown Hill

Stoke Golding

W.Bromage

CHAPTER XI

Bosworth Field

Henry of Richmond was the acknowledged representative and heir of the Lancastrian royal house, through his mother, the Lady Margaret, the undoubted heiress of John of Gaunt. In fifteenth-century circumstances, the circumstances exposed in this book, a woman could hardly have been advanced as standard-bearer of a party—the example of Margaret of Anjou had not been propitious —much less as queen regnant to the throne. The Lady Margaret seems to have recognised this and contented herself with doing all she could for her son—she had an able, politic, Beaufort head as well as a pious Lancastrian heart.

Henry was also now the candidate of the dissentient Yorkists, of the Queen-dowager's party, the Woodvilles and all those who had risen against the tyrant in the autumn of 1483. But the de-cision would be made, as usual, by people in the middle, those who were as yet uncommitted, the Stanleys in their dominant po-sition in the North-West and North Wales, the Percies in the far North.

Henry's great weakness was that he was unknown in England— he would never have been brought forward if Richard had been content to remain Protector and done his duty by his nephews. The Lancastrian claimant had never been seen there, except when, as a boy of fourteen, he had been brought to Court by his uncle Jasper to receive the blessing of his uncle, the sainted Henry VI, during the Re-adeption of 1470-71. Ever since then Henry had been an exile in Brittany, watched over as a valuable pawn on the diplomatic chessboard, in the triangular game played by England, France and the independent duchy under its last duke, Francis II. Henry was inured to insecurity and danger—it was his daily por-tion. He was a Welshman, of that less familiar but recognisable

type, unimpassioned, cool and calculating. He had been well educated and brought up; one of his tutors afterwards said that never
had he known a boy so quick at learning. He was still better
educated in the uses of adversity: he was secretive and shrewd,
with none of the extrovert Yorkist overconfidence in life, the
bonhomie of Edward IV, the blunt impulsiveness of Edward's
father, Richard of York. Henry, above all things, kept his own
counsel, a rather silent man, an introvert with a far-seeing look
in the luminous, intelligent, but deep-sunken eyes one sees in the
Torrigiani bust of him. The ingrained sense of insecurity com-
pensated itself in his addiction to money—overcompensated itself, for in the end he became miserly. He left a large treasure,
for his son Henry VIII to spend, who took after his grandfather
Edward IV—and that is a clue to *him*. The secret Henry VII is
less obvious and more interesting: he was made to be a founder
of a dynasty.

Born on the feast of St. Agnes the second, 28 January 1457,
Henry was now a man of twenty-six, some four years Richard's
junior. Under the careful, almost paternal tutelage of Jasper,
Henry had kept himself unmarried, free for whatever might betide
in England. And now he was publicly pledged, in all solemnity,
to marry Elizabeth of York, already eighteen and marriageable,
to end the dynastic discord in England for good.

It would seem that a most important lesson had been learned
by Jasper and Henry from the failure of 1483—namely to make
their ancestral base in Wales the springboard for their blow at
Richard in the heart of his kingdom. It was a much better strategic
conception, indeed there had been no strategic conception at all
in the widespread movements against Richard all over the South,
all confusion and no unity. In Wales the Tudors would be on
sure ground; they would find their own following awaiting them
there, and in case of defeat a line of retreat still open to them.
Moreover, there Henry would be able to make decisive contact
with the Stanleys. Already Wales was in expectation of his coming;
there was a tradition that there he was known by the magic name
of Owen, with its living memories for the Welsh, and the bards
were singing that the Black Bull of Anglesey would vanquish the
White Boar (i.e., Richard's cognisance). "When wilt thou, Black
Bull, come to land?" sang the leading bard, Lewis Glyn Cothi.

"How long shall we wait? On the feast of the Virgin, fair Gwynedd [North Wales] in her singing watched the seas."

The time would not be long now.

The disturbances of that autumn were more widespread and damaging than has been altogether realised, and they had their sequel in a state of virtual hostilities at the western end of the Channel. All Breton ships and goods in West Country ports were seized; the Duke of Brittany on his side armed his subjects and kept a watch on his coasts. From the scraps of evidence that remain the Cornish gentry were generally disaffected. The lands of the Arundells were given by Richard to the horrid Tyrrell; Dynham got many of the Courtenay lands, the predatory Bodrugan shared in the share-out.[1] When a truce with Brittany was made Richard entered on a diplomatic campaign to get Henry surrendered: he offered the whole annual revenues of the earldom of Richmond in return for him.

These efforts and the constant watch that had to be kept made for crushing expense. The Croyland chronicler tells us that, though Richard had got through without having to fight a battle, it was "at an expense not less than if two armies had fought hand to hand."[2] A good deal of the confiscations went to Richard's northern adherents on whom he depended, to the disgust of "people in the South, who daily longed more and more for the hoped-for return of their ancient rulers, rather than the present tyranny of these people."

In January the one Parliament of Richard's brief reign met. An immense act of attainder was put through, no less than a hundred persons being named; this served to bring home all the more the widespread extent of the disaffection. Even so, concessions had to be made. Richard did not dare to drive the Stanleys into open revolt; so the Lady Margaret was spared the full consequences of attainder: she was given in custody, along with her lands, to her husband, who had not committed himself and remained Steward of the Household. Richard had to affect a confidence he did not feel; as More says, with large gifts he procured unsteadfast friendships. Tyrrell, however, was faithful, and was rewarded by a private act of this Parliament, of which Catesby was Speaker.

Richard went out of his way to abolish benevolences, which he could ill afford, in order to purchase popularity.

This was followed by an extraordinary royal letter to the bishops for the promotion of morality and the suppression of vice: "our principal intent and fervent desire is to see virtue and cleanness of living to be advanced, increased and multiplied, and vices and all other things repugnant to virtue, provoking the high indignation and fearful displeasure of God, to be repressed and annulled."[3] On his northern progress Richard had been careful to restore to the priory at Pontefract twenty acres of land that Edward IV had annexed, "calling to remembrance the dreadful sentence of the church of God given against all those persons which wilfully attempt to usurp unto themselves, against good conscience, possessions or other things of right belonging to God and his said church, and the great peril of soul which may ensue by the same."

It takes no very subtle knowledge of psychology to penetrate the inwardness of these pronouncements: the need for propitiation. There may well have been an element of remorse, with the suspicious insistence on the word "conscience." As More tells us, "I have heard by credible report of such as were secret with his chamberers that, after this abominable deed done [the murder of his nephews], he never had quiet in his mind, he never thought himself sure. . . . He took ill rest a nights, lay long waking and musing, sore wearied with care and watch, rather slumbered than slept, troubled with fearful dreams—suddenly sometimes start up, leap out of his bed and run about the chamber—so was his restless heart continually tossed and tumbled with the tedious impression and stormy remembrance of his abominable deed."[4] Richard did what he could to assuage the pangs of conscience: he had founded a chantry at Middleham, a college of priests at All Hallows, Barking, beside the Tower; he proposed to found another at Barnard Castle, which he had originally shared with Clarence. At York he apparently intended an unexampled foundation—no less than a hundred priests to say Masses for his soul. No doubt he felt he needed them.

We must not overlook the many charitable acts for which he was responsible, the efficiency of his administration and even the reforms in it if he had had time, his constructive intentions merely adumbrated.

In February, Richard's son, Edward, was declared heir apparent to the Crown. In March, after the Parliament, all the lords, spiritual and temporal, knights and gentlemen of the household remaining in London were called on—though it was exceptional—to swear to the succession. The Croyland chronicler tells us that they were assembled "at the special command of the King in a certain lower room near the passage which leads to the Queen's apartments. And here each subscribed his name to a kind of new oath, drawn up by some persons to me unknown, of adherence to Edward, the King's only son, as their supreme lord, in case anything should happen to his father."[5] This was before Richard and his Queen set out on a northward progress to survey the state of his kingdom.

Alas for his hopes!—in April the boy, for whom all had been done, died at Middleham. Richard and Anne heard the news at Nottingham, the strategic centre where they remained for a month in case of invasion. Both of them were distracted by grief at the news—the Croyland chronicler may well have been an eyewitness: "you might have seen his father and mother in a state almost bordering on madness, by reason of their sudden grief . . . this only son, in whom all the hopes of the royal succession, fortified with so many oaths, were centred."

What was to happen now in the bosom of Richard's family, struck by this blow of fate? What was to happen to the succession?

At first Richard declared Clarence's boy, Edward of Warwick —Edward was becoming an unlucky name to bear—his heir and successor. But Warwick's blood was attainted by the attainder of his father, Clarence, and he may have suffered from some physical and mental debility. In any case, for the sake of consistency or a better candidate, Richard switched to his sister's son, John de la Pole, Earl of Lincoln, a young man of twenty, and declared him his heir. Lincoln was residing with Warwick at Sheriff Hutton in Yorkshire, as head of the Council of the North. Richard now made him nominally Lieutenant of Ireland, and gave him the reversion to the Lady Margaret Beaufort's estates.

And what of Edward IV's queen and daughters, who had remained all this while in sanctuary?

Richard was well able to appreciate the latent danger of a marriage between the heir of Lancaster and the heiress of York. He had used the opportunity of the meeting of Parliament to induce the Queen-dowager, with the most solemn assurances, to come out of sanctuary with her daughters. No one would have trusted his word by itself, so he swore an oath before the lords spiritual and temporal, and the lord mayor and aldermen of London, giving his word as a king, that "if the daughters of Elizabeth Grey, late calling herself Queen of England [she had been Queen for twenty years], that is to wit, Elizabeth, Cecily, Anne, Catherine and Bridget, will come to me out of the sanctuary of Westminster, and be guided, ruled, and demeaned after me, then I shall see that they shall be in surety of their lives . . . nor them nor any of them imprison in the Tower of London or other prison . . ."[6] Fancy any king having to give such an oath before such witnesses! . . . it in itself is eloquent of the atmosphere of distrust in which Richard lived, moved and had his being. In return Richard assured their mother, "Dame Elizabeth Grey," a good annual income and marriage portions for her daughters. What else could the poor woman, in her bleak situation, do but accept? She was probably reduced to poverty, living on the charity of the monks, with no hope of the future, after the collapse of the autumn before.

Some prospect now opened before them, for her daughters if not for her. After the agonies and the anxieties of that summer, the invasion not having materialised, Richard kept Christmas at Westminster with much splendour. Edward's eldest daughter was given a leading place at Court, arrayed like Queen Anne herself, with whom her dresses were exchanged. Perhaps this was a measure of necessity, but spectators suspiciously wondered whether he meant to make her a queen. They knew of Henry's solemn engagement to marry her and the threat this portended to Richard.

Queen Anne was not a good life actuarially, and Polydore Vergil has the story that Richard abstained from her bed and complained of her sterility, then spread a rumour of her death, which caused her to fear that he meant to bring it about. We do not have to credit this story of Richard's treatment of his wife— though it has its value as showing that people thought him capable of anything. True it is that Queen Anne did die not long after, on 16 March 1485, and Richard certainly entertained the thought of marrying his niece then. The rumour of it gave the gravest anxiety to Henry in Brittany—if it proved possible it would be the most effective way of frustrating his plans. He even began to turn his mind elsewhere for a match.

It proved politically impossible in England for Richard to marry his niece. His closest supporters, Ratcliffe and Catesby, intimated to him that his North Country following would never stomach such a match, that if he pursued it they would believe that he had poisoned the Queen for the purpose. These councillors, on whom he depended, told him plainly that if he did not publicly disclaim the intention the North would no longer stand by him. They even called in the aid of twelve doctors of divinity to support their view against marriage within such a prohibited degree. So Richard had to endure the humiliation of swearing yet one more public oath before the mayor and citizens of London, a little before Easter 1485, in the hall of the knights of St. John at Clerkenwell. Here he made the required denial "in a loud and distinct voice—more, however, as many supposed, to suit the wishes of those who advised him to that effect than in conformity with his own."[7] He followed this up by writing to the mayor and aldermen of faithful York to explain himself; and since he could not now marry Elizabeth he sent her to Sheriff Hutton, as far out of Henry's way as possible.

All this time, in spite of the blows rained upon him, Richard had to affect an appearance of confidence, though "trusting few of such as were about him." The country was alienated from him; the administration churned on, but there was only his inner circle of agents he could rely on, the small band who fought for him and most of whom fell with him at Bosworth. The case of a Wiltshire gentleman, William Collingbourne, attracted much attention that summer. He had been a gentleman of Edward IV's household and then became an officer of Richard's mother, the slandered Duchess of York. He so much hated the tyrant that he entered into conspiracy with a group of his friends to bring Henry in at Poole. A powerful commission was got together for his treason-trial, but what attracted still more attention was the rhyme he had fixed on the door of St. Paul's—it circulated all over England:

> The Cat, the Rat, and Lovell our Dog,
> Ruleth all England under a Hog.

That hit off the inner ruling group, Catesby, Ratcliffe and Lovell, while the Hog was Richard, whose cognisance was a boar. That August he had remained on in London for the translation of Henry VI's body from humble Chertsey to the new glories of St. George's at Windsor—more propitiation; all to no purpose: no one was moved, except Henry.

That summer in Brittany, Henry had a narrow escape from Richard's frantic efforts to get him. He had offered Henry's protector, the Duke, a bribe in vain. Then Francis had a lapse into mental illness, and his Treasurer, Pierre Landois, thought to make profit for himself by surrendering Henry to the English king. Besides, Henry's following was becoming inconveniently large—gentry from the western counties, even sheriffs, were crossing the Channel to him: altogether there were several hundred English folk, a considerable number of them persons of quality. Somehow Morton in Flanders heard of what was intended and sent a trusty priest, Christopher Urswick, to warn Henry just in time. Henry sent Urswick on to the French king to ask permission to move into France. Meanwhile Jasper Tudor conducted the leading persons of Henry's suite towards the frontier on the excuse of paying a visit to the Duke, who was staying there. To avoid suspicion Henry remained behind; two days later he absconded with only five servants, changed clothes with one of them in a wood and crossed the frontier in disguise. Only an hour later Landois' horsemen, sent to bring Henry back prisoner, reached the frontier too late.

The English left behind at Vannes were in despair for his safety, but at that moment the Duke recovered, was displeased at his minister's behaviour and advanced the money for Henry's following to join him at the French Court sojourning further up the Loire. To the French, Richard was the enemy—they had ceased making the payments agreed on at Picquigny even before the death of Edward IV, who had intended to renew the war. The French Council thereupon decided to advance Henry the money to array his men and to raise a body of mercenaries—some eighteen hundred men under the expert Philibert de Chandé—for the invasion. From France, Henry launched his indictment of Richard as a homicide—psychological preparation for the campaign—

writing to his supporters and friends in England as their rightful king "under our signet": "being given to understand your good devoir and entreaty to advance me to the furtherance of my rightful claim, due and lineal inheritance of that Crown, and for the just depriving of that homicide and unnatural tyrant, which now unjustly bears dominion over you. . . ."[8] Everyone knew that Richard *was* a homicide: it was unnecessary for Henry to add anything, or further besmirch the dignity of the Crown, once the issue had been decided at Bosworth.

With invasion imminent and a general state of emergency Richard issued commissions of array for nearly every county, since he did not know where the blow would fall. The expense of all this forced him to go back on his word to abolish benevolences and, though he would not use the name, to resort to the same device, to raise money by forced loans. Distrust sapped the ground from under his feet, people were escaping to Henry, prosecutions for treason multiplied. When a member of the prominent Clifford clan, Sir Roger, was being drawn through the City for execution on Tower Hill, his people nearly succeeded in rescuing him. Then, a matter of far more significance, the leading Lancastrian noble, the Earl of Oxford, persuaded his keeper, one of the Blounts, governor of Hammes Castle, to go over with him to Henry; a Devon Fortescue, the porter of Calais, aided and abetted their escape. This was a most important accession, for Oxford came next to Henry and Jasper in rank and was a more experienced commander in the field.

All was ready for Henry to repeat the venture of the founder of his house, Henry of Lancaster, in 1399. There were, however, marked differences: Henry Tudor claimed to be king by right, Bolingbroke had not begun by claiming the kingship. Then, too, however uncertain the chances of war—and Richard was a far more experienced soldier—Henry Tudor's political prospects already looked better than Bolingbroke's had done. The Tudors could expect a welcome from Wales, though its loyalty would have to be ensured by their presence. Henry was in touch with the most powerful figure in West Wales, Rhys ap Thomas, who was pledged to him; he had hopes of Sir Walter Herbert in South Wales. He was in touch with the Stanleys, with whom North Wales, Cheshire and Lancashire would march; then, more like 1399, it seems that the Earl of Northumberland had a secret understanding with Henry. So far as preparations could go, the plans had been well laid this time. Before leaving France, Henry had handed over two Yorkists, Dorset and Bourchier, who had shown themselves undependable, as pledges for the loan advanced him by the French—a characteristically astute move: Henry would be a good politician.

Richard took up his station again at Nottingham, the strategic centre from which to move best to any point of attack—and with his faithful Yorkshiremen at his back. In June he renewed his proclamation against Henry, who "is descended of bastard blood both of the father's side and of the mother's side, for the said Owen the grandfather was bastard born, and his mother was daughter unto John, Duke of Somerset, son unto John, Earl of Somerset, son unto Dame Catherine Swinford, and of her in double adultery gotten, whereby it evidently appeareth that no title can nor may be in him, which fully intendeth to enter this realm purposing a conquest."[9] As we have seen, Richard was very keen on bastardising everybody. He called on "the natural and true subjects" of the realm "like good and true Englishmen to endeavour themselves with all their powers for the defence of them, their wives, children and goods" to rally against the invader. The appeal was of no force coming from him; men had to be pressed into service. A later phrase from the chronicler Hall would seem to express Richard's bitter contempt—"an unknown Welshman, whose father I never knew, nor him personally saw."[10]

The unknown Welshman embarked from Harfleur—familiar territory to his Lancastrian predecessors and forebears—on 1 August 1485; his forces were small, some two thousand altogether.[11] The very smallness of Henry's forces meant that he would have to depend on the country's revulsion from Richard. A victory would be not so much Henry's work as Richard's defeat, the defeat he had brought on himself, when he could perfectly well have ruled the country with its good will as Protector for his nephews.

Henry, having very fair weather and "a soft southern wind" with him, arrived at Milford Haven a little before sunset on 7 August. On landing he knelt down, kissed the ground, and began the Psalm *"Judica me, Deus, et decerne causam meam."* Here in Pembrokeshire they were in Jasper Tudor's country, indeed his earldom, where Henry had been brought up as a boy. They moved on to Haverfordwest, the county town, where they were well received. The inhabitants of Pembroke sent their submission, asking pardon for former offences and declaring their readiness to serve Jasper as their earl. While Henry was on his way to Cardigan there was an alarm that Sir Walter Herbert had a large force to withstand them at Carmarthen. Henry sent out scouts and found that all was quiet. Indeed, one of Herbert's captains, Richard Griffith, came over with his men, shortly followed by Evan Morgan with more. "Thus Henry went forward without stay almost in any place," and furnishing himself with the supplies left at various points to resist the invaders. He had reached an understanding with Rhys ap Thomas, the leading figure in West Wales, to whom Henry promised the Lieutenancy of South Wales on his victory. They decided to follow different routes with their forces—a wise decision to spare the countryside and keep Welsh and French from quarrelling on the march.

Henry seems now to have moved up the coast north to Aberystwyth—there is a tradition at the delightful manor-house of Wern that he spent a night there on his way.* This northern route enabled him to receive a reinforcement from north-west Wales, Tudor country and the old Glendower stronghold; and turning east to make contact with the Stanley lordships of Yale and Bromham. He sent messages to his mother, the Stanleys, Talbots and other promising adherents, and so came out of Wales at Shrewsbury, to be joined on the way by Rhys ap Thomas, as good as his word. Somewhere along the route they picked up a recruit called David Cecil, a younger son of the little manor-house of Alltyrynys, and carried him with them to Bosworth Field.[12] This was the origin of the fortunes of that family, alongside the Tudors. Shrewsbury opened its gates to Henry, as it had not done for Buckingham, whom it delivered up to Richard's vengeance.

Richard does not seem to have heard of Henry's landing until 11 August; caught by surprise at these well-concealed movements

---

* I am grateful to Mr. Goronwy Rees for taking me to that remote spot, where I learned the tradition.

through Wales, having relied on Rhys ap Thomas and Herbert to oppose any landing in that area, Richard now sent out urgent messages for the nobles of the realm to join him with all their powers. Norfolk and Surrey, Northumberland and the Stanleys prepared to march with their forces to the focal point.

We have a close-up of the emergency in Norfolk's letter to John Paston, "letting you to understand that the King's enemies be a-land, and that the King would have set forth as upon Monday, but only for Our Lady Day. But for certain he goeth forth as upon Tuesday. . . . Wherefore I pray you that ye meet with me at Bury [St. Edmunds], for by the grace of God I purpose to lie at Bury as upon Tuesday night, and that ye bring with you such company of tall men as ye may goodly make at my cost and charge, beside that ye have promised the King. And I pray you ordain them jackets of my livery, and I shall content you at your meeting with me. Your lover, J. Norfolk."[13] Richard was furious at the news that the invaders had reached Shrewsbury without resistance. This in itself was enough reason to suspect treachery, but the attitude of the Stanleys gave the gravest cause for anxiety.

Early in the year Lord Stanley had asked leave to absent himself from Court to visit his family; he had been absent from his post for months when Richard required him to attend or to send his son and heir, Lord Strange, instead. This Stanley did, just before news came of Henry's landing. Stanley's brother, Sir William, was Chamberlain of North Wales and Henry's route had passed along the borders of his jurisdiction. Suspicious and alarmed, Richard summoned Lord Stanley, head of the family, to Nottingham at once. Lord Stanley replied that he was ill of the sweating sickness. At the same time his son made an attempt to escape, but, recaptured, confessed that his uncle, Sir William Stanley and Sir John Savage were in league with Henry. These were immediately proclaimed traitors, and Richard threatened those who did not come to his aid with death and confiscation— hardly a mood to inspire confidence at such a moment.

Beyond Shrewsbury, Henry was joined by Sir Gilbert Talbot, of that famous name, with some five hundred men. At Stafford, Henry had a preliminary meeting with Sir William Stanley, who came with a small retinue and then returned to his soldiers whom he was assembling. Lord Stanley was at Lichfield with two or three thousand men. Before Henry's approach Lord Stanley withdrew further down Watling Street to Atherstone, where evidently it was arranged that Henry should meet his stepfather. Henry camped a night outside the walls of Lichfield and next day was honourably received within the little city with its spires.

One night on the road to Tamworth, Henry had an adventure, which he must have related to Polydore himself. He was in great anxiety, since he could not assure himself of Lord Stanley, whose son Richard was keeping as a hostage and would certainly kill if Stanley came out openly on Henry's side. Deliberating over this Henry got left behind with a party of only twenty, while his army went forward. Night fell; Henry's party lost track of the army and did not know where they were. The rumor was that Richard was near at hand with a large army; so, not daring to inquire the way for fear of betrayal, they spent the night, full of apprehension, at a small town some distance from camp. The army was in no less alarm; but, when he caught up in the grey of the morning, Henry improved the occasion by reporting that he had gone out of the way to receive a message from supporters who could not yet declare themselves, and that it had been very encouraging.

Henry left the army again to pay a secret visit to Lord Stanley and Sir William at Atherstone, where these two were encamped with the Stanley forces of some three thousand. The three men met in a little close, where they took each other by the hand and were glad to see each other. Then they took counsel together "in what sort to arraign battle with King Richard, whom they heard to be not far off." A little before the evening of the same day Henry received a significant accession of strength from a number of deserters from Richard. Two important captains whom he had summoned from London with Brackenbury, but whom he distrusted—Sir Walter Hungerford and Sir Thomas Bourchier—left Watling Street at Stony Stratford and struck across country to join Henry. Next day Sir John Savage came in, with Sir Brian Sanford, Sir Simon Digby and a considerable number of other deserters with "a choice band of armed men." All this put Henry in good hope.

Richard was moved to anger at learning that his great enemy had thus reached the centre of his kingdom unopposed. At first he had been disinclined to regard the threat as serious, Henry's forces were so small—Richard considered it too rash a venture. Now, however, he had gathered a large army, ten thousand to Henry's five, and moved out of Nottingham south to Leicester to intercept Henry, a long array strung out along the road, himself in the middle on a splendid white courser, cavalry on either side. On Sunday, 21 August, Richard marched out of Leicester in pomp, wearing a crown, or circlet round his helmet, that all might recognise him. Norfolk and his son Surrey were with him, with their East Anglian contingents, Northumberland with his large body of men from the Borders, Richard's faithful York-shiremen and his inner circle of henchmen with the forces they had raised.

The King's host marched to intercept the invaders at a point near Market Bosworth, some dozen miles west of Leicester. There they encamped for the night, probably in the rolling country near Sutton Cheney giving good views out over the flat country which Henry was approaching. Henry encamped that night on the plain of White Moors, about three miles from Richard's position. The curious horseshoe-shaped Ambien Hill thrust out a spur between the two armies. One would not have thought Henry's position a good one, except that his much smaller army was protected by a marsh between him and Ambien Hill. Today, when one goes over the ground it is cut up by hedges and fences; then it was all open country and the marshy ground more extensive. Otherwise the landscape has not changed. The Stanleys were moving into the best position to intervene, while still appearing uncommitted "in the mid way between the two battles," i.e., armies. Evidently Henry was expecting the Stanley forces of some three thousand to join in with him to complete the array—there would then be less disparity between the two armies. It appears that Sir William had the active command of the Stanley forces.

The Croyland chronicler tells us that Richard awoke before dawn, no breakfast prepared for him nor were any chaplains present to say Mass. He declared that he had had a restless night disturbed by dreams, and presented an even paler and more haggard appearance than usual. (The more rational Renaissance mind of Polydore Vergil declared that he believed it to be no dream, but a bad conscience, "a conscience guilty of heinous offences.") Richard is reported to have declared that whichever side won would prove the destruction of the kingdom; for, if he won, he would wreak vengeance on his enemies, and no doubt his adversary would do the same. He proceeded to draw out his army to its impressive full length along the ridge of Ambien Hill, with Norfolk leading the van. Norfolk had had a warning rhyme nailed on his gate the night before he set out towards his master:

> Jack of Norfolk, be not too bold,
> For Dickon, thy master, is bought and sold.

However, Richard's duke proceeded to be bold on the day— and paid the penalty. Richard himself was in the centre. Northumberland asked to remain posted in the rear on the ridge overlooking Lord Stanley's force—there was another who evidently intended to wait and see how things would go in this extraordinary battle, where so many were waiting on events and wondering what others were going to do.

Before launching the attack Richard sent a message to Lord Stanley ordering him to join in against the enemy without delay, and threatening that, if he did not, his son should be beheaded. To this Stanley replied that he would not, and that he had other sons. Richard gave the order for Lord Strange to be beheaded, but found that his subordinates were against carrying the order out. This must have confirmed his fears, that he was no longer in command of his fate, that there were people on the field who would betray him, as indeed was the case.

Henry also was kept in anxiety as to what Lord Stanley would do. After the conference at Atherstone, Henry was in better heart; but in the morning when he sent to Stanley to join forces with him and set the soldiers in array, he got a dubious reply, that Henry should set his own folks in order while Stanley would come to him well prepared in time. Henry was "no little vexed" with this and even "somewhat appalled," but had to be content with it and set about ordering his men. Since his forces were now so many fewer than he had expected—clearly he had expected the Stanleys to take their place in the line—he made "a slender vanward for the small number of his people." In front he placed his archers under Oxford's command; on the right, to defend them, Gilbert Talbot with his force; on the left, Sir John Savage. Henry himself, "trusting to the aid of Thomas Stanley, with one troop of horsemen and a few footmen, did follow." Clearly he had expected to post the Stanleys with himself in the centre. He had the marsh for defence on his right, and the sun at his back—so he was looking north towards Ambien Hill, where Richard's forces, more than twice Henry's five thousand and long drawn out, made an imposing sight.

Nevertheless Henry gave the word, and when his men had passed the marsh Richard commanded his troops to attack. There was first an exchange of arrow-shot, then hand-to-hand fighting. Oxford was so much outnumbered that he gave the order that his men were not to go above ten foot from their standards, and thus make a strong stand, no scattering. (A lesson Oxford had learned from his own experience at Barnet.) Richard's troops suspected some stratagem, and paused in the fight—"many with right good will, who rather coveted the king dead than alive, and therefore fought faintly."[14] Seeing this hesitation, Oxford with Talbot and Savage, on the wings, closed in in wedge formation and renewed their attack with determination. The fighting here was now fierce, and it must have been at this point that Norfolk and some of Richard's best chiefs were killed. The news that Norfolk was dead and his son Surrey captured was brought to Richard. At the same time the fatal significance of Northumberland's equivocal stand was brought home to him: the whole of the rearward of his army was standing idle and taking no part in the action.

Richard must have been in despair at the treachery about him, but he had the courage of despair and would rather die than fly the field. Intelligence was brought him that Henry was posted not far off with his small troop, while the battle between the two vans raged hotly. The King made in that direction and assured himself that it was Henry posted by his standard. Richard paused for a last drink at the spring that is still known as Dickon's Well, and then charged straight for Henry's bodyguard. In the fury of his onslaught he killed Sir William Brandon, Henry's standard-bearer; the powerful Sir John Cheney was unhorsed. The fight waxed furious, Henry's guard put up a tougher resistance than was expected; the issue in general was still undecided and Henry's

troops wearying, when Sir William Stanley, seeing that this was
the moment, brought his forces into action.

This decided the battle. Richard himself was surrounded and
killed, fighting manfully in the midst of his enemies. His van must
have been caught in flank by the Stanleys, and this now enabled
Oxford "to put to flight them that fought in the forward, whereof
a great many were killed in the chase. But many more forbare
to fight, who came to the field with King Richard for awe and
for no goodwill and departed without any danger, as men who
desired not the safety but destruction of that prince whom they
hated."[15] We learn that there was a very great number of captives,
"for when King Richard was killed, all men forthwith threw away
weapon and freely submitted themselves to Henry's obedience;
whereof the most part would have done the same at the beginning,
if for King Richard's scurriers [scouts], scouring to and fro, they
might so have done." The action had lasted not more than two
hours, but the chase continued southward to Stoke Golding—
the church spire of which one sees from the ridge of Ambien Hill.

The losses were heavy in Richard's immediate circle, those
who had stuck by him through thick and thin, his active agents:
besides his Duke of Norfolk, Lord Ferrers, Sir Robert Brackenbury, Sir Richard Ratcliffe and John Kendall, the King's secretary,
were killed. Sir William Catesby was caught, and executed
a couple of days after at Leicester. He was given time to make his
will: he hoped that the new king would be good to his children,
"for he is called a full gracious prince, and I never offended him
by my good and free will."[16] He ended with a reproach to the
Stanleys: "my lords Stanley, Strange and all that blood, help
and pray for my soul, for ye have not for my body, as I trusted in
you." That would suggest that he had been a means of saving
Lord Strange's life from Richard, hoping for a *quid pro quo*.

Richard's body was treated with great indignity. Perfectly naked,
it was trussed over a horse's back, head and arms dangling on
one side, legs on the other. Passing over a bridge the head
was bruised against a stone. It was brought to the church of the
Grey Friars at Leicester, where it was exposed for two days so
that people might see that he was dead. A king's body would
never have been treated in this way if he had not been what he
was.

After the battle Henry moved south towards Stoke Golding. Richard's crown, or circlet, which was found among the spoils of the field, was brought to Henry, and set on his head by his step-father, Lord Stanley, who had brought him quite enough anxiety already. However, Henry was jubilant, "replenished with joy incredible"; he took up his station on a little hill, known still as Crown Hill, to commend his soldiers, order that the wounded be attended to, the slain buried, and to give thanks to the nobles, gentlemen and captains for their efforts. The soldiery acclaimed him, "King Henry! God save King Henry!"

They marched into Leicester to rest and recuperate for a couple of days, and so down Watling Street, much trampled in these wars, to London.

The lurid drama of Richard's brief reign was over.

CHAPTER XII
Tudor Sequel

The sequel to Bosworth was the whole Tudor age—which, without it, might never have been as it was. Of course, Richard III—considering what he was and the general distrust and detestation of him on account of his great crime—might have been overthrown at some other time in another way. On the other hand, if Edward IV had lived his full span, or Richard done his duty by his brother's children, the Yorkist line would in all probability have gone on and the whole surface appearance of English political history would have been different—not perhaps the permanent course of the country, for that is determined by deeper forces and factors.

It is not, however, the business of the historian to consider probabilities and might-have-beens, but facts. The fact is that Henry won at Bosworth, or, rather, that Richard was betrayed (as the city chronicler of York has it) and defeated: Henry became king, proved that he knew how to keep the throne, reconciled the lines of Lancaster and York by his marriage to Elizabeth of York, and his line, through their daughter Margaret of Scotland, has been there ever since. As Professor Chrimes says, "the Crown *has* remained to the heirs of Henry's body ever since, though not in his heirs male only."[1] The direct line of the Tudors came to an end with Henry's grand-daughter, Elizabeth I—she once referred to him as "my good grandfather"—in 1603. Then the Stuarts came in from Scotland to unite the kingdoms, the fruit of Henry's long-sighted marriage of his daughter Margaret to James IV. From Henry VII, through that marriage descend also the royal houses of Bavaria and Italy, both of which—from a legitimist point of view—come in the line before the fortunate Hanoverians, in whom the succession was determined, after James II, because they were Protestants.

Henry VII was nothing if not a founder.

What kind of man was this whom the event at Bosworth projected into our history, so unexpectedly, so suddenly, yet so decisively?

Polydore Vergil, who knew him, describes Henry's appearance as it was towards the end of his life—he was only fifty-two when he died, worn out by the job of kingship. "His body was slender but well-built and strong; his height above the average. His appearance was remarkably attractive and his face was cheerful, especially when speaking; his eyes were small and blue, his teeth few, poor and blackish; his hair was thin and grey; his complexion pale."[2] If we can judge from his death-mask at Westminster, his countenance depicted both his ancestry and his character very well. His long head resembles that of his French grandmother, Catherine of Valois; but the lower part of his face has the strong, set chin, the rather ascetic mouth, of his Beaufort mother; then there are the Welsh high cheek-bones, the deep-set eyes. Bacon is perceptive in describing his countenance as "reverend, and a little like a churchman."[3]

There is no eroticism in this cool, controlled, rather sad face. The chief affection in his life was for his mother, whom he "reverenced much, heard little . . . for he was governed by none."[4] After the family affairs of the two Yorkist kings, it is a relief to observe the terms on which Henry was with his mother. She writes to him, "my own sweet and most dear king and all my worldly joy, in as humble manner as I can think I recommend me to your Grace, and most heartily beseech our Lord to bless you."[5] Or, "my dear heart, I will no more encumber your Grace with further writing in this matter." Or, "my dearest and only desired joy in this world . . . At Calais town, this day of St. Agnes, that I did bring into this world my good and gracious prince, king, and only beloved son." Henry's Lancastrian title came through her: she was the heiress of the house of Lancaster; but England was not yet ripe for the rule of a woman, and the only claim she made was to sign herself, a little improperly, "Margaret R." She qualified this, however, by subscribing herself, "your humble servant, beadwoman [prayer-woman], and mother."

It is worth observing, too, after Edward IV and Richard III, that Henry was morally respectable, like his Lancastrian predeces sors, Henry IV, Henry V and Henry VI. Bacon observes that "towards his queen he was nothing uxorious, nor scarce indulgent; but companionable and respective, and without jealousy."[6] He adds that nevertheless, "she could do nothing with him," that is to say that she had no political influence. Her volatile intriguing mother, Elizabeth Woodville, Henry took an early opportunity of popping into Bermondsey nunnery, where she was best off. These two, his own wise and devout mother and his dutiful wife, kept rather in the background, were the only women in Henry's life.

We come upon their appearance in his privy purse expenses— as near as we get to Henry's personal life. There are his visits to his mother at Collyweston in Northamptonshire, payments to her chaplain for Masses, to a priest of hers "for singing before our Lady of the pew" or to "my lady the king's mother's poet."[7] As to the Queen, we hear of a corporas-cloth for the altar in her chapel, frontlets (possibly frontals for the same), furs for her person, for her disguising (i.e., a masque), her fiddler, her surgeon, her debts—a very large sum of £2,000, which is to be repaid. Then there are the children: a tippet of sarcenet for young Henry, Duke of York, money for him to play at dice with, a lute for Margaret, in 1502 a large sum for the state-funeral of Henry's eldest son, Prince Arthur. But for these accounts we should not have known that the third son of Owen Tudor and Henry V's queen, another Owen and Henry VII's uncle, continued into his reign, an elderly monk of Westminster. In 1498 the King gave him £2 "in reward"; four years later Morgan Kidwelly, one of Henry's Welsh servants, was paid for burying the old man, who was given a knell from the tower of St. Margaret's, Westminster. There was a link with all the Welsh and Lancastrian past.

Thus Henry kept touch with the past of which he had known so little, so much of his life having been spent in exile. He began well as a reconciler, treating Richard's nephews, Lincoln and the later Suffolk, in friendly fashion and welcoming them to Court. Henry was quick to redeem Dorset and Bourchier, the pledges he had left behind in France; we find the King losing to Dorset at the butts, i.e., at archery, or at tennis, i.e., the old game of real tennis; there are payments to Suffolk's minstrels and Northumberland's players. So far from being ashamed of his ancient Welsh lineage, Henry was proud of it; there are frequent gifts to Welshmen on St. David's Day, or for making rhymes, or to Welsh harpers. An intimate servant of Henry's in his first years was the Cornishman, Sir Richard Edgcumbe, to whom he entrusted important missions, to Ireland, Scotland and Brittany, where he died. A Cornish Treffry was Groom of the Household or of the Chamber—we find a payment to him for the carriage of carpets, evidently when the King was removing from one residence to another. Along with these small items there are large ones for the palace Henry was building at Sheen, to become Richmond, after his earldom, for finishing King's Chapel, and building Henry's splendid fane at Westminster. Along with these are endearing items, to a woman who brought the King cherries and strawberries, another who gave him posies. He kept several fools, "the foolish Duke of Lancaster," the Spanish fool and Thomas Blackall. Uncle Jasper, now promoted to the famous Lancastrian title, Duke of Bedford, sends his tumbler, or the Earl of Oxford his juggler, to entertain the King. Henry has his dogs: there are payments for a wether slain by his spaniels, a colt by his greyhounds. There are his frequent losses at cards—evidently his gains would not appear in the accounts. These simple entries serve to offset Bacon's dismissive, "for his pleasures, there is no news of them."

Henry kept a pet monkey. Once the monkey destroyed the King's memoranda-book, in which he noted down everything and everybody in businesslike fashion—the destruction gave a good deal of pleasure to the courtiers who observed it. The presence of the ape gives point to Henry's famous reproof to the Irish lords for supporting Lambert Simnel, the joiner's son, who was made to claim the Crown as young Richard of York or alternatively Clarence's son, Warwick: "My masters of Ireland, ye will crown apes at last"—one can see Henry pointing to his pet.

The accounts show frequent payments for binding books. Bacon tells us that "he was rather studious than learned, reading most books that were of any worth in the French tongue"—a convincing touch for someone who had spent his formative years in France. And he was ready to learn from his experience abroad: to offset the insecurity amid which he lived and moved, he introduced a bodyguard after the French model. Hence the yeomen of the guard, who are still with us in their red Tudor livery, flat pancake hats and halberds—the beefeaters at the Tower, a familiar relic of Henry VII to thousands who would not recognise his noble work at Westminster or know what he did for his country.

Even his privy purse expenses reveal that he was a chief patron of the early voyages to America, in particular of John Cabot, and did far more in this respect than the extravagant, navy-minded Henry VIII. This is not our theme, but we may note briefly the number of payments for ships going towards "the new-found isle," i.e., Newfoundland; to "men of Bristol that found the isle"; to "merchants of Bristol that have been in the Newfoundland"; to one that brought hawks from there, and the Portuguese that brought Henry popinjays and cats of the mountain.

Unlike the two Yorkist brothers Henry was not a soldier, and was constitutionally inclined to peace. This was what the country needed above all—a pacifier; indeed Henry's combination of qualities was providentially that best suited to the requirements of the historical juncture at which he lived—as again with his granddaughter, Elizabeth I, and her time. He had plenty of courage, but it did not lead him to aggression, as it did with his militant son, who did not take after him but after his Yorkist grandfather, Edward IV. Everything in Henry VII's make-up was geared to politics, business, affairs. Polydore Vergil speaks of his prudence, his caution and wisdom: "his mind was brave and resolute and never, even at moments of the greatest danger, deserted him. He had a most pertinacious memory."[8] No one dared to try and get the better of him through deceit or guile.

This does not mean that Polydore is uncritical: he strongly disapproves of Henry's avarice, which grew upon him with the years. Both Morton, whom Henry made his Chancellor and Archbishop of Canterbury, and Sir Reginald Bray, his chief confidant in so far as he had one, got the blame for this so long as they lived; when they were dead it was seen that they had been restraining influences—neither of them feared to withstand the King or tell him exactly what he thought. It is all of a piece psychologically: Henry was overcompensating the insecurity in which he had been nurtured. His suspiciousness was also part of this. Bacon says, "he was indeed full of apprehensions and suspicions. But as he did easily take them, so he did easily check them and master them; whereby they were not dangerous but troubled himself more than others. . . . He was a prince sad [grave], serious and full of thoughts and secret observations; and full of notes and memorials of his own hand, especially touching persons, as whom to employ, whom to reward, whom to inquire of, whom to beware of, what were the dependencies, what were the factions, and the like: keeping, as it were, a journal of his thoughts."[9]

Polydore tells us that he was a just man, who cherished justice above all things—in that, like his great-uncle Henry V—that he vigorously repressed violence and manslaughter, and upheld the rule of law. This was just what the country cried out for—and, though he never won popularity, "he was greatly regretted on that account by all his subjects."[10] He made it his business to bring the internal faction-fighting to an end: it was a lifelong task, and he had many interferences in performing it, especially at the beginning. But he won through, and well before the end attained a European reputation for wisdom and statecraft, gaining the admiration of his fellow-rulers for "his universal insight into the affairs of the world."[11] Bacon justly sums up his character as a ruler: "he was of an high mind, and loved his own will and his own way: as one that revered himself and would reign indeed. Had he been a private man he would have been termed proud; but in a wise prince it was but keeping of distance: which indeed he did towards all, not admitting any near or full approach either to his power or to his secrets."

In short, Henry from the first knew how to be a king; the decision at Bosworth had done well for the country.

It was all achieved by sleepless assiduity, an incessant attention to affairs. "For never prince was more wholly given to his affairs, nor in them more of himself; insomuch as in triumphs of jousts and tourneys and balls and masks (which they then called disguises) he was rather a princely and gentle spectator than seemed much to be delighted." What Henry enjoyed was the business of kingship. We know with what care he supervised every department of government, with what special interest he watched over the nation's accounts, initialling page after page of financial records himself. For all his medieval attachment to religion—and he was a secret almsgiver to priests for the benefit of his soul's salvation—Henry was much of a modern man. With him we were moving out of the Middle Ages: he was a business man.

After Bosworth and a couple of days' rest at Leicester, Henry made his way to the capital—new and unfamiliar territory to him, so he needed to go all the more carefully. However, after the nightmare they had been through, people gave the victor of Bosworth a warm welcome, setting out food and drink along the highways where his forces passed. As soon as he could Henry dismissed his foreign mercenaries. He made his ceremonial entry into the City on 3 September 1485, though an outbreak of sweating sickness postponed the coronation till 30 October—performed by Archbishop Bourchier, who had seen and lived through so much. Meanwhile Henry had summoned Elizabeth of York to come up from Sheriff Hutton, and put out a proclamation declaring his intent to fulfil his promise to marry her. To assure opinion that he came as a reconciler he published a general pardon to all who would come in and submit to his obedience. Henry was sparing of honours at his coronation: his immense indebtedness to his uncle Jasper, who had kept the Lancastrian cause going all through its worst days, was recognised by the re-creation of the Bedford dukedom for him. Henry's step-father, Lord Stanley, had the Lancastrian earldom of Derby re-created for him. Sir William Stanley was made lord chamberlain and richly rewarded with grants and lands. The earldom of Devon was revived for Edward Courtenay of Boconnoc, head of the family.

Then Henry was ready to meet Parliament. In his own eyes, as the Lancastrian heir, he was the right heir to the throne. Without going into the rights and wrongs of the succession disputed by the Yorkists, Parliament enacted sensibly and empirically that the inheritance of the Crowns "be, rest, remain and abide in the most royal person of our now sovereign lord, King Henry VII, and in the heirs of his body lawfully coming, perpetually with the grace of God so to endure, and in none other."[12] And so it has remained. As against the immense act of attainder that Richard put through after Buckingham's rebellion, Henry was content to attaint only a score of the leading persons who had fought against him at Bosworth. This aroused much apprehension, and "there was many gentlemen against it, but it would not be, for it was the king's pleasure."[13] Henry was already determined to settle things his own way: this measure put these people and their estates at his mercy—it was taking a high line to regard those who had

fought against him at Bosworth, including Richard, as rebels.
But now Henry could hope to win the residue over by exercising
clemency, which he proceeded to do in his own time and at his
own pace. There was no clemency for the memory of Richard III.
Mr. Armstrong points out that the act of attainder specifically
includes among the charges against Richard the "shedding of
infants' blood." That was enough: everyone knew what it referred
to. It was "an abnormal formula" in itself; but it was an abnormal
circumstance: it was, quite simply, the deed that had cost Richard
the throne.*

On his side the new king exacted a solemn oath from Lords and
Commons and all the knights and squires of the household to put
a stop to the lawlessness engendered by the wars. Laws were
enacted against "maintenance and livery," the maintaining of numbers of armed retainers wearing their lord's badge, that phenomenon so much to the fore ever since the breakdown of royal authority under Henry VI, which had made the raising of private armies
easy. There were further enactments against interference with
the regular course of justice, the bribing of juries, unlawful assemblies. All this was really directed against the independent power
of the great lords, which had made the Wars of the Roses possible
and kept them going. The middle classes of the nation, people in
general, were heartily sick of them. What was new was that here
was a king who did not belong to the type, and was going to
make it his business to reduce these people, even when they were
his own partisans—like the Earl of Oxford—to order.

Having reached that understanding to chart a new course—in
which the Tudors always would be supported by the Commons
and the middle classes of society—before Parliament dispersed it
showed its anxiety to ratify the new deal, by reconciling Lancaster and York, in petitioning Henry to proceed to his marriage.
The King was now ready to do so, having settled things his own
way and shown that he had no mind to enter upon his reign as
his wife's "gentleman-usher," any more than William III would do
in 1688. Without waiting for the papal dispensation—for Henry
and Elizabeth were of kin—he married her on 18 January 1486.
He did not have her crowned for nearly two years, not until No-

* C. A. J. Armstrong, "An Italian Astrologer at the Court of Henry VII,"
Italian Renaissance Studies, ed. E. F. Jacob, 448–49.

vember 1487—a very pointed way of making his point, that the Crown was his, not hers. Henry was undoubted master. When the papal Bull came, which had been carefully negotiated, it not only recognised his title and the validity of the marriage, "to avoid the effusion of Christian blood" and to establish peace, but it categorically denounced all who should oppose him as rebels and threatened them with excommunication.[14] The fact that the papacy was prepared to underwrite the settlement showed that in its view Bosworth was no "mere incident in the intestine strife": it had settled something.[15] And so it proved.

It is not my purpose to write the story of the Tudor age, or even of Henry's successful reign that gave it its start, but to confine myself to the restricted theme, the rather squalid tale, of the *sequelae* to the long duel between the houses, the last sputterings out of the fire that was started in 1399.

After settling matters thus to his liking in London, Henry set out on a progress to the North, to show himself to the country that had never seen him, in particular in the northern capital which had long been at Richard's bidding. To underscore his point yet once more Henry made the progress on his own, without his Queen: he was not willing to receive the country's obedience, or even seek popularity, on her account. He was well received in the eastern counties, and spent Easter religiously at splendid Lincoln. He had no sooner arrived at York than the city was full of the rumour that Lord Lovell had gathered a large number of men at Middleham and was marching on the northern capital. It was very alarming, for Henry had no army with him, merely his bodyguard and retinue ill equipped to fight. However, speed was essential: Henry sent everything he had against the rebels, and made up for lack of equipment by arming his force with pardons. The dissemination of these did the work for him. Lovell fled by night into hiding in Lancashire; his men disbanded and submitted; Humphrey Stafford was taken at Culham, near Oxford, and beheaded, his brother pardoned.

The King completed his progress in peace, crossed over to the western side of the country to Worcester, where he received the welcome papal Bulls confirming both his marriage and his title. And so to Bristol, acquainting himself with the country as he went, back to Richmond and thence down the Thames to Westminster. In the autumn he took Elizabeth with him on a hunting tour westward and into the New Forest. Here at Winchester their first child was born, 20 September 1486, precisely eight months after the wedding. Around the old West Saxon capital there lingered very early memories and ghosts, even an Arthurian aura. The child was baptised Arthur in the cathedral the Sunday after his birth, and the genealogists duly traced his descent back to Cadwallader and the early British kings. To Henry everything was politics: the name was a reminder of his own ancient lineage from kings before ever the English had come to the island. It was to reconcile Wales at last, after all that she had suffered earlier in the century: whatever trouble Henry and his dynasty had in the century to come, Wales gave none.

Next year, 1487, Henry encountered serious trouble, the first and perhaps the gravest crisis of his reign. In Margaret, dowager Duchess of Burgundy, Edward IV's sister, and thus Henry's aunt by marriage, he had an inveterate enemy. For the next decade Margaret, a dowager with a plentiful dower and having little else to do, made Flanders a welcome refuge for dissident Yorkists and a base for attempts to attack Henry's settlement of affairs in England. Bacon, who had no addiction to women, describes the situation concisely: "this princess, having the spirit of a man and malice of a woman, abounding in treasure by the greatness of her dower and her provident government, and being childless and without any nearer care, made it her design and enterprise to see the majesty royal of England once again replaced in her house."[16] Polydore Vergil gives us Henry's own view of the matter when he says that "Margaret was not indeed unaware that the house of York had been almost utterly destroyed by her brother Richard, but she was not satisfied with the hatred which had almost obliterated the family of Henry VI, nor mindful of the marriage which finally united the two houses of York and Lancaster. She pursued Henry with insatiable hatred . . . and never desisted from employing every scheme which might harm him as the head of the other faction."[17] After all, Henry had been on the throne for only a year; her brothers had held it for twenty-five. If Henry could upset that with one battle, why could not she? The event was to show that Bosworth had meant more than just one more battle in the Wars of the Roses.

After Bosworth the Duke of Suffolk, married to Richard's sister, and their son the Earl of Lincoln, whom Richard had named his heir, quickly submitted to Henry, were well received and well treated. But early in 1487 trouble raised its head; Elizabeth Woodville must have had something to do with it, for in February, Henry deprived her of her lands, which he settled on his Queen, and retired the mother to the convent at Bermondsey on a small pension. Shortly after Lincoln absconded to Flanders to plot with his aunt and Lord Lovell. Meanwhile at Oxford a promising scheme had been excogitated. A naughty priest named Simmons had picked up a joiner's son, one Lambert Simnel, whose good looks win Bacon's susceptible commendation: "a comely youth and well-favoured, not without some extraordinary dignity and grace of aspect."[18]

Simmons trained his good-looking youth to impersonate Clarence's son, Warwick. When the rumour went round that Warwick had been put to death in the Tower, Simmons saw that his moment had come. He took Lambert off to Ireland, where Yorkist sympathy still prevailed. The all-powerful Fitzgeralds fell for this nonsense, and Lambert was crowned as Edward VI with a diadem borrowed from a statue of the Virgin. The plotters in Flanders decided to join in the scheme that promised so well. The Duchess Margaret provided the money to raise no less than two thousand German mercenaries under a redoubtable captain, Martin Schwarz.

Henry was extremely disturbed to think that so obvious a deception should blow up into a threat of such proportions. He expected the invasion to come in the eastern counties, opposite the coast of Flanders, and accordingly spent Easter at Norwich, devoutly visiting the shrine at Walsingham. All was quiet. On his return to London, Henry had Warwick publicly shown through the streets of London, to be "wondered upon"—as Richard had not been able to produce the Princes from the Tower. On the Sunday Warwick was produced at Mass in St. Paul's, where Henry arranged for him to greet many important persons, particularly those whom he suspected. It must have had some effect—though, people being what they are, some said that the real Warwick was bogus, and the bogus one in Dublin the real thing.

The blow fell from Ireland, where Henry's enemies concentrated under the banner of the joiner's son. (Lincoln, and his aunt Margaret, knew the truth of the matter very well, but determined to use the deception to advance Lincoln to the throne.) Henry had taken up his station at Nottingham—as Richard had done in the hour of danger—when the invaders landed in Lancashire, crossed over to Yorkshire to pick up recruits and came down the Fosse way to Newark. Here Henry was waiting for them just north of the Trent crossing by a village called Stoke, where he drew up his army in the usual three-column formation. Lincoln and Schwarz fought with desperate courage, the German mercenaries fighting with their congenital stubbornness and showing themselves as good as the English. The Irish contingent was no less spirited, but, having no armour, suffered heavily. It seems that only Henry's van was engaged, for he had a decisive advantage in numbers. The resistance was bitter and the engagement lasted somewhat longer than Bosworth. When Henry saw the rebel line being broken he gave orders to spare Lincoln's life, in order to find out from him who else were involved in conspiring against him. But in the fighting Lincoln was killed, as well as Schwarz, Sir Thomas Broughton and Sir Thomas Fitzgerald. The fate of Lord Lovell has always been a mystery. He was last seen swimming his horse across the Trent; but at his delightful house of Minster Lovell, now a ruin, beside the clear waters of the Windrush in that lovely Oxfordshire valley running up to Burford, there has long been the tradition of a seated skeleton of a man in a vault below, evidently long shut up there. At any rate Richard's faithful follower disappeared from view, and, equally curiously, his name was accidentally omitted from the list of Yorkists attainted after the battle.

Among these were the Cornish Yorkists Sir Henry Bodrugan and John Beaumont. All the names recited in the Act are those of knights and gentlemen, the only peer being Lincoln himself, against whom the reproach is delivered, "nothing considering the great and sovereign kindness that our sovereign liege lord that now is at divers sundry times continually showed to the said late earl. . . ."[19] It seems that these people in proximity to the succession simply could not resist the temptation to try for it: the wine went to their heads and turned into blood.

Stoke was actually the last battle in the Wars of the Roses and, for all Henry's politic wisdom in playing down the threat to him, it had been a real crisis from which he was glad to be delivered. In much relief of mind he went on to Lincoln to give thanks in the cathedral, and sent his standard to rest before the shrine at Walsingham. He gave the likely young lad Simnel a job as a turnspit in his kitchen, and later promoted him to be his falconer, keeper of the King's hawks., The lad's patron, the intriguing Simmons, was consigned to perpetual imprisonment. Henry had surmounted the first big challenge of his reign, but he well knew how much disaffection there was about and that only sleepless watchfulness would see him through. In this respect his reign bears some resemblance to that of the founder of his house, Henry IV. They were both careworn, conscientious men, bearing a load of anxiety. Both were successful in the end in rooting their dynasty. Henry Tudor was luckier in that his happy marriage united both lines of Lancaster and York. On the other hand, through the accidents and strains of the fifteenth century, the Lancastrian line had become very sparse, where the Yorkist—in spite of both Edward IV and Richard III's depredations upon their own family—was prolific. Lincoln was one of seven brothers, sons of Richard III's sister; there were other sisters in addition to the sisters of Henry's Yorkist queen, and the children they would bear. This meant that the challenge of the White Rose, latent or overt, would sputter on under the Tudors.

Though we must confine ourselves to this theme, perhaps we may interpolate that Henry followed Edward IV's example with a very successful stroke against France in 1492. Impossible to go into the complex story of the triangular conflict over the independence of Brittany which led to its union with the French crown—the upshot was that Henry got a large grant from Parliament to lead a powerful army to France. He captured Boulogne, and then did what Edward IV had done at Picquigny in 1475—allowed himself to be bought off, by the Treaty of Etaples, for a large sum to cover his outlay for aid to Brittany as well as arrears due under the Treaty of Picquigny, and a useful pension of £5,000 a year, which went on being paid all through his reign and until 1511. This business deal was unpopular in England, but Henry knew that a solid peace was better than the intermittent fever of war. And, after all, it was no other than the warrior Edward IV had done before him. It was not the only respect in which Henry took a leaf out of Edward's notebook: Henry was—in his direct administration, the use he made of his household for the purpose, in the personal scrutiny he gave to all departments of government —Edward's apt successor. Though he could not command Edward's popularity, he did not have Edward's weaknesses, and in the end was all the more successful.

During the decade after the battle of Stoke the challenge continued from a combination of Yorkist disaffection in Ireland with the support of the dowager in Flanders, who might have put her wealth to better and more enduring uses. This combination made possible the fabulous career of Perkin Warbeck as an impostor. For six years, 1491 to 1497, he remained a thorn in Henry's side, giving him ceaseless anxiety and trouble. It is extraordinary that it should have been so, all the more that the deception originated in much the same way as Lambert Simnel's—one would think that people would have learned! Warbeck was really the son of a respectable citizen of Tournai, who had travelled a good deal in Europe for various masters in trade. He was in Portugal as servant to the wife of Sir Edward Brampton, Edward IV's Jewish merchant; thence he went to Brittany and so to Cork. There the citizens, seeing this personable youth dressed in his master's silks, insisted on recognising him first as Clarence's son and then as Edward IV's younger son supposed to have escaped murder at the hands of the murderers of his elder brother, Edward V. Poor Perkin insisted that it was not so, and took his oath before the mayor to the contrary. But the enlightened citizenry of Cork would take no denial, and the whole boring story began all over again— at least it was very boring to Henry VII. (He had reason to agree with the Liberal publicist—"the longer one lives the more one sees that things really are as silly as they seem.")

Whatever the citizens of Cork thought, the Fitzgerald Earl of Kildare was not going to be made a fool of a second time. He protested to Ormonde, "I am accused to the King, as I understand, that I should have lain with the French lad that was supported with your cousin and mine, the Earl of Desmond, and that I should aid, support, and comfort him with goods and messages.

Whereas I never lay with him, nor aided, comforted, nor supported him with goods nor in none other manner wise, as the lords of this land have certified his highness at this time."[20] It was not until Warbeck crossed to Flanders and was taken up and coached for his part by Margaret that he began to have political significance. By 1493 Henry, whose intelligence service was admirable, knew all about Perkin Warbeck, his origins and story.

What Henry wanted most of all to uncover was the number of Yorkist irreconcilables about him. His chance came when Sir Robert Clifford decamped to Flanders as their emissary to concoct plans with Margaret for joint action with Perkin as their figure-head. Henry bribed Clifford back with a pardon, with all the information he needed and rather more than he liked. In consequence Henry was able to pounce suddenly in 1495 on the nest of Yorkists before they could get moving—two Ratcliffes, Lord Fitzwalter and Robert Ratcliffe, Sir Simon Mountford, Sir Thomas Thwaites, the Dean of St. Paul's—William Worsley—and others. Most of the group, we observe, were North countrymen. The clerics involved in this treason were pardoned, the rest brought to book.

What disturbed Henry most of all was that his mother's brother-in-law, Sir William Stanley, was implicated. Stanley had decided the issue at Bosworth and been well rewarded: he had been made lord chamberlain, he had been given large grants of land and offices, he was the richest commoner in England. There was the rub: apparently he aspired to the royal earldom of Chester—his brother had been rewarded with that of Derby—and considered that his rewards were not commensurate with his services at Bosworth. The King was greatly grieved to find disaffection in so near a quarter, and, though he had suspected Stanley for some time, was reluctant to proceed against him. Stanley was a very proud man and made a full confession expecting leniency. The King was anxious not to offend Stanley's brother, Derby, whose loyalty was beyond suspicion; on the other hand, Sir William enjoyed great authority and this made leniency all the more dangerous—it would encourage others. Henry took the decision: Stanley was condemned and beheaded. Thus the conspiracy was nipped in the bud before Perkin could move. With Margaret's support he made a demonstration off the coast at Deal that summer: he landed two or three hundred men, who were rounded up or dispatched; himself did not dare to land.

Instead Perkin made for the south of Ireland, where he recruited some support, and thence to Scotland, where he was welcomed, relations with England being in a hostile phase. James III even gave "the Duke of York" a cousin of his own, Lady Catherine Gordon, in marriage. Next year, 1497, the Cornish rose in their remote peninsula against the taxation imposed for the Scottish war: they said that events on the Scottish Border were no concern of theirs, and they were a poor people unable to support these impositions. They marched under their leaders all the way up the south of England, without pillage or rapine—unlike the Northerners—to receive their quietus at Blackheath. Henry was lenient in dealing with these poor folk—with the result that when Perkin landed near Land's End in September they were ready to rise again and march with him. This time, after an assault on the gates of Exeter in vain, they got only as far as Taunton when the royal forces closed in on them, and Perkin fled to sanctuary at Beaulieu.

Brought before Henry, Perkin made a full confession of his imposture, which is corroborated by the letter which Perkin wrote to his mother from Exeter, whither he was conducted in the King's entourage.[21] This time Henry did not spare the West Country, but he made it take its punishment in cash not in blood: severe exactions were made upon the offending western counties. It all added to Henry's accumulating treasure, reinforcing security, detracting from popularity. We find traces of these events in Henry's privy purse expenses: payments for Perkin's horsemeat, moneys paid out to bring his wife, the Lady Catherine, from St. Michael's Mount to Court, where she was kindly taken into the Queen's household.

Henry was at last in a position to expose the imposture practiced upon—or, rather, for their own ends accepted by—so many people. He made the most of it: Perkin was publicly exhibited in Westminster and in the streets of London. He solemnly swore that the Duchess Margaret knew as well as himself that he was not King Edward's son. Now that Henry had emerged unscathed from her intrigues, triumphant over his internal enemies, even Margaret was compelled to write and ask pardon for her offences—Henry had tactfully kept her name out of his public indictments. It was the end of her attempts.

Poor Perkin had ceased to serve these grand people's purposes. Or not quite. Henry was ambitious to secure his dynasty by a marriage of his heir, Prince Arthur, to Catherine, daughter of Ferdinand and Isabella, most successful of contemporary rulers, the creators of the new Spain. The Spanish monarchs had constantly been pressing him to make an end of the last male heir of the house of York, and his own dynasty secure, before they would marry their daughter into it. Perkin was used once more for the purposes of high politics. Spirited and not unwilling, he was trapped into attempting an escape from the Tower and taking Clarence's son with him. Poor young Warwick gave his consent. They were then both caught. Perkin and his abettor, the mayor of Cork, were hanged. The Earl of Warwick was led out from his lodging in the Tower between two men and beheaded, 29 November 1499. At the next tide following his body was borne up the Thames to Bisham Abbey where he was buried among his Montagu ancestors. Thus perished the last direct male heir of the Yorkist line.

It was none the less a crime for being a judicial one, and it exacted its penalty, for—unlike his son—Henry was a humane man. It is said that he was troubled by it on his death-bed. It certainly brought him only the more unpopularity—even his official historian, Polydore Vergil, expresses his condemnation of the deed. What adds to the pathos is that Warwick was an innocent in both senses of the word. Imprisoned from the age of eight both by Richard and Henry, the boy grew up, it was said, "unable to discern a goose from a capon." Nevertheless, he had to be got rid of to make Catherine of Aragon's marriage secure. Next year the Spanish envoy was able to report that never had England been so tranquil and obedient, that now there remained not "a drop of doubtful royal blood," and that he "must forbear from importuning them any more on this subject, as he has written so oft concerning the execution of Perkin and the son of the duke of Clarence."[22] Catherine's marriage to Prince Arthur could now go forward. She herself, in all her later troubles with Henry VIII, was convinced that it was because her marriage had been made in blood.

With this exception Henry VII's treatment of sprigs of the house of York is in marked contrast to that of his son, Henry VIII. The question had its difficulties and complexities, its ups and downs in accordance with changes in the political situation. So long as these persons were loyal and did not lend themselves to conspiring against the régime, Henry treated them well and even, though always watchful, with some confidence. But if they escaped abroad they might always be used by the country's enemies; they then became a danger and might well be guilty of treason. Even so Henry was patient, and gave these people plenty of rope—quite unlike his son with his tiger's pounce.

Take the father's treatment of Suffolk: this was Edmund de la Pole, next brother to Lincoln who had been killed at Stoke and became therefore Richard III's heir. Henry made him welcome at Court, where he was given a foremost place proper to his rank in all the ceremonies. On his father the Duke's death the son agreed to accept the rank of Earl, on the ground that the reduced revenue would not support the dignity of a dukedom. In return, and for £5,000 Henry restored to him a portion of the family lands forfeited by his brother's attainder.[23] This may have rankled; in any case Suffolk was not the kind of man to whom Henry could entrust high office. In 1498 he killed a man in a brawl, and though the King pardoned him he resented the fact that he was put through a common court of justice. I fear that he had a high Yorkist temperament. In 1499 he absconded from the country, went to stay with the horrid Sir James Tyrrell at Guines and then on to St. Omer. "As the Netherlands were the nursery of Yorkist plots Henry might have been pardoned if he had adopted stern measures."[24] Instead of that he allowed Suffolk back again—it was very politic of him, for thus he gained ever more information about the nuclei of disaffection to his rule. (It was the way his grand-daughter Elizabeth behaved later, putting up with a good deal of treachery and disloyalty around her, so long as it did not turn active.)

Next year when Henry crossed to Calais for his interview with the Archduke Philip he took Suffolk with him. But in the summer of 1501, embarrassed with heavy debts, Suffolk fled abroad again, taking his brother Richard—this time to Henry's enemy, the

Emperor Maximilian. Here he assumed the title of duke and was generally known abroad as "the White Rose," as successive Yorkist pretenders were styled. Henry reacted to this by having the de la Pole brothers attainted, sending a third brother, William, to the Tower where he spent the rest of his life—he lived to nearly the end of the next reign. The King reaped the reward of his earlier patience, for he was now able to deal with the other members of this circle of Yorkist disaffection. Tyrrell at last paid the penalty for his crimes. Polydore Vergil tells us positively, "he was that James to whom King Richard gave the business of arranging the deaths of the innocent sons of King Edward, which he carried out. At that time James could, without danger to his own life, have spared the boys, rescued them from death and carried them to safety, for without doubt all the people would have risen in arms to defend them."[25] (Perhaps that was expecting too much—a piece of hindsight on Polydore's part: it was only after the murders that people saw what a monster Richard was.) Along with Suffolk's brother, Lord William Courtenay, who had married Edward IV's daughter Catherine, was taken into custody, where he remained until Henry's death. Evidently his patience had uncovered a whole nest of aristocratic Yorkist malcontents.

Henry remained ever on the watch, and at length his patience was rewarded by an accident. In 1506 the Archduke Philip and his wife Juana—Catherine of Aragon's sister—were forced by storm to take refuge at Weymouth on their way from Flanders to Spain. They were well entertained by Henry at Windsor, but he took the opportunity to extract a very favourable commercial treaty out of Philip and to get the White Rose surrendered to him. Philip stipulated that Suffolk's life be spared—and so it was until Henry VIII's French war, when that Henry took the opportunity of Suffolk's brother Richard's fighting with the French against his own country to have Suffolk executed, on his old attainder, in 1513. It is not to be supposed that Suffolk, whose light-headedness brought these troubles on the brothers, was much of a loss to anyone.

His brother, Richard, who succeeded to the style of "the White Rose," was a more appealing and even a romantic character.

17

He was a professional soldier who saw service all over the Continent. At Aix in 1504 he was left behind for a time as a pledge for his brother's debts; he then went off fighting in Hungary, later in Germany. During Henry VIII's first French war he entered French service; in 1512 he commanded a force of German Landsknechts in the invasion of Navarre, in 1513 he was in the field against Henry VIII himself—which gave the excuse for Suffolk's execution. Next year he was planning a descent on England, when peace was made; again in Henry's second French war, in 1522–23, Richard was planning to invade once more. His plans and hopes were put an end to at the disastrous battle of Pavia in 1525, where he was killed fighting on the French side. An old painting in the Ashmolean at Oxford shows his body stricken in the thick of the fray, *"Le Duc de Suffolk dit Blanche Rose."*

There remained only William, the lifelong prisoner in the Tower, for whom one feels sorriest of all. He inherited the good looks of his family. Before Suffolk brought these troubles down upon them, an Italian visitor had observed young Lord William making a success of things at Henry VII's court. He was then, 1496–97, about eighteen and was very handsome; he was being ogled by a rich widow, and, having been left very poor by the disaster his uncle Richard had brought upon his house, young William did the sensible thing and married the lady. "This old woman knew how to play her cards so well that he was content to become her husband and patiently to waste the flower of his beauty with her, hoping soon to enjoy her great wealth with some handsome young lady."[26] One sees that he was an authentic sprig of his house. The lady was the daughter of Lord Stourton, already twice widowed—so that, in addition to her dower she would have her widow's thirds from her two previous husbands. If only Suffolk had not been such a fool it is just possible that William might have made a success of his life. His wife lived on until 1521; he survived in the Tower until 1539—one finds Henry VIII providing rather handsomely for his clothing, gowns furred with fox or black boge, doublets of black velvet, black satin or damask, silk points and girdles, numerous shirts and shoes and slippers.[27] After all, was he not Henry's cousin? There were, of course, no children of the marriage, and with him the male line of his family became extinct.

The Tudors were not without their own family troubles—first and foremost, the difficulty they had in keeping going, like the Lancastrians, as against the proliferation, the sheer vital statistics, of the Yorkist stock. In 1495 Jasper Tudor, to whom so much had been owed, died. In the autumn of Bosworth he had married Queen Elizabeth Woodville's sister Catherine, widow of the Duke of Buckingham. They had no children—not that Jasper had any claim to the throne. That was in Henry alone, by right of his mother. In 1500 Henry's youngest son, Edmund—called after Henry's father, by a familiar Beaufort name—died at Hatfield.

What was more serious was that the eldest son and heir, Prince Arthur, on whom so many hopes were fixed, was of delicate health. A principal diplomatic objective of Henry's was to match him into the Spanish royal house, with a large dowry. This took years of negotiations, since foxy Ferdinand was a match for Henry —though ultimately Henry won the game. Catherine of Aragon was a girl of fifteen when she arrived in England in 1501. Prince Arthur was nine months younger. They were married at St. Paul's, on 14 November, but the Council objected to their cohabitation as yet on the ground of Arthur's youth and delicacy. Henry did allow them to keep house together at Ludlow Castle; they had five months together, when Arthur died, 2 April 1502. Catherine always maintained subsequently that the marriage never had been consummated.

Henry and his queen were at Greenwich when the news of Arthur's death was brought to him. Deeply grieved he sent for Elizabeth to help him to share the sorrow.[28] She came and comforted him as best she could, reminding him that his mother had had one only child, and yet God had preserved him and brought him where he was. God had yet left him a fair prince and two princesses, and "we are both young enough." She reminded him that he was known for prudence and wisdom all over Christendom and that he should take this grief accordingly. Henry was grateful and thanked her. But when the Queen retired to her own chamber, she was so overcome that her attendants had to send for the King to come and comfort her. "Then his grace of true gentle and faithful love in good haste came and relieved her," reminding her of the grounds of consolation she had given him.

This is the only close-up of their life together that we have;

it shows the terms of mutual affection, sympathy and trust that this Lancastrian and this Yorkist were on, and that theirs was a true union. There was never a murmur of any infidelity or unhappiness between them. It is clear that Elizabeth of York had neither the politic head of Henry's mother, nor the busy intriguing nature of her own mother: she was entirely domestic. She had the good looks of her family, was tall and fair, with long golden hair; from her effigy at Westminster one sees an entirely feminine face, rather long with regular features, as against the strong, square, ascetic features of Henry's mother.

It seems that in this year Elizabeth was already ill. Early next year she gave birth to another child, which died, and she herself died a few days after, on her birthday, 11 February 1503. She was thirty-eight. There seems to have been only one opinion of her gentleness and goodness: where Henry elicited respect, but no affection, she won people's love. The young Thomas More wrote his best poem in her memory:

> Where are our castles, now where are our towers?
> Goodly Richmond, soon art thou gone from me;
> At Westminster, that costly work of yours,
> Mine own dear lord now shall I never see.
> Almighty God, vouchsafe to grant that ye
> For you and your children well may edify.
> My palace builded is, and lo now here I lie.[29]

Henry survived his wife only six years. During the latter half of his reign he "was grown," in Bacon's phrase, "to such a height of reputation for cunning and policy that every accident and event that went well was laid and imputed to his foresight."[30] In this year he secured the Scottish marriage for his daughter Margaret, which ultimately brought the Stuarts to the English throne and secured the union of the kingdoms. He betrothed his other daughter Mary to the Archduke Charles, who became the Emperor Charles V. Here things worked out contrary to Henry's expectations. After his death, rejected by Charles she was married by her brother to the ageing Louis XII of France; she was said to have danced him off his feet in a matter of months, and then married for love—and greatly to Henry VIII's chagrin—Charles Brandon, who became Duke of Suffolk. From that marriage descended the

Greys, who were next in succession to the Tudors after the Scottish line. The Scots kept it, at any rate in their descendants.

The problem was what to do with Catherine of Aragon after Arthur's death. Henry thought of marrying her himself; but he was ageing, and this would have needed a prodigious papal dispensation. There was difficulty enough in procuring a dispensation to marry her to her brother-in-law, young Henry, and the troubles multiplied later. Henry VII died in 1509. Polydore Vergil tells us that in each of the last three springtimes of his life he was prostrated by fever: it looks as if he was of a consumptive turn. He was fifty-two when he died. Polydore adds that he wore himself out by his incessant application to all the details of government. It may justly be said that, like Henry IV, he was unlamented; it may also be said that he had equal reason for satisfaction: each had founded a dynasty.

People thought that, when Henry was out of the way, with his grasping concern for money, his constant supervision of the details of government, his eye on everything so that nobody could get away with anything, and was succeeded by a golden youth of eighteen, it would be a golden age. We recall Erasmus' enthusiastic expectations of such a youth, or Giustiniani's description of him coming in from tennis, the red-gold hair, the fair complexion, the glowing skin showing through his cambric shirt. Henry had the looks, the physique, the temperament of his Yorkist ancestors. Not quite so tall as his grandfather Edward IV, he was yet six feet and correspondingly broad and big, good-looking when he was young and before, like Edward, he grew fat. Henry VIII took after his grandfather even in his gestures: he had the same habit of putting his arm familiarly around a man's neck. Where, with Edward IV, it was a mark of genuine geniality, for he was a *bonhomme;* with Henry VIII it could not be relied on: he was a *faux bonhomme.* Sir Thomas More was not taken in by this appearance of familiarity. When congratulated by his son-in-law Roper on the King's treating him with such familiarity in his garden at Chelsea, More replied that if his head would purchase the King a castle in France it should not fail to fall.

There were other Yorkist characteristics that came out more and more in Henry VIII as he grew older and, accustomed to have his own way, was confronted with any opposition, overt or latent, evident, suspected or merely contingent. Again, he was not an introvert like the Lancastrians, but an extrovert in touch with life at many points, physical and sensual, an out-of-doors man, given to sports and athletic prowess when young, responsive to a wide range of women, a gifted musician, keen to shine as a soldier, creator of the royal navy, personally interested in everything that related to ships and shipbuilding. Henry VIII had an obvious, outgoing, formidable personality that impressed itself upon his time and upon posterity; and, whatever he did, he always commanded popularity, like his grandfather, and unlike his father who better deserved it.

We have seen that Henry took the opportunity of Richard de la Pole's treason to execute Suffolk in 1513. In 1521, with less excuse, he brought the princely Buckingham to the block. Edward Stafford, third duke, was the son of Richard III's Buckingham and descended from Edward III's youngest son, Thomas of Woodstock. He provided yet another case of how dangerous it was in those times to be a descendant of Edward III. He seems to have been a man of unattractive character, both harsh and weak, haughty but vacillating. Immensely aristocratic and with many quarterings, he was formidable only by his great wealth, his wide lands and connections. He was one of the old great nobles who did not relish the new directions of Tudor policy, with its appeal to the middle classes of society, an anti-feudal, more modern outlook. Buckingham was betrayed by his own intimates, the silly prophecies he listened to about his becoming king one day. It did not altogether amount to treason, but was construed as such— the cruel doctrine of constructive treason that was used by Henry to keep the path clear of persons too near the throne. Buckingham's downfall used to be blamed, unfairly, on Wolsey; we now know that it was Henry himself who pressed the matter home. Its real inwardness was that in 1521 Henry had no heir of his own to the throne other than the sickly Mary, and Catherine of Aragon was unlikely to produce any more progeny.

That factor indeed was what opened the floodgate of the Reformation. If Henry had not been under the necessity of producing a male heir, and so of getting rid of Catherine, it would not have taken precisely the form it did. With the crisis of the Reformation in England—the dissolution of the monasteries, the revolt against the new deal in the Pilgrimage of Grace—the distaste, the disaffection among the old noble families made itself evident. Cardinal Pole, Clarence's grandson, through his mother Margaret, Countess of Salisbury—the unfortunate Warwick's sister, made himself the European spokesman of the conservative reaction against Henry's course. With his book *Pro ecclesiasticae unitatis defensione,* he pilloried Henry before the bar of European opinion, over the divorce, the act of Supremacy, the breach with Rome, the attack on the Church, everything.

Henry tried to get the Cardinal assassinated. Frustrated in that he got back at his family. In any case, Henry told the French ambassador, Marillac, for a long time he had intended to extirpate the whole house of the White Rose. Now he had his chance. Lord Montagu, the male head of the Pole family—Clarence's grandson, and Henry Courtenay, Marquis of Exeter—Edward IV's grandson, were condemned to death in 1538 by a court of their peers for correspondence with "the King's great enemy." The Countess of Salisbury was imprisoned for two years in the Tower before she was dragged out to a barbarous beheading on the scaffold. In the last months of Henry's life, the last affair he concerned himself with was to bring Norfolk and his son, Surrey, to book for the latter's quartering of the royal arms in the manner of an heir-apparent to the Crown. Surrey was descended from Edward III through Thomas of Woodstock and from Edward I through his Mowbray ancestors. He had already been warned, but, mad with aristocratic pride and insolence, would give no heed, was condemned, and beheaded on Tower Hill. His father Norfolk's attainder passed both Houses of Parliament on 27 January 1547, and was awaiting the royal assent when the old tyrant died next day.

Norfolk thus survived to pass the six years of young Edward VI's reign in the Tower and be delivered at Mary's accession. With him was Edward Courtenay, the Marquis of Exeter's only son and Edward IV's great-grandson. He had been a prisoner in the Tower ever since his father's fall in 1538, and emerged, somewhat light-headed, into the light of day. Queen Mary re-created the earldom of Devon for him, and treated him with every favour, except the last. She refused to consider seriously the young man's aspirations for her hand; rejected in that quarter he entered into the Wyatt conspiracy with the hope of getting the heir-presumptive, Elizabeth. He was lucky to get off with his life; sent back to the Tower, he was rusticated to Fotheringhay, that old stronghold of his Yorkist ancestors. With his death, unmarried and without issue, at Padua in 1556, all serious Yorkist aspiration towards the Crown, which had caused so much bloodshed and suffering, was at an end.

And we are on the threshold of the happier prospects of the Elizabethan age.

CHAPTER XIII

The Mirror of Literature

These dramatic events—from the revolution of 1399 all the way through the Wars of the Roses to Bosworth—bore an extraordinarily rich harvest in literature. Not only in contemporary ballads and topical verse as events unfolded; subsequently these provided the matter for the most important works of the new humanist history and biography, of traditional narrative poetry, of both Elizabethan historical writing and chronicle plays on the stage culminating in Shakespeare's history-plays. It is as if the interest in the astonishing story of the previous century, with its sombre, blood-stained happenings, gripped the public mind more and more as the Elizabethan age ripened to its own achievement. Of course, the conflict between Lancaster and York provided fine material for histories and plays; but it takes more than that to account for it. It is part of the heightened self-awareness, the consciousness of the past as part of present experience, that is signally characteristic of the Elizabethan age. Shakespeare himself, like all the greatest creative writers, was a backward-looking man, inspired by the past.

Some of these works, especially those that are contemporary with the events they describe or comment upon or those that are fairly near in point of time, have their primary interest as historical sources. They are usually material for literature, rather than literature itself. We are not concerned here with historical sources as such—though we have sometimes had occasion to discuss them in relation to critical events—but rather with the reflection of events in literature, the picture of them painted in the public mind, in that collective memory which is the literature of a people.

We may observe that the significant additions to sources in our time—notably the discovery of Mancini's history of Richard

III's usurpation and the publication of *The Great Chronicle of London*—no less than the critical discussion of Sir Thomas More's *Richard III*, all corroborate and strengthen the traditional views of the age as they have broadly come down to us. With some few corrections in detail, though with—let us hope—rather more subtle psychological perceptions, we can appreciate that the traditional picture is in keeping with the best scholarship and the conclusions of common sense.

The London chronicles, perhaps the most important of original authorities as a whole for our period, take shape at its very beginning, virtually with the Revolution of 1399.[1] By definition their perspective is that of London, happenings away from London are rather out of view, or away on a hazy horizon. On the other hand, the capital is the scene upon which most of the important happenings are projected. The attitude of the citizenry, a *bourgeois* point of view, even though muted, in this age of Bastard Feudalism —when the public scene was dominated by the deplorable doings of the nobility—offers an incisive comment, a promise of better things, a more orderly and better governed society. These London chronicles, of which *The Great Chronicle* is the most ample representative—with its new and useful information for the two Yorkist reigns—can be said to have their artistic counterpart in Hall's influential history, with his middle-class point of view enthusiastically endorsing Tudor government and its systematic reduction of the old nobles' place in society. Not a town cat mewed when their heads fell.

This development in historical literature reflected changing social circumstances. The monastic chronicle may be regarded as the characteristic expression of the Middle Ages in historical writing. The Latin tradition continues but it is being displaced by English, just as the contemporary Latin poetry is much inferior to English in quantity and quality. Nevertheless, a late representative of the *genre*, the continuation of the Croyland chronicle, gives us our best account of Richard III's seizure of the Crown in 1483 and "seems to be written from personal knowledge."[2] The writer, who was a king's councillor, a doctor of canon law, employed by Edward IV on an important diplomatic mission, "clearly believed that Richard was responsible for the death of his nephews." John Warkworth in his chronicle does not accuse Richard of the killing of Henry VI's son at Tewkesbury, and there is no reason why we should; but he makes it perfectly clear that "in his lifetime he [Richard] was suspected of the murder of Henry VI."[3]

The numerous versions extant of the London chronicles show that they were in great request, that there was a growing demand for historical reading. There was a higher standard of literacy than is popularly supposed, as we might have realised from the expressiveness and vivacity of those correspondences that have fortunately, but accidentally, been preserved—of the Pastons, Plumptons, Celys, Stonors. The desire for educational progress is to be marked in Henry VI's great foundations of Eton and King's College at Cambridge, in Chichele's of All Souls and Waynflete's of Magdalen at Oxford, as of Lady Margaret Beaufort's later, of St. John's and Christ's at Cambridge; and no less among the London citizens in the founding of four grammar schools.

The continuation of the *Brut* was the most popular history of the time, the first of our printed histories. "It is a somewhat remarkable illustration of the growing strength of the English language and of the wider interest in English history that the only continuous chronicle of the early fifteenth century should have been composed in the popular speech."[4] And we can already "trace in the *Brut* the germs of that opinion which in the hands of the Elizabethan historians and dramatists made Henry V the national hero and the struggle of Lancaster and York the theme of a national cycle of tragedies." The Tudor historians Hall, Stow and Holinshed—the three pre-eminent creators of the literary history of the fifteenth century—all made greater use of these original authorities, chronicles, contemporary pamphlets, histories, biographies, than has fully been realised. To these the admirable Stow, with his antiquary's zeal, added the search of original records and documents. The discovery of *The Great Chronicle* has confirmed Stow's excellence and reliability in the use of original material; his use of the then unpublished *History of the Arrival of Edward IV* and of the continuation of the Croyland chronicle gave his account of the reign of Edward IV original value. So that, altogether, the use Shakespeare made of the Tudor historians in their transmission from the original authorities has had "an abiding effect in the formation of popular opinion on the character of the fifteenth century."[5]

In the course of this book we have given many illustrations of the transference of history into literature—on the wing, as it were, in the case of ballads. It so happens that two Bosworth ballads come out of the circle of the Stanleys, composed by persons in their service; they give us some authentic strokes and some historical information we get nowhere else. Here is what *The Rose of England*, allegorical in form, tells us of Richard III and the destruction he wrought within his own family:

> Then came in a beast men call a Boar
> And he rooted this garden up and down;
> By the seed of the Rose he set no store,
> But afterwards it wore the crown.
>
> He took the branches of this Rose away
> And all in sunder did them tear;
> And he buried them under a clod of clay,
> Swore they should never bloom nor bear.[6]

The ballad gives us an account of Henry's rejection at first at Shrewsbury:

> At that time was bailiff in Shrewsbury
> One Master Mytton in the town.
> The gates were strong and he made them fast
> And the portcullis he let down.
>
> And through a garret of the wall
> Over Severn these words said he,
> "At these gates no man enter shall."
> But he kept him out a night and a day.

Apparently it was upon Sir William Stanley's instructions that the gates were opened to Henry, who afterwards pardoned the bailiff for his loyalty to his charge.

There are further touches that seem authentic enough:

> At Atherstone these lords did meet—
> A worthy sight it was to see,
> How earl Richmond took his hat in hand
> And said, "Cheshire and Lancashire, welcome to me!"

And here is the experienced commander, Oxford—the Blue Boar —at Bosworth:

Then the Blue Boar the vanward had:
He was both wary and wise of wit;
The right hand of them he took
The sun and wind of them to get.

A much more important Bosworth poem is *The Song of the Lady Bessy,* i.e., Elizabeth of York. Sir Charles Firth describes it as "well constructed, vivid, dramatic, and marked by an epic breadth of treatment."[7] It is valuable for the indications it gives us—we have hardly any other information—of the efforts against Richard culminating in Bosworth, the contacts between the Stanleys and Henry abroad, the plan to marry Elizabeth to him. It begins with Richard's plan to marry his niece himself, and Elizabeth in her distress appeals to Lord Stanley for help. Stanley owed her father obligations—Edward IV had given him the grant of the Isle of Man and other lands and offices—and she relied on this for succour. Rather than marry the murderer of her brothers she would kill herself.

Stanley is greatly afraid—he knows that Richard would halt at nothing—and hesitates; the poem re-creates the atmosphere of terror, "fields have eyes and woods have ears." In the end he consents and messages are sent out to the circle, Stanley's brother, Sir William, at Holt Castle, his nephew Sir John Savage and his friend Gilbert Talbot.

Sir John Savage is your sister's son,
He is well beloved within his shire—

apart from this we had not known of the relationship. The friends are bidden to London to take counsel with Lord Stanley—and we do know that the Lady Margaret raised large sums in London to aid her son's project; they are to come in disguise, avoiding their usual inns on the way, and when they meet to sit with their backs to the bench. In London they meet thus at an inn in the suburbs and the resolution is taken to send Humphrey Brereton to Henry in Brittany.

Brereton may be the author of the poem, for it is a good Cheshire name and the poem is full of personal touches. Brereton does not know Henry—how few had seen him up to this date!—but the porter who admitted him into the abbey of Bégrames (or

Bégars), where Henry was residing, described the "Prince of England" as he was, shooting at the butts with three lords, dressed in black velvet:

> "A wart he hath," the porter said.
> "A little also above the chin.
> His face is white, his wart is red,
> No more than the head of a small pin."

Another version describes Henry as of "long visage and pale": there is the authentic Lancastrian face, none of the masculine beauty of Edward IV. Other touches reveal inside information among the Stanleys: for example, when Stanley said farewell to his son, Lord Strange:

> My son George by the hand I hent [held]:
> I held so hard forsooth, certain,
> That his foremost finger out of the joint went.
> I hurt him sore, he did complain.

This was meant for a token another day, when he should return in disguise as a merchant of Kendal. This was fanciful; as Firth says, the poem "probably contains a certain number of true facts handed down by tradition, yet at the same time, owing to the scantiness of the other evidence about the conspiracy against Richard, it is impossible to determine exactly where the fact ends and the fiction begins."[8]

Of Bosworth we have an authentic touch, when King Richard "hoveth upon the mountain," i.e., Ambien Hill, where his long-drawn-out van made a fine sight. The poem tells us that it was Sir William Harington, of that devoted Yorkist family, who interceded with Richard for Lord Strange's life, and that it was Harington who tried to get Richard to mount horse and fly, when he saw the battle going against him. But Richard would not hear of flight:

> Give me my battle-axe in my hand,
> And set my crown on my head so high,
> For by him that made both sun and moon,
> King of England this day will I die.

We know that Henry had some artillery with him at Bosworth: the poem mentions

> The shots of guns were so fierce.

And, in fact, the cannon-balls of "serpentines" have been found on the field. As Richard's dishonoured body enters Leicester, it is greeted with the taunt:

> "How like you the killing of my brethren dear?
> Welcome, gentle uncle, home."

Yet a third Bosworth ballad also comes out of the Stanley circle, emphasising as they all do how much Henry owed his victory to that family. The interest of this poem to us is more confined to topographical details; for example, Sir William Stanley left after his first preliminary meeting with Henry,

> And came again by light of day
> To the little pretty town of Stone.

Ambien Hill that dominates the battlefield is described once more as a mountain; and it was upon another hill opposite that Henry was crowned with Richard's circlet after the battle.

From Bosworth ballads to Polydore Vergil's *Anglica Historia* is to move from medieval England into the light of Renaissance Europe. Polydore was one of the most eminent scholars in England during his long residence of nearly fifty years, from 1502 onwards. An Italian by origin he brought to Gothic England the new critical standards of the Renaissance. In applying them to the traditional myths of early British history—Brutus, Aeneas, the fall of Troy, Arthur and the rest of it—he later incurred the ire (and abuse) of patriotic Tudor scholars, such as Leland. Polydore achieved the first modern English history with critical standards, the first to break the long tradition of medieval annalistic chronicle and write a critical history that was also a composed work of art. And his influence, in spite of the snarls of the inferior, was immense. He was a leading authority for the historian Hall, and through him Polydore's picture of the fifteenth century passed into the English tradition. When we come, at the end of the Elizabethan age, to Bacon's famous *History of the Reign of King Henry VII*, it was directly based on Polydore.

He was in the best position for writing about these events: as a critical scholar and historian of the first rank, as an outsider coming from a more sophisticated civilisation and himself not involved in these controversial issues, and also as the first to write about them. Henry VII was more responsive to and interested in the new Renaissance trends than he has been given credit for, when one considers his patronage of Torrigiani and other artists, of the Genoese Cabots for the new voyages of discovery, of Polydore, Carmeliano and other scholars. After all, Henry had spent fourteen formative years of his life in France, was sympathetic to French ideas of government and preferred to do his serious reading in French.

In 1506 Henry asked Polydore to undertake his history of England, and Polydore spent twelve years upon it. In addition to his critical use of the old authorities—and he pays tribute to the excellence of the best monastic chroniclers, William of Malmesbury and Matthew Paris—Polydore took the trouble to consult everyone he could who had been concerned in recent events. This would naturally include Henry himself, and such very well-informed persons as the diplomat Christopher Urswick, and Polydore's fellow ecclesiastics at St. Paul's. Hence it is that Polydore is able to tell us so much about Henry's affairs in Brittany, his invasion and the events of the reign. He is our only real authority for the battle of Bosworth: we must go to him for the fountain-source. It is probable that Henry gave him his information—the battle is certainly viewed from that side.

Polydore, as an outsider, reveals no particular prejudice—except when he comes to Wolsey (everybody seems to have been prejudiced against Wolsey). It is true that Polydore regarded Richard as a monster; but, after the murder of the Princes, everyone did. As Kingsford sums up, from the beginning of Edward IV's reign Polydore's history "begins to assume something of the quality of an original authority"; and "of the latter part of Richard's reign Polydore has given an account of great original value."[9]

We have already seen that the discovery in our time of Mancini's work on Richard's usurpation corroborates Polydore, and quite independently; for Mancini was in England during the critical months of Edward IV's death and Richard's take-over, April to July 1483—nine years before Polydore came to the country. Mr. Armstrong tells us that Mancini, "who was writing a treatise and not a diary, hid himself most conscientiously behind the facts he related. He was still more scrupulous in avoiding considerations foreign to his matter, and in refusing to use historical data as excuse for ethical reflection. . . . The moral impartiality of Mancini lends added weight to his statements."[10] Again, Mancini "never discloses the sources of his information . . . but there is reason to believe that what he wrote was either from his own observation or drawn from close witnesses." For example, he probably "derived his knowledge of Edward V's ability to understand refinements of literature from Carmelianus, who had himself addressed the young Edward in most elevated tones."[11] Even Mancini's silences testify to his reliability: "any account of Richard would have been of the greatest value to us, but this honest silence enhances the worth of Mancini's other statements."

Neither Polydore nor More can have known of Mancini's work, but it corroborates both their accounts.

Since More was a writer of genius and one of the grand figures in the English tradition, his *History of King Richard III*—sometimes known as a history of King Edward V—has had a great impact on the public mind and notably on Shakespeare. It must be remembered, however, that it was an experiment, or an exercise, and that it is only a first draft, uncorrected, full of gaps of names or dates or things that escaped More's memory at the time to be filled in later, and also with some errors of detail that are perfectly understandable in these circumstances. As Pollard says, "such errors were inevitable in a work derived almost exclusively from oral tradition dating from nearly thirty years before; and it must be remembered that More, if ever he intended *Richard III* to be published, never revised it or intended it to be published as he left it."[12]

On the other hand, herein lies the work's value: it is a historical exercise, written *pari passu* in English and Latin, in writing down instalments as More remembered them of the dramatic events of Edward's death and Richard's seizure of power. A number of the speeches are written up in dramatic form; the work is in every sense unfinished, it ends abruptly with Morton persuading Buckingham to revolt against Richard. We can only deplore that it is an unfinished fragment, More has so much to tell us that comes from people concerned in those happenings. As Pollard tells us, it is not only from Cardinal Morton that More could have learned what took place, there was his own father who knew what was thought and observed in the City at the time; or there was his own bishop, Fitzjames, "who had been chaplain to Edward IV, treasurer of St. Paul's almost throughout Richard's reign, almoner to Henry VII."[13] There were those respectable, well-informed men, Bishops Foxe and Warham, or More's family connections, William Roper, "Richard III's commissioner of array for Kent and Fitzjames's successor as attorney-general," or Sir John Cutte, whom More succeeded as under-treasurer: "Cutte could have given More no little information about Richard III: he was that king's servant and receiver of Crown lands . . . and third husband of Warwick the Kingmaker's niece, Lucy Neville," hence a cousin of Richard's queen. There was no lack of people who knew what had happened; but it was too appalling and too dangerous to write it down.

More was appalled by the story, but got most of it down—as Erasmus said of him, a man of exquisite scrupulousness of conscience, More "always had a peculiar loathing for tyranny."[14] We can say of him that he fixed one tyrant in literature, but was himself fixed by another. (We must not forget that Henry VIII was Richard's great-nephew—he had the same hard-heartedness and, though he did not kill children, was a cruel man.) A closer study of More has revealed in how many respects he has subsequently been corroborated in details, where his memory or that of his informant was not at fault, from the documents. More wrote his book about 1513, the period when he also wrote his *Utopia*. At this time there was an awkward reminder of Buckingham's fate in 1483. In February 1514 Henry VIII still had no child, and Buckingham's son remarked that "if anything but good should happen to the King, he, the Duke of Buckingham, was next in succession to the crown of England."[15] A few years more and the Duke would pay for that with his life. The whole subject of the succession was still a dangerous one, and More dropped his pen.

However, though unfinished, More had written a masterpiece, one of the first works of modern historical art. And since he was a genius, as well as a saint, the work has never ceased to make its impact, it has so much life and power, such a passionate loathing of evil. Polydore is "coolly detached and rationalistic, where the *Richard* is essentially dramatic"; however, they come to the same thing where Richard is concerned.[16] With More's more subtle perception of character, he adds the hypocritical, the play-acting, element to Richard's role—the citing of Hastings' private life at the time of his murder, the persecution of kindly Jane Shore, the trumping up of the weapons as if captured from the Woodvilles on Richard's entry into London, the feigned reluctance before the citizens to take the Crown. All this added a dimension to Richard's constricted, tormented, inhuman personality: it received a further reverberation in the mind of Shakespeare.

Edward Hall stands in marked contrast to More: the son of Protestant Reformers, the enthusiastic, patriotic Henrician, whose hero Henry VIII could do no wrong, against Henry's most eminent victim, who died for the unity of Christendom. It was, of course, a hopeless cause, and Hall wrote of its martyr, surely this man was "the foolishest wise man, or the wisest foolish man" to do so. Hall was an eminently sensible man, where More was an exquisitely sensitive one—though as Lord Chancellor he did burn people for their beliefs. Nevertheless these two so different men are at one in their view of Richard III.

Hall's famous chronicle covers much the ground of this book, the history from 1399 onwards. Its subject is described in its full title: "the union of the two noble and illustrious families of Lancaster and York, being long in continual dissension for the Crown of this noble realm, with all the acts done in both the times of the princes, both of the one lineage and of the other, beginning at the time of King Henry IV, the first author of this division, and so successively proceeding to the reign of the high and prudent prince King Henry VIII, the indubitable flower and very heir of both the said lineages."[17] The lay-out of the story can be seen from the expressive titles of the various books, beginning with "an introduction into the division of the two houses of Lancaster and York." There follow: "the unquiet time of King Henry IV, the victorious acts of King Henry V, the troublesome season of King Henry VI, the prosperous reign of King Edward IV, the pitiful life of King Edward V, the tragical doings of King Richard III, the politic governance of King Henry VII, the triumphant reign of King Henry VIII." These epithets are well considered and sum up the reigns very concisely.

Hall, born in 1499, came of a Shropshire family but spent most of his life in London where he became common serjeant of the

City and died in 1547. He thus represents in all its fulness, its
rumbustious vitality, the middle-class point of view of the London
citizenry. There was no doubt that they were with Henry VIII and
his Reformation course; Hall expressed it with gusto and conviction, with the result that in 1555, when Mary found herself strong
enough to embark on the persecution of the Protestants, the book
was called in and burned. There is some difference of style between the earlier books, where Hall is resting entirely on his
authorities and writes in a puffed-up alliterative style which he
considers in accordance with the dignity of history and that of the
contemporary period of which he was an eyewitness. He has all
the characteristic *engoûment* of the time for ceremonies and
pageants, culminating in the extravagant splendour of the Field
of the Cloth of Gold. Creighton thought that "his power of describing the action of a mob is admirable."[18]

Hall's tone is that of a brusque common sense, a point of view
wholly devoted to the new deal, and therefore anti-ecclesiastical,
anti-Catholic. Thus he shared and did much to perpetuate the
Londoners' bias in favour of "good Duke Humphrey of Gloucester" against Cardinal Beaufort, a much better servant of his country. Nothing any cardinal did could be much good in Hall's eyes.
He also adumbrated and developed the prejudiced view of Suffolk
carried on by the Londoners as the lover of Margaret of Anjou,
and this is what is carried forward into Shakespeare's *Henry VI*.
Shakespeare read Hall with avidity and profit, taking the colour-
ing of his themes as well as many telling details into the plays.

For Hall was himself an artist—the personality of the man
comes through his work and keeps his book alive where the impersonal are dead and forgotten. One recognises him in touch
after touch: he is never afraid to speak his mind. After the lapse
of centuries one can still agree with him about the "foolish and
fantastical persons" who foretold ill to Henry IV for rewarding
Archbishop Scrope with his deserts. Or there is Hall's comment
on Kent, with its oblique glance at the absurd Nun of Kent who
brought so many good people into trouble—"which county in
ancient time hath not been dull in setting forth of new fantastical
fantasies." Or there are such vivid pen-portraits as that of Richard
III—Hall would have known people who knew him:

When he stood musing he would bite and chew busily his nether lip . . . beside that the dagger that he ware he would, when he studied, with his hand pluck up and down in the sheath to the midst, never drawing it fully out. His wit [intelligence] was pregnant, quick and ready, wily to feign and apt to dissimule; he had a proud mind and arrogant stomach, the which accompanied him to his death, which he rather desiring to suffer by dint of sword than being forsaken and destitute of his untrue companions would by coward flight preserve and save his uncertain life. Which by malice, sickness or condign punishment might chance shortly after to come to confusion.

It is convincing and just: a portrait of a psychotic type.

Early in Elizabeth's reign Hall became the prime source for an influential best-seller, *The Mirror for Magistrates,* in which the striking stories of the previous century were told in verse. A corporate work, it was the scheme of a group of young Edwardians on their way to becoming Elizabethans: persons belonging to Edward VI's Court or household. The leading spirits were William Baldwin, who wrote plays for the revels, and George Ferrers, master of the King's pastimes. They recruited other contributors such as Thomas Phaer the translator, a Welshman who wrote the poem about Glendower, Thomas Chaloner who became a diplomatic envoy, and Thomas Sackville who ended up as Elizabeth's Lord Treasurer. The book went from edition to edition, from 1559 up to 1587, being expanded with each. A Cornishman, Humphrey Cavell, was brought in to write the story of Michael Joseph the blacksmith, leader of the rising of 1497. Other contributors came to include John Dolman, who wrote the story of Lord Hastings' fall, and Thomas Churchyard.

The book belonged to the familiar type of Lydgate's *Fall of Princes:* the didactic purpose was to learn from the warning examples of history and preach the doctrine of obedience upon which the Tudors were so insistent. We have seen from the distractions of the previous century how necessary this was and how salutary to din it in. To readers of this book the stories will be familiar—from the downfall of Richard II's Chief Justice, Sir Robert Tresillian, of Richard's uncle Gloucester and Richard himself, up to the fate of Buckingham, of Collingbourne, of Jane

Shore and even, a last addition, of Wolsey. The poems are traditional in form, continuous with the fifteenth-century jog-trot usual
for the narration of topical or historical events. The book is distinguished by Sackville's "Induction," perhaps the finest of early
Elizabethan poems. Sackville was also part-author of *Gorboduc,*
first of Elizabethan tragedies, precursor of an immense harvest to
come. With these works we watch the bridge being formed from
the dramatic treatment of historical material, "histories" as they
were apt to call them whether in prose or verse, to the drama
proper and full-fledged history-plays.

The influence of *The Mirror for Magistrates* upon subsequent
writers and dramatists must have been very considerable. It was
one of the most popular of literary media in impressing upon
people's minds the dominant Tudor view of the fifteenth century.
Nor was it much out, except for the idealisation of "good Duke
Humphrey," and its flagrant injustice to Suffolk and Margaret of
Anjou.

The two leading Elizabethan chroniclers of English history,
John Stow and Raphael Holinshed, offer almost as much of a
contrast as Polydore Vergil and Edward Hall. Again the first,
Stow, is more impersonal and objective, practising his own precept
that "in histories the chief thing that is to be desired is truth."
Stow's real passion was antiquarianism; his chief admirer in our
time does not claim that he was a great historian but that his
Annals, "a chronologically exact narrative . . . was the best history of England which had appeared up to his death."[19] Its value
is largely due to the conscientiousness with which Stow went to
original sources and records, some of which he was the only
scholar to use. He had much less Protestant prejudice than Hall or
Holinshed, indeed in his own day he was thought to have too much
sympathy for the old faith, the old customs and ceremonies. It
must be admitted that the *Annals* is dull reading, where Hall and
Holinshed are both more lively and exciting, and so have exerted
a far greater influence upon the poets and dramatists.

Holinshed, whom we really ought to call Hollingshead, had the
luck to come out first: "the first complete history of England of
an authoritative character, composed in English and in a continuous narrative to appear in print."[20] The work of collaborators,

it was the second edition, of 1587, that had such a prodigious influence, first and foremost upon Shakespeare. For him Holinshed's chronicles constituted a prime source of material not only for medieval history, and thus the history-plays proper, but also for the mythical pre-history of Britain with *Macbeth, King Lear* and *Cymbeline*. The volume of 1587 came out at a providential moment for the actor with the ambition to be a dramatist: he saw in it at once a rich quarry for future plays.

This second edition was edited by the admirable Exeter antiquarian, John Hooker, who inserted some lively West Country touches. Shakespeare characteristically did not fail to make good use of one of these. Richard III says towards the end of his career:

> When last I was at Exeter
> The mayor in courtesy showed me the castle,
> And called it Rougemont. At which name I started,
> Because a bard of Ireland told me once
> I should not live long after I saw Richmond.

It is well known how sometimes Shakespeare simply transposes Holinshed's prose into blank verse; perhaps less well that "Holinshed copied Hall's prejudices rather than Stow's impartiality, and the colour which he thus gave to his narrative reappears naturally in Shakespeare's plays, and has in consequence been stamped on popular opinion."[21] Holinshed himself occasionally inserts a telling personal touch. In his later years he was steward to the Warwickshire family of Burdet—hence no doubt his suggestion of the story of Sir Nicholas Burdet, killed at Pontoise in 1441, for *The Mirror for Magistrates*. When he comes in his chronicles to Bosworth he is able to tell us of the great marsh on Henry's right "at this present by reason of ditches cast it is grown to be firm ground."[22] It is, however, still marshy in parts today.

The Elizabethan age was to an extraordinary degree a historically-minded age, while in it verse was as popular as prose. So that it is hardly surprising that so many of the poets and dramatists turned more and more to history. A successor to *The Mirror for Magistrates* in popularity was William Warner's *Albion's England*. This work, in jogging fourteeners, begins with the mythical history of Britain but comes down to the "dissension and union of the two lineages Lancaster and York." In the edition of 1589 there is inserted a large plate illustrating their descents "until the uniting of the same" in Henry VIII, who visibly represented both. Warner's work, which went on being added to with each edition, was not only popular but highly thought of in its day and by people with antiquarian tastes, like Lamb, since. It is more difficult for us to appreciate such beauties as this:

> Shall Tudor from Plantagenet the Crown
> by craking [croaking] snatch?

The poet Daniel was interested in history all his life, and towards the end of it, not content with his contributions in verse, published a prose *History of England*. Miss McKisack pays tribute to him as "a natural historian, endowed with a rare sense of the past and with an intuitive understanding (almost unique in that age) of the limitations of historical knowledge."[23] Earlier, in 1595, Daniel published his long, though unfinished narrative poem *The Civil Wars*, which was in time to influence Shakespeare's *Richard II*, then being written.

The poem covers the period from the Revolution of 1399 but breaks off with Warwick and Clarence's disgust at Edward IV's marriage to Elizabeth Woodville. Daniel describes his purpose to be—

to show the deformities of civil dissension, and the miserable events of rebellions, conspiracies and bloody revengements, which followed as in a circle upon that breach of the due course of succession by the usurpation of Henry IV. And thereby to make the blessings of peace and the happiness of an established government in a direct line the better to appear. I trust I shall do a grateful work to my country to continue the same unto the glorious union of Henry VII, from whence is descended our present happiness.[24]

Daniel's chief sources were Froissart, Polydore Vergil and Hall. From his sonnets, which are in some ways close to Shakespeare's, we see that he was rather in tune with the early Shakespeare. And just as Shakespeare drew upon Daniel's poem for his play, so later Daniel made changes in his text from reading Shakespeare. The poem in its gentle, ambling measure gives an unexciting reflection of those stormy passages of history in its still waters. It is not without charm, intuitive understanding, wisdom; but it is without passion—one thing of which the fifteenth century had a superfluity. Perhaps Drayton's comment is in place:

> . . . Some wise men him rehearse
> To be too much historian in verse.
> His rhymes were smooth, his metre well did close,
> But yet his manner better fitted prose.

Drayton's interest in history was no less great than Daniel's and he gave it even more extended expression in his verse. Where Daniel's is the poetry of reflection and has a certain philosophical cast, Drayton's is the poetry of action, as we see at its most concise in his stirring *Ballad of Agincourt:*

> Fair stood the wind for France,
> When we our sails advance,
> Nor now to prove our chance
>   Longer will tarry;
> But putting to the main
> At Caux, the mouth of Seine,
> With all his martial train,
>   Landed king Harry. . . .
>
> Upon St. Crispin's day
> Fought was this noble fray,
> Which fame did not delay,
>   To England to carry:
> O, when shall English men
> With such acts fill a pen,
> Or England breed again
>   Such a king Harry?

Such a poem is but the crest of the wave of popular ballading which the heroic events of the previous century gave rise to with the Elizabethans. In the anonymous play *Edward IV* there appears a three-man's song which may have given Drayton a cue:

> Agincourt, Agincourt, know ye not Agincourt?
> Where the English slew and hurt
>   All the French foemen . . .

This period was of special interest to Drayton as it was to many Elizabethans, particularly towards the end of the century. Of *England's Heroical Epistles*, significantly the most popular of his works, nearly a half are concerned with subjects from it: Queen Isabel and Richard II, Queen Catherine and Owen Tudor, Eleanor Cobham and Duke Humphrey, William de la Pole and Queen Margaret, Edward IV and Mistress Shore. Later, Drayton devoted most of a volume to a long poem, "The Miseries of Margaret," which again displays not only the glow of action but the response to landscape and topography of the author of *Polyolbion*. Drayton was not only indebted to Holinshed and Hall for his history, but owed something to Shakespeare's *Henry VI* plays, as also to *Henry V* for his Agincourt works. For, at the end of his life, he returned to the theme with his long poem "The Battle of Agincourt," to which he devoted most of another book.

Drayton was one of the contributors to the play *Sir John Oldcastle*. Only the First Part of that survives, the Second is missing. Dr. Tillyard tells us, not very specifically, that it is "a good specimen of wholesome Elizabethan stuff. But there are scenes in it exceptional in their weightiness"—presumably Drayton's.[25] That a Second Part was called for can be regarded as an indication of its popularity. Nor were these themes popular only with London audiences. One of the most admired of academic plays was Thomas Legge's Latin play, *Richardus Tertius,* performed in the hall of St. John's at Cambridge in 1579.[26] It deserved its fame, it is written with such verve and passion—it should be given a revival in our time, either in the original or in a verse translation. Here is the beginning of Richard's long soliloquy on his approaching fate:

> *O saeva fata semper, O sortem asperam*
> *Cum saevit et cum parcit ex aequo malam*
> *Fortuna fallax rebus humanis nimis*
> *Insultat, agili cuncta pervertens rota . . .*

The battle of Bosworth is suggested in a classical and formal manner on the stage, rather than acted out in the Gothic manner of English history-plays. It ends with the symbolic crowning of Henry, and "an epilogue, wherein let be declared the happy uniting of both houses, of whom the Queen's Majesty came and is undoubted heir, wishing her a prosperous reign."[27] The play was evidently written with a royal visit to the university in mind. It is pleasant to think that the youth who played the part of Edward V was Lord William Howard, great-grandson of Richard III's Duke of Norfolk. The dramatic subject had such appeal that in the next decade, in 1586, Henry Lacey wrote another play under the same title in imitation of Legge's.

It may perhaps be easier to exhaust the reader than the subject, so prolific was the progeny of fifteenth-century history in sixteenth-century literature. The concentration of interest is particularly marked in the last years of Elizabeth I's reign when the question of the succession was in everybody's mind again. These are the years of Shakespeare's tetralogy: *Richard II*, 1595, *1 & 2 Henry IV*, 1597–98, *Henry V*, 1599. In London people were conscious of Essex as another popular Bolingbroke—and what would happen on the Queen's death? In 1599 John Hayward produced his *First Part of the Life and Reign of King Henry IV*. It extended only to the end of the first year of his reign, that is to say, it is a history of the Revolution of 1399. Equipped with a too laudatory, and possibly pointed, dedication to Essex it gave great offense to the Queen and Hayward was imprisoned in the Tower for it. John Chamberlain indicates the suspicions it gave rise to: "here hath been much descanting about it, why such a story should come at this time, and many exceptions taken, especially to the Epistle," i.e., the dedication to Essex.[28] In 1601 came Essex's disastrous attempt to do a Bolingbroke.

The peaceful settlement of the succession in 1603 in James I, the great-grandson of Henry VII's daughter Margaret, did not quench people's interest in our themes, either in prose or in verse. Sir John Beaumont as a Leicestershire man and an inhabitant near by was well acquainted with the site of Bosworth, and devoted a long poem to it, with a tribute to the new king now uniting two nations. *Bosworth Field* was published posthumously:

> The winter's storm of civil war I sing
> Whose end is crowned with our eternal spring,
> Where Roses joined, their colours mix in one,
> And armies fight no more for England's throne.

Though less pretentious, it is a superior work to the somewhat rebarbative poem of the same period, *The Ghost of Richard III*, by Donne's friend Christopher Brooke, published in 1614. Thomas Gainsford published his poem *The Vision and Discourse of Henry VII concerning the Unity of Great Britain* in 1610 and followed it in 1618 with *The True and Wonderful History of Perkin Warbeck.* From the latter and from Bacon's *Henry VII* John Ford derived much of his material for his play *The Chronicle History of Perkin Warbeck,* though his interest in the subject may have come partly from his being a West countryman.

With Bacon's masterpiece the Tudor picture was transmitted to the following age. And so, in essentials, the sensible tradition stands.

CHAPTER XIV

Shakespeare's Vision of the Conflict

We are now in a better position to appreciate that Shakespeare's spreading concern with this subject did not originate with him but was the crest of a wave in the continuous and growing interest in the story of the previous century. This crest was reached in the 1590's; the momentum was even speeded up as the 1590's advanced and the new century began with the tragedy of Essex's fall. There was the widespread growth of the Elizabethan interest in history in itself to go upon; there was the natural response to the stage to the public interest, the "unusual public interest in the matters treated in such plays."[1] In addition to this, there was an inner excitement, as the Queen's long reign drew to its close, in the dangerously disturbing question of the succession, matters that had involved depositions of kings, civil dissensions and war. The more dangerous these subjects the greater their fascination for the public. There is plenty of evidence of how these things went together: the "popularity" of Essex and the consciousness that he might make another Bolingbroke, the comparison of the Queen's last years with Richard II's, her awareness of what people were saying and her acute sensitivity to it; the censorship of the deposition scene in *Richard II*, the putting on of the play by Essex's followers on the eve of his rising, Hayward's imprisonment for his *Henry IV*.

Shakespeare stood in a close relationship to all this through his acquaintance with Southampton, Essex's chief supporter. Moreover, the most popular of dramatists was the most sensitive to the public demand. On the other hand he could be trusted not to affront authority, but to preach sound doctrine in his plays, for he was above all conservative in his view of social order and a conformist. We are all familiar now with Shakespeare's emphasis on the necessity of authority and obedience to keep society together, "the thoughts that, as his maturest as well as his earliest works show, habitually occurred to him at the mention of lawlessness and civil disorder."[2] His interpretation of the events we have been dealing with in this book is the traditional, common-sense one. But over and above that, or beneath and underlying it, is the note of urgency and conviction: "his thought gives the whole dreadful pageant a significance and depth of meaning unsounded by Marlowe"—or anyone else for that matter. We have come to understand better, in the tragic circumstances of our own time, the pure political understanding he had, the firm comprehension of the facts of society—which should hardly be a matter of surprise in anyone with such a grasp of human nature. We have also come to understand better—what should never have been in question— how much reading and reflection went into his plays, the range of sources he used as well as the effectiveness and speed with which he searched them. We know now, for example, that he was by no means wholly and solely dependent on Holinshed for his knowl- edge of English history, that for the *Henry VI* plays he followed Hall rather than Holinshed, that for *Richard II* he used not only these but Berners' Froissart, Daniel's *The Civil Wars* and the anonymous *Woodstock* play. He picked on whatever was relevant.

Here we are not concerned with the whole vision of England's past of this most historically-minded of dramatists, but simply with the restricted theme of his view, his portrayal, of the dynastic conflict.

He devoted two quartets of plays to the subject. It was the first to occupy his mind as a dramatist; the plays he wrote on it formed his first original contribution, and not the least vital, to the English stage—that of the chronicle-play, in which the historical theme is more important than the individual characters as such. This is true of the three parts of *Henry VI*, with which Shakespeare had his first success and made his name. These plays were written in 1590–91, and were followed after an interval—when Shake- speare was occupied, during the plague years 1592–93, mainly with writing for his patron, Southampton, his long narrative poems and the Sonnets—by the noticeably more mature *Richard III* in 1593. This first quartet may be regarded as dealing with the Wars of the Roses, beginning with the loss of the English dominion in France and ending with Bosworth. Shakespeare's second quartet begins with *Richard II,* of 1595, and is completed by the trilogy of the two parts of *Henry IV* and *Henry V,* in 1597–99.

Falling between Shakespeare's two tetralogies comes the interesting anonymous play *Woodstock*—one more evidence of the appeal of these subjects to the public. The play is much influenced by the Second Part of *Henry VI*—one more tribute to the popularity of those plays. And it offers a link between the two groups, for something of *Woodstock* is reflected again in *Richard II.* Who can have written it?[3] How much we should like to know! For it has something of Shakespeare's grasp of historical situation and political sense, a plain homely realism and a sense of humour taking after the Jack Cade scenes of *2 Henry VI.* The main theme of the play is the relationship between the young king, led away by flatterers, and his uncle, Thomas of Woodstock, who is an idealised "good Duke Humphrey," standing for plain, honest dealing and the good of the country as against both favourites and factions. The date of the play, then, must be between 1591 and 1595.

For chronological order and the sake of the theme we must begin with the second quartet, for the story begins with the unlawful deposition of Richard II, the Revolution of 1399, which unleashed the fell consequences that filled the succeeding century with alarms and troubles. In no play does Shakespeare adhere more closely to his historical sources than in *Richard II;* the result is that, apart from anything else, the play can be read as very fair history. Shakespeare has poeticised the personality of Richard and viewed him with more sympathy than he deserved as a king; for, as a king, it was his business to rule justly and effectively, and he completely failed in his task. On the other hand, his fate, even historically, demands our sympathy: it was a terrible price that the King paid for his inadequacy—as a man, he might have passed well enough.

Viewing the sequence of events with the advantage of hindsight, would it have been better to have kept Richard II with all his faults? At least he would have followed a policy of peace with France. Beyond that, we see that our question, like most historical hypotheses, is a nonsense question; for it was in fact impossible to keep Richard on the throne. Political decisions are made on the basis of facts; Richard had lost control of events, and Bolingbroke seized control of them. Events swept them both off their stance, one to his fall, the other to the throne he had not originally sought. So both are, in a sense—unless they abdicate their part in the human process—prisoners of historical circumstance. Thereby hangs their tragedy; for harm will be done, and ill deeds bring their consequences.

The deposition not only struck at the basis of monarchy, and therefore the constitutional system, but something deeper, the sacramental idea implicit in medieval monarchy. Today we can understand the rationale of this in anthropological terms: the necessity of the sacramental, the numinous, in holding society together since human beings are so little rational. The divinity that doth hedge a king is indeed Shakespeare's chief emphasis: it is remarkable, in comparison with that how little he makes of the "legitimist" argument that March, representing the senior line, was Richard's true heir. That is not Shakespeare's theme: his theme is Bolingbroke's wrong-doing in usurping the throne, the retribution upon him, the sins of the fathers visited upon the children to the third and fourth generation.

Richard II begins where Hall's chronicle begins—with the quarrel between Mowbray and Bolingbroke which tempted Richard to get rid of them both and unleashed the train of consequences that led to his deposition. In the very first scene the "glorious worth" of Bolingbroke's descent is underlined as dramatic preparation for what is to come; there is his popularity and his careful cultivation of it for future use, as against Richard's light-headed carelessness, his head turned by flatterers, his refusal to give heed to good advice—all historically true—culminating in his flagrant injustice to Bolingbroke. This cut at a no less fundamental root for society than kingship, the security of property, the magnate's right to his own land.

But when Richard's throne is usurped by another the security of society itself, in modern terms, is undermined; in medieval terms, it is an offence against God. In the play the Bishop of Carlisle, who in historic fact was the one person to make a solemn protest in Parliament, says:

> And if you crown him, let me prophesy,
> The blood of English shall manure the ground,
> And future ages groan for this foul act. . . .
> And in this seat of peace, tumultuous wars
> Shall kin with kin, and kind with kind confound.

Bit by bit the whole of society is affected by the division that ensues. As Froissart says, "what nobleman liveth at this day, or what gentleman of any ancient stock or progeny is there, whose lineage hath not been infested and plagued with this unnatural division?"[4] Or rather, as we have seen the historian put it, the fracture in society gave the opportunity for all the strains and tensions, the feuds and conflicts, to break out. Just as

> Not all the water in the rough, rude sea
> Can wash the balm off from an anointed king—

so also, for all who were involved in the deposition, water cannot wash away their sin. They will pay the penalty in their own blood—which flowed freely enough, as we have seen, in their own generation and the two following.

We see Bolingbroke's own retribution worked out in the story of his reign—Hall's "the unquiet time of King Henry IV"—in the two parts of the play of that name. The very first lines strike the note:

> So shaken as we are, so wan with care,
> Find we a time for frighted peace to pant,
> And breathe short-winded accents of new broils
> To be commenced in strands afar remote. . . .

In fact Henry IV was for ever disappointed of his hope of transmuting the civil broils at home into a Crusade abroad, of making retribution in that form. His reign was filled from end to end with unquiet and unease; never any peace of mind or body, for when he had surmounted the worst dangers threatening him, the combination of the Percies with Glendower and the Welsh resistance, Henry was henceforth, though not old, an exhausted and sick man.

Shakespeare expanded a few hints in the chronicles to make in these two plays a main theme of the discord between King Henry and Prince Hal. We have seen how it was in historic fact; in the

19

drama the effect is immensely heightened—it becomes the main stuff of the two plays—for it adds yet another dimension to the retribution upon Henry: he sees his son, keeping the company he keeps and going the way he seems to be upon, becoming another Richard. The usurper of Richard's throne, now himself an anointed king, warns his son of such conduct:

> The skipping king, he ambled up and down
> With shallow jesters and rash bavin wits,
> Soon kindled and soon burnt, carded his state,
> Mingled his royalty with capering fools,
> Had his great name profanèd with their scorns. . . .

Henry is afraid that his heir will go the same way and lose the throne he himself had secured with such care.

Much of the action of these plays, necessarily foreshortened and telescoped for dramatic effect, is taken up—as indeed Henry's reign was—with the risings against his unsteady throne. The Percies regret that ever they made Henry king; here is Hotspur:

> My father gave him welcome to the shore,
> And when he heard him swear and vow to God
> He came but to be duke of Lancaster. . . .
> My father, in kind heart and pity moved,
> Swore him assistance and performed it too.

This is a fair version of the actual event. Then Henry could reply, as he does in the play:

> Though then, God knows, I had no such intent
> But that necessity so bowed the state
> That I and greatness were compelled to kiss.

That also is just: having put his hand to the plough, he could not turn back; he was caught in the toils of historic circumstance as fast as Richard—unless he too were to abnegate. (And what then? We are up against the nature of historic, i.e., human, action. The choice is, either to withdraw altogether—and that is a form of action—or else to go on.)

In the Second Part of *Henry IV* the actual crisis of the reign is past—as it was in fact with the battle of Shrewsbury—but Henry is a man exhausted and ill, with his son anxious to take his place and govern before his father is dead. That was true enough, too, as we have seen. But the philosophic issues raised by participation in political action are weighed by the King *dans les intermittences du coeur:*

> O God! that one might read the book of fate
> And see the revolution of the times . . .

(Perhaps, if one could, one might withdraw altogether.) There is the bitterness of irony in the changes time brings: Henry says:

> O, if this were seen,
> The happiest youth, viewing his progress through,
> What perils passed, what crosses to ensue,
> Would shut the book, and sit him down and die.
> 'Tis not ten years gone
> Since Richard and Northumberland, great friends,
> Did feast together, and in two years after
> Were they at wars. It is but eight years since
> This Percy was the man nearest my soul,
> Who like a brother toiled in my affairs,
> And laid his love and life under my foot. . . .

And now! . . . both Hotspur and his father, who made Henry king, meet their death in arms against him.

So much for historic action. It makes one sympathise with Falstaff, taking no part in it at the battle of Shrewsbury, and shamming dead:

> The better part of valour is discretion, in the which better part I have saved my life.

And, contemplating Hotspur's dead body:

> To die is to be a counterfeit, for he is but the counterfeit of a man who hath not the life of a man. But to counterfeit dying, when a man thereby liveth, is to be no counterfeit, but the true and perfect image of life indeed.

Which is the more philosophic spirit? Which the more philosophic part?

Yet, generation after generation, youth cannot but be tempted by the temptations of action. We might take the most wonderful scene in these two plays, and one of the most unforgettable in Shakespeare—that in which Prince Hal comes to his father sleeping and, thinking it the sleep of death, puts on his father's crown—

as an epigraph on all the action of this book. We have seen how one after the other of them—Bolingbroke, and then Richard of York, then his sons Edward IV and Richard III—could not resist the glamour of the Crown, gave their lives for it or were worn out by its burden; and this was true of the claimants and pretenders no less than, in another sense, of Richard II and Henry VI, both victims. When Henry IV awakes and finds the crown gone from his side, he recalls his son with the reproach:

> Dost thou so hunger for mine empty chair
> That thou wilt needs invest thee with my honours
> Before thy hour be ripe? O foolish youth!
> Thou seek'st the greatness that will overwhelm thee.

Hall the chronicler wondered what were Richard III's thoughts as he went down into the dust at Bosworth.

We have seen that there is some warrant for Shakespeare's symbolic, non-historical scene here: Prince Henry wanted to assume the Crown before his father's death. (The son, too, was a victim: dead, worn out with the French campaigns, at thirty-five.) Still Henry IV had cleared the way for his son's quiet occupation of the throne, by his life of care, the burden of retribution he had borne:

> For all the soil of the achievement goes .
> With me into the earth. It seemed in me
> But as an honour snatched with boist'rous hand,
> And I had many living to upbraid
> My gain of it by their assistances,
> Which daily grew to quarrel and to bloodshed,
> Wounding supposèd peace. All these bold fears
> Thou see'st with peril I have answerèd.
> For all my reign hath been but as a scene
> Acting that argument: for what in me was purchased
> Falls upon thee in a more fairer sort;
> So thou the garland wear'st successively.

Though Henry V succeeded quietly as the second monarch of the Lancastrian house, there was a sputter of a challenge remaining over from what his father had had to endure, in the Cambridge-Scrope conspiracy on the eve of setting out for the Agincourt campaign. The intention of Richard of Cambridge—father of Richard of York, be it remembered—was to put his brother-in-law, the third Earl of March, Richard II's heir, on the throne. Actually, March always accepted the country's verdict on Richard in 1399 and lived a loyal subject of the Lancastrians. The conspiracy is dealt with in Act II, Scene 2 of the play.

The first act is taken up with the diplomatic negotiations with France, or rather, the diplomatic preparations for war. Internal peace having been secured, the long war with France can be resumed. Not merely piety but historical accuracy compels me to absolve Archbishop Chichele, founder of my college at Oxford, from Shakespeare's charge of inciting Henry V to war with France to divert the Commons from attacking the Church. Henry V needed no encouragement from anyone: he was a man bent on pursuing his own ends, very much his own master.

Shakespeare's portrait of Henry V is the traditional one, dear to the Elizabethans, of the hero-king. As such he was so popular a figure that there were at least two plays about him, in addition to Shakespeare's; to one of these, *The Famous Victories of Henry V,* Shakespeare's plays on both Henry IV and Henry V are indebted for some touches. The younger Henry's character was a Tudor commonplace from Hall onwards:

> This Henry was a king whose life was immaculate and his living without spot. . . . This prince was a captain against whom fortune never frowned nor mischance once spurned. . . . This justiciary was so feared that all rebellion was banished and sedition suppressed. . . . He was merciful to offenders, charitable to the needy, indifferent [impartial] to all men, faithful to his friends, and fierce to his enemies, toward God most devout, toward the world moderate, and to his realm a very father. What should I say? He was the blazing comet and apparent lantern in his days; he was the mirror of Christendom and the glory of his country; he was the flower of kings past, and a glass to them that should succeed.[5]

We observe that there is not a word of criticism of the Napoleonic adventure into which he led his country—once he embarked on it, neither could he extricate himself: he too was caught in the web of historic circumstance. All this goes straight into Shakespeare's heroic drama, a different kind of play from the Henry IV plays with their true dramatic conflicts: *Henry V* is more of a pageant. Henry's prayer before Agincourt does reflect back, however, to his father's sin in usurping the throne:

> Not today, O Lord,
> O not today, think not upon the fault
> My father made in compassing the Crown. . . .

This is not a theme of the play, any more than it was of the reign. So long as the house of Lancaster was successful it could maintain its hold on the throne, and even for some time after its evident failure with Henry's son, so strong was the impulse and prestige the father gave to it. The theme of the play is rather that which we have been observing in practice all through this book: the responsibilities of rule, the burdens, obligations, duties of kingship, its essential role in society, and when it fails society itself is sick. "Upon the king," Henry meditates before Agincourt,

> Upon the king let us our lives, our souls,
> Our debts, our careful wives,
> Our children, and our sins, lay on the king!
> We must bear all.

Shakespeare's human sympathies saw the other side to this in the protest of the common soldier:

> But if the cause be not good, the king himself hath a heavy reckoning to make, when all those legs and arms and heads, chopped off in a battle, shall join together at the latter day and cry all, "We died at such a place."

It remains all the more curious that no reflection is made, even indirectly or by implication, upon Henry V for leading his country into the ultimate impasse of the French war. His was the responsibility: if he had not left his son with the impossible legacy of a kingdom in France to lose, his house might never have lost the English throne and there would have been no Wars of the Roses.

Shakespeare's trilogy on the long reign of Henry VI gave him his first success and made the foundation of his career in the theatre. In the Epilogue to *Henry V,* a sonnet spoken by the Chorus (probably played by Shakespeare himself), he refers to the frequent performances the *Henry VI* plays had had:

Henry the Sixth, in infant bands crowned king
   Of France and England, did this king succeed:
Whose state so many had the managing
    That they lost France and made his England bleed—
Which oft our stage hath shown. . . .

The loss of France is the subject of the First Part, which is planned as a kind of portico to the Second and Third Parts depicting the internal strife of the Wars of the Roses; the whole structure completed by *Richard III,* which has always maintained its place through the centuries as one of his most popular pieces.

The main source for this first quartet was Hall's chronicle. The extent of Shakespeare's debt to Hall has come to be realised only in our own time: he was "so intimately familiar with Hall that in any one of these four plays he ranged widely over the whole of Hall's history, picking up phrases and incidents freely, and weaving them into his more limited structure."[6] In reading Hall, it must have struck the young actor-dramatist what a magnificent scheme for a sequence of plays Hall provided—the book was already almost a drama in itself. From it Shakespeare took the dominant general idea that gave structure to the whole scheme and made the welter of the fifteenth century intelligible: internal divisions and dissensions in England lost France and then well-nigh lost England herself. It all went back to the original sin of Henry IV and was redeemed only in the fourth generation by the union of Lancaster and York in the Tudors. This was the traditional view of the sixteenth century and there was everything to be said for it—in any case William Shakespeare was never a man to challenge the traditional view.

Moreover, a popular playwright, he was quite naturally bent on success with the public; so his plays are intensely patriotic, they have the overemphasis, the naïve jingoism to our ears, of the years immediately succeeding the Armada. In these circumstances the loss of France posed a ticklish problem to the ambitious beginner. The theme of war in Normandy had its contemporary appeal, with Essex's romantic expedition in 1591—in which the young Southampton was so anxious to serve[7]—and the dramatist had the aid of the reverberations and the long memories which that theme aroused in a London audience. Marlowe's friend, Nashe, testified to it at the time:

How it would have joyed brave Talbot—the Terror of the French
—to think that after he had lain two hundred years in his tomb
he should triumph again on the stage, and have his bones new
embalmed with the tears of ten thousand spectators at least—at
several [different] times—who, in the tragedian that represents
his person, imagine they behold him fresh bleeding.[8]

This clearly refers to the First Part of *Henry VI,* where Talbot
is treated as the hero of the war in France. Everything is done by
the tactful dramatist—not the least of whose characteristics proved
to be his unfailing tact—to make the defeat palatable, to put it
right with the audience. Joan of Arc was victorious, but her
victories were due to her sorcery, in addition to her patriotic
courage, of course—and this was the traditional view of her that
had come down in the chronicles. The English were being driven
out of France—but every time there is a battle on the stage the
English beat the French. It is really too simple. But it was undoubtedly successful theatre, and that is what a play is for.

Other mitigations were thoughtfully provided for the audience.
There was Burgundy's treacherous desertion of the English alliance
to help to account for the defeat—that would appeal to London
memories kept going by the ballads. There was the struggle between factions at Court, in particular for the appointment as
Lieutenant in France—and that had been true enough. Shakespeare took over from Hall the traditional view of "good Duke
Humphrey," who had been displaced by the Cardinal—a cardinal
was never a popular bird with Elizabethans. Then there was the
French marriage of Henry VI to Margaret of Anjou, to which the
English imputed much of the troubles that followed—again, as we
have seen, with some reason. There are appeals to the traditional
English contempt for the French, however absurd, going back to
the Hundred Years' War—and the Elizabethans were apt to be
as xenophobic as people at such stages and times usually are.
Or we have a personal bid from Shakespeare, an appeal to the
rising popularity of the hopeful young Elizabethan hero, Essex.
When the bodies of Talbot and his son are carried off the stage,
Sir William Lucy (ancestor of the Charlecote family Shakespeare
knew, a nice Warwickshire touch) says:

> But from their ashes shall be reared
> A phoenix that shall make all France afeared.

For all the immaturities and inconsistencies of a prentice-work, of which we have not got a very satisfactory text, one cannot but be struck by the dramatic effectiveness of *1 Henry VI*, the conciseness with which the historical events of twenty years are drawn together, the rhythmical antiphony of the first two acts answering each other. It is a remarkable achievement of construction for a beginner, foreshadowing the still greater one he brought off with the trilogy as a whole. This was clearly in mind; this introductory play is an integral part of a planned tetralogy. There are sufficient references forward and backward to keep the whole history, as it is going to unfold, in mind. And this is the purpose of Shakespeare's chief inventions. The Temple Garden scene, with the plucking of the roses red and white as badges of the houses of Lancaster and York, has no warrant in history; it is put into the play as preparation for the wars to come in the succeeding plays. Similarly with the build-up Shakespeare gives to the character of York, and giving him a victory over Joan of Arc which is quite unhistorical: it is to provide him with a foundation for his part in the future, as Protector and in the Wars of the Roses, which he may be said to have started.

In the Second and Third Parts of *Henry VI* the scene is transferred almost wholly to England and we watch the working out of the internal broils and the loss of France in civil war on English soil. It begins with Henry's disastrous marriage to Margaret, sealed with the loss of Maine and Anjou, goes on to make a theme of the rivalry between York and Somerset, and the larger conflict between "good Duke Humphrey" and Cardinal Beaufort. In the end the "good Duke" is murdered in his bed by Beaufort's machinations, in accordance with the popular tradition, though there is no reason to suppose that Humphrey suffered anything other than a stroke: it was enough to put paid to his useless career. Everyone agrees that the Jack Cade scenes exhibit Shakespeare already in full and mature control of his hitherto unexampled powers of rendering the realistic, and un-self-conscious, humour of the "illogical classes." The play ends with York arriving from Ireland to challenge the throne and his victory at the first battle of St. Albans. The Wars of the Roses have begun.

There is thus a heightening of tone with the Third Part of *Henry VI* that makes it at once more sombre and more lurid, and brings it close in its effect to the horrors of *Titus Andronicus*. The dominant image is that of the slaughter-house—which would have been closely familiar to an Elizabethan glover's son— and England was a slaughter-house in the latter half of the fif- teenth century, at least for the royal houses and the nobility con- cerned in their conflict. Shakespeare has even darkened the pic- ture, both for dramatic effect and also as a consequence of the conciseness with which he has got those crowded decades into five acts.

The play begins with York's occupying Henry's throne at West- minster, his rejection by the Lancastrian lords and the compro- mise by which Henry is to retain the Crown for life while York rules and is to succeed after Henry's death. Margaret, who is a dominant figure in this play, refuses to accept this, and York and his son are killed at Wakefield. One alteration here is very effective —the taunting of York by crowning him with a paper-crown before he is done to death. There is a great deal of mutual taunting, of an almost ritual, sacrificial character, in the play; and though grievous and harassing to a modern ear, there is no doubt, from recent productions of the play, of its terrible effectiveness. Our century has the worst of all reasons for understanding its blood- lust and blood-guiltiness so much better than the civilised nine- teenth century: Victorian critics could not believe their ears.

In one of these mutual tauntings Edward of York reproaches Margaret with having let loose the flood:

> For what hath broached this tumult but thy pride?
> Hadst thou been meek, our title still had slept,
> And we, in pity of the gentle king,
> Had slipped our claim until another age.

We have seen that, historically, there was something in that: if the Frenchwoman had known how to treat York decently he might never have challenged the throne. There follows Towton and the ruin of the Lancastrian house. On that battlefield Henry reflects on the body of the son killed by the father in that strife dividing families:

> O that my death would stay these ruthful deeds!
> O pity, pity, gentle heaven, pity!
> The red rose and the white are on his face,
> The fatal colours of our striving houses. . . .

And so to Edward IV's assumption of the Crown, his temporary loss of it at the hands of Warwick, the battles of Barnet and Tewkesbury, the killing of Prince Edward and then of his father, Henry VI, in the Tower.

Once again, the moral is not only that of Hall but one that evidently meant something strongly for Shakespeare himself, for it is enforced in play after play in the early 1590's:

> Why, knows not Montagu that of itself
> England is safe, if true within itself?

This is followed by a contemporary reference that would appeal to the audience just at that juncture:

> 'Tis better using France than trusting France:
> Let us be backed with God and with the seas
> Which he hath given for fence impregnable:
> In them and in ourselves our safety lies.

Yet underneath these surface sentiments, obvious enough, another dimension is suggested by the meditations of Henry on the purposelessness of so much of human action. This must have spoken, from a deeper level, for William Shakespeare. Here is the senseless to-and-fro of battle, like the ebb and flow of the war itself:

> Now sways it this way, like a mighty sea
> Forced by the tide to combat with the wind;
> Now sways it that way, like the selfsame sea
> Forced to retire by fury of the wind:
> Sometime the flood prevails, and then the wind;
> Now one the better, then another best;
> Both tugging to be victors, breast to breast,
> Yet neither conqueror not conquerèd:
> So is the equal poise of this fell war.

It must often have seemed in those ill decades—

> All pity choked with custom of fell deeds—

as if there were no end to it.

And yet, an end was on the way, though no one could have foreseen it—perhaps that was the most dramatic thing about it. No one could have foreseen that the end would, paradoxically, be precipitated by the malign character and the monstrous deeds of Richard III. Everyone—except his little group of faithful agents, Catesby, Ratcliffe, Lovell, Jack of Norfolk—turned against that; and that united the country to end the conflict.

This is already in view and effectively prepared for in this play. Shakespeare adopts the traditional view that Richard of Gloucester had long meditated his blood-stained march to the throne; that he and his brothers killed Henry VI's son at Tewkesbury, that he then killed Henry in the Tower, was responsible for Clarence's death, before culminating his crimes with the murder of his nephews. As we have seen, it is not known that he had any part in the killing of Prince Edward, and he was not responsible for Clarence's death. He certainly supervised the dispatch of Henry VI, but that would have been on Edward IV's orders; and he indubitably made away with his brother's children. As for his design on the Crown, it is unlikely that he seriously contemplated it until the sudden illness and death of Edward IV in 1483 unexpectedly opened the way.

Already Richard is the practised hypocrite of More's portrait of him, the dissembler of Hall's description, "wily to feign and apt to dissimule," and as we have observed him acting a part, in actual fact, in his seizure of power in 1483. Shakespeare names him a play-actor, when he comes to kill King Henry:

> What scene of death hath Roscius now to act?

Suddenly, with his long soliloquy in Act III, Scene 2, we are confronted with the realisation of the conscious, Machiavellian villain Richard of Gloucester is to become:

> Why, I can smile, and murder while I smile,
> And cry "Content" to that which grieves my heart,
> And wet my cheeks with artificial tears,
> And frame my face to all occasions. . . .
> I can add colours to the chameleon,
> Change shapes with Proteus for advantages
> And set the murderous Machiavel to school.

From the *Henry VI* plays to *Richard III* we move from promising (and successful) prentice-work to a masterpiece. The years 1592–93 were the turning-point in Shakespeare's life: with his friendship with Southampton came his introduction into an aristocratic circle of refined sensibilities and tastes, that helped to bring out all his potentialities. In this warm clime his genius rapidly ripened. Many have noticed the startling change from the early formal comedies, *The Comedy of Errors* and *The Two Gentlemen of Verona*, to the inspiration, the free flow of genius, of *A Midsummer Night's Dream* and *Love's Labour's Lost*. Similarly with the step from the *Henry VI* trilogy to the last play in this series, the *Richard III* of 1593. We are in a different dimension, where "history tends to pass into tragedy, becoming less of a fateful pageant and more the adventure of an individual soul."[9]

As we have observed in the realm of historical fact, too, we are moving from the medieval to the Renaissance world. The world of medieval belief did impose some inhibitions, some restraints if only upon the conscience; with Richard III all inhibitions were removed, he was resolved to set conscience at nought: in his very first speech, setting the tone of the play,

> I am determinèd to prove a villain.

The first act rapidly foreshortens the events of the last years of Edward IV's reign to set the scene. Richard has sown the seeds of suspicion that sends Clarence to the Tower; he meets Anne Neville, widow of Prince Edward, escorting as mourner the body of Henry VI, and brazenly wooes her. Queen Margaret comes back from banishment, a kind of Cassandra, to act as chorus to the fell deeds of Richard upon his own house and work out her revenge for her. For all the liberties that Shakespeare has taken with the history to make the drama there are detailed touches caught up which we recall from the chronicles: the bleeding of Henry's body upon the pavement, Richard's aristocratic contempt for the new-sprung Woodvilles:

> Since every Jack became a gentleman,
> There's many a gentle person made a Jack.

The act ends with the intensely imaginative and effective scene of Clarence's murder in the Tower. We see Richard as the full-fledged hypocrite Shakespeare developed out of More's portrait of his character:

> I am too childish—foolish for this world.

> Because I cannot flatter and look fair,
> Smile in men's faces, smoothe, deceive and cog,
> Duck with French nods and apish courtesy,
> I must be held a rancorous enemy.
> Cannot a plain man live and think no harm,
> But thus his simple truth must be abused? . . .

Actually, in historic fact, Richard was but a ham-actor, for everybody saw through his acting; it was his power, the terror he inspired, that was persuasive.

In the second act Edward dies, regretting Clarence, with the authentic touch—

> But for my brother not a man would speak.

Richard's seizure of power is set in train with the interception of the young king on his way to London. Richard's mother, the Duchess of York, laments:

> Accursèd and unquiet wrangling days,
> How many of you have mine eyes beheld!
> My husband lost his life to get the Crown,
> And often up and down my sons were tossed,
> For me to joy and weep their gain and loss.
> And being seated, and domestic broils
> Clean overblown, themselves the conquerors
> Make war upon themselves, brother to brother,
> Blood to blood, self to self!

It is a fair summing up: Shakespeare leaves it to the women to make the sensible comment on this world of male action.

The long third act, with its rapid seven scenes, sees the unfolding of Richard's plot, and his capture of the throne. We have the divided Councils, the sounding out of Hastings by Catesby, the sensational scene in the Tower when Richard sent for the strawberries from Bishop Morton's garden while he made the final arrangements to arrest Hastings:

> My noble lords and cousins all, good morrow.
> I have been long a sleeper, but I trust
> My absence doth neglect no great design
> Which, by my presence, might have been concluded.

The act ends with Buckingham's presentation of Richard to the mayor and citizens, with the reluctant Protector appearing aloft between two bishops with a prayer-book in his hands, evidently abstracted unwillingly from his devotions.

The fourth act sees Richard, crowned and married to Anne, sending Tyrrell to murder his nephews. Dighton and Forest, the murderers, are described as "fleshed villains"—this is More's phrase, we remember, "fleshed in murder." This is followed by a ritual scene in which the three women, old Queen Margaret, the Duchess of York and Edward IV's queen, recite the litany of their griefs. Margaret, like a *revenante,* recites:

> Bear with me: I am hungry for revenge,
> And now I cloy me with beholding it.
> Thy Edward, he is dead, that killed my Edward;
> Thy other Edward dead to quit my Edward;
> Young York he is but boot [thrown in], because
>   both they
> Matched not the high perfection of my loss.
> Thy Clarence, he is dead, that stabbed my Edward;
> And the beholders of this frantic play,
> Th' adulterate Hastings, Rivers, Vaughan, Grey,
> Untimely smothered in their dusky graves.

And so on . . . On Anne's death Richard makes interest with Elizabeth Woodville to marry her daughter, Elizabeth. The Stanleys send their message to Henry of Richmond overseas; Henry makes his first attempt, Buckingham's founders.

In act five Buckingham is led to execution in the market-place at Salisbury upon All Souls' Day. Henry lands at Milford, is welcomed by the country and, to Richard's surprise and rage, succeeds in penetrating to the heart of England without impeachment:

> Thus far into the bowels of the land
> Have we marched on without impediment.

The two armies reach Bosworth Field; the preparation for the battle is the best and most elaborate in all these plays, though there is the least fighting. We must remember that the Elizabethans loved battle-scenes on the stage, few as the actors must have been, there was the business and bustle of marching to and fro, the banners and flags, the clash of arms and braying of trumpets. The appeal of the scene to us is an inward one: the symbolic representation of Richard's crimes in the appearance of the ghosts of Henry VI and his son, of Clarence, Rivers, Grey and Vaughan, Hastings, the smothered Princes, Richard's dead wife and Buckingham—the melancholy procession that visits Richard's tent, when the lights burn blue, in the night before Bosworth. Richard's last night on earth, the torment of his smothered conscience, is marvellously realised and brought to life. At various junctures in the play he is specifically named a "homicide," four times in fact, lastly by Henry in his oration to his soldiers—just as, historically, Henry named him in his proclamation to the country:

> truly, gentlemen,
> A bloody tyrant and a homicide:
> One raised in blood, and one in blood established.

Henry has the last word on the fratricidal war:

> England hath long been mad, and scarred herself.

There must be a new beginning:

> And then, as we have ta'en the sacrament,
> We will unite the white rose and the red.

Shakespeare's first masterpiece has always held the stage and never lost its appeal for the public through the centuries. In the name-part it provides a superb rôle for energetic actors, as we see all the way from Burbage to Olivier. In his own day Burbage was perhaps most famous for his creation of this rôle, as the stories about him would seem to indicate. In the next generation a guide showing people around the field of Bosworth could easily slip into saying that it was Burbage who cried out, "A horse, a horse! my kingdom for a horse!" The story is told in "Iter Boreale," the delightful poem by Richard Corbett describing a summer jaunt into the Midlands with three of his Christ Church companions.

> Mine host was full of ale and history,
> And on the morrow when he brought us nigh
> Where the two Roses joined, you would suppose
> Chaucer ne'er made the *Romaunt of the Rose*.

> Hear him. "See ye yon wood? There Richard lay
> With his whole army. Look the other way,
> And lo where Richmond in a bed of gorse
> Encamped himself o'er night and all his force.
> Upon this hill they met." Why, he could tell
> The inch where Richmond stood, where Richard fell.[10]

But most of the host's information seems to have come from the favourite play:

> Besides what of his knowledge he can say
> He had authentic notice from the play:
> Which I might guess by mustering up the ghosts
> And policies not incident to hosts,
> But chiefly by that one perspicuous thing
> Where he mistook a player for a king,
> For when he would have said King Richard died
> And called, "A horse! a horse!" he "Burbage" cried.

It provides us with a pretty instance of the shaping, continuing influence Shakespeare was going to exert upon the English mind in the conception of its own past. The great Duke of Marlborough admitted that Shakespeare's plays were all the history he had ever read. With so perceptive and sympathetic a mind for guide, a great master in the understanding of human nature to make the past intelligible, a dramatist with a penetrating insight into society and politics, anyone deriving his view of the whole story from Shakespeare would not be far out.

EPILOGUE

Before the Elizabethan age was over, and before Bacon magistrally fixed the traditional portrait of Henry VII with his *History*, the tradition was challenged and Richard III found a defender in Sir George Buck. Buck was Master of the Revels, but he also had antiquarian and scholarly interests. He was descended from a Yorkshire family that had lost its possessions for fighting on Richard's side at Bosworth, so Buck had a motive for his work of piety. This describes it, for, though it is not a foolish work, in it Richard can do no wrong.

This uncritical, even laudatory attitude is singularly unpersuasive. From the very first, with Richard's first steps to seize power with the capture of Edward V at Stony Stratford and the Queen's hurrying with young Richard of York into sanctuary, we are told that she "out of a pretended motherly care, rather indeed her policy, would not let him stir from her to see the King."[1] Even Buck cannot justify Richard's murder of Hastings—the turning-point in the *coup d'état*—"generally supposed much affectionate to the Protector." Of course Buck accepts Richard's bastardising of Edward IV's children and the view that his wife was unworthy to be a king's wife "by reason of her extreme unequal quality." This was the snobbish attitude of the old aristocrats towards her, which Buck was continuing; we have seen that through her mother, the widow of Henry V's brother, Bedford, she came from one of the noblest families in Europe, and neither the one consideration nor the other has anything to say to the legitimacy of her marriage.

When it comes to Richard's murder of his nephews, all that Buck can say is that in a Roll of Parliament "there are arguments to be gathered that the two sons of King Edward were living in the time of this Parliament [1483], which was at the least nine months after the death of their father and six months after King Richard."[2] We see that this is a vague and baseless supposition. Upon it Buck bases an argument that "if King Richard suffered them to live so long, there is no reason why he should after make them away." All the indications point to Richard having had them done away with in August, 1483; he had the strongest motive to clear them out of the way for himself and his own son. The cause of Buckingham's turning against Richard was his "reformation of an ill government and tyranny"—we see the usual reversal of common sense with such people.

Perhaps it is unfair to recall that poor Buck ended up out of his mind.

Buck's arguments—if such we may call them—were taken up in the eighteenth century by Horace Walpole, in his *Historic Doubts on the Life and Reign of King Richard the Third*. Horace was a whimsical, paradoxical, wholly delightful creature, a cultivated dilettante whose lifelong occupation was to *épater le bourgeois*. We can sympathise with his inflection, though we must not do so at the expense of truth. He was out to challenge received opinions, especially if they were popularly held—several times in his work there are contemptuous comments on the views of the mob and those who carry "mob-banners"; he too was an aristocrat—but it sometimes happens that received opinions and traditional views are right, popular or not.

Horace starts from the point of view that "all very ancient history, except that of the illuminated Jews, is a perfect fable."[3] Now we know. The whole of the *Cambridge Ancient History* is in vain. When we come to English history, "if we take a survey of our own history and examine it with any attention, what an unsatisfactory picture does it present to us! How dry, how superficial, how void of information! How little is recorded besides battles, plagues and religious foundations!" It is left doubtful which of these the Whiggish sceptic deplored most. As for the historians, they are no better regarded: "so incompetent has the generality of historians been for the province they have undertaken . . ." This was said of the age that produced Gibbon, Hume, Robertson, Madox and the fine achievements of the English topographical historians.

Here was a *littérateur* come to put them right. "Many of the crimes imputed to Richard seemed improbable; and, what was stronger, contrary to his own interest." Here is an unintelligent foundation for a defence of Richard, for it was strongly to his interest to get his nephews out of his way. We need not suppose that he was guilty of all the crimes imputed to him: the murders of his nephews and of Henry VI are quite enough. We see that Walpole's was a light-weight affair: whether he has unravelled that dark period his readers must decide—"nor is it of any importance whether I have or not. The attempt was mere matter of curiosity and speculation." That puts it in the right perspective.

Horace objected equally to the views of Sir Thomas More and Francis Bacon: "the most senseless stories of the mob are converted to history by the former; the latter is still more culpable: he has held up to the admiration of posterity and, what is worse, to the imitation of succeeding princes, a man whose nearest approach to wisdom was mean cunning, and raised into a legislator a sanguinary, sordid and trembling usurper."[4] We see that this is merely juvenile and silly. But Horace had the sense to insist that he had no positive conclusions of his own to offer concerning Richard: "I have ventured to establish no peremptory conclusion of my own." Of course not: it is impossible to give any account either coherent in itself or consistent with the facts other than that on which the historians are agreed.

Horace involved himself in some controversy with the most philosophical intelligence among the historians of the time. It is obvious that Hume did not take Walpole very seriously. In reply Horace was surprised that "the best reasoner and greatest sceptic amongst them has for once listed under such mob-banners." Hume was as enlightened a sceptic as ever Walpole was; only he had more justice of mind: he was capable of appreciating More's "probity and great sense." Horace disliked the saint. However, in a further reply to the cleric who was President of the Society of Antiquaries, Horace emphasised once more that he had only expressed his doubts: "it is a subject of no consequence; I expressed my doubts on it; I concluded doubting."[5]

In some circumstances the propagation of doubt, where there is no need for it, is as absurd as the assertion of nonsense itself. We do not have to go to novelists for our history, or to societies that exist to propagate a preconceived point of view for any justice of mind. It is the business of the historian simply to seek and establish the truth of the matter. No reputable historian has ever thought Richard other than guilty; to suppose otherwise is contrary not merely to completely consistent tradition, but to all the evidence that exists and to common sense.

NOTES

PROLOGUE

1. S. B. Chrimes, *Lancastrians, Yorkists and Henry VII*, 176–77.
2. Ibid.
3. Ibid.
4. Ibid., 178.

CHAPTER I

1. M. McKisack, *The Fourteenth Century, 1307–1399* (The Oxford History of England), 385.
2. Ibid., 407.
3. Ibid., 412.
4. Ibid., 444.
5. Ibid., 459.
6. *Chronicon Adae de Usk, 1377–1421*, ed. E. M. Thompson, 151.

CHAPTER II

1. *Chronicon Adae de Usk, 1377–1421*, ed. E. M. Thompson, 158.
2. Walsingham, from G. E. C., *The Complete Peerage*, I, 244.
3. J. Tait, "Did Richard II Murder the Duke of Gloucester?", T. F. Tout and J. Tait, *Historical Essays*, 193 foll.
4. *Chronicon*, 169–70.
5. Ibid., 164.
6. Ibid., 182.
7. Ibid., 187.

CHAPTER III

1. *Chronicon*, 200–2, 298.
2. E. F. Jacob, *The Fifteenth Century, 1399–1485* (Oxford History of England), 30.
3. *Chronicon*, 220.
4. Ibid., 229.
5. C. L. Kingsford, *Henry V*, 47–49.
6. Jacob, 56.

7. Ibid., 73–74, 78.

8. Kingsford, 3.

9. Jacob, 90.

10. Kingsford, 61.

11. These are examined in detail by Kingsford in his introduction to his edition of *The First English Life of King Henry the Fifth,* xviii foll.

12. Ibid., xxvii–xxviii.

CHAPTER IV

1. Jacob, 121.

2. R. H. Robbins, ed., *Historical Poems of the XIVth and XVth Centuries,* 47.

3. Ibid., 136.

4. The story is referred to at least as early as 1429 in a poem by John Audelay:

> His [Henry VI's] father, for love of maid Catherine,
> In France he wrought torment and teen [grief]
> His love, they said, it should not been,
>   And sent him balls him with to play.
> Then was he wise in wars withal
> And taught Frenchmen to play at the ball. . . .

Robbins, 109.

5. Ibid., 142.

6. Kingsford, 142.

7. J. H. Wylie and W. T. Waugh, *The Reign of Henry the Fifth,* III, 86.

8. Ibid., 93, 95–96.

9. Kingsford, 220.

10. Kingsford, 307–8.

11. Jacob, 182.

12. Kingsford, 310.

13. Jacob, 193.

14. *Dict. Nat. Biog.,* under "Henry Beaufort."

15. Wylie and Waugh, III, 338.

16. Jacob, 200.

17. Ibid., 201.

18. Wylie and Waugh, III, 424.

CHAPTER V

1. Jacob, 200, 201, 202.

2. J. H. Ramsay, *Lancaster and York,* I, 340.

3. *Dict. Nat. Biog.*, under "Henry VI." I am indebted to this excellent article by T. F. Tout, from which other quotations come.

4. Robbins, 362.

5. Ibid., xxvi.

6. K. H. Vickers, *Humphrey, Duke of Gloucester*, 205.

7. Jacob, 244.

8. Ramsay, I, 389.

9. A. H. Burne, *The Agincourt War*, 240.

10. Ramsay, I, 398.

11. Ibid., I, 404, 405.

12. Jacob, 248.

13. Tout, loc. cit.

14. Ramsay, I, 425, 427, 428.

15. Jacob, 256.

16. Tout, loc. cit.

17. Jacob, 261, 262.

CHAPTER VI

1. Jacob, 471.

2. Vickers, 271.

3. Robbins, 176.

4. Vickers, 277.

5. Jacob, 475.

6. Ibid., 477.

7. *Dict. Nat. Biog.*, under "Margaret of Anjou," by T. F. Tout.

8. Ibid.

9. Ibid.

10. Jacob, 323, 325, 330.

11. Ibid., 320.

12. Robbins, 135.

13. Ramsay, II, 102.

14. Ibid., 107.

15. J. Gairdner, ed., *The Paston Letters* (ed. 1904), II, 162.

16. Robbins, 186.

17. Jacob, 492, 493.

18. Robbins, 187–89.

19. Ibid., 63.

20. Jacob, 505.

21. Ramsay, II, 156.

22. Jacob, 506.

CHAPTER VII

1. Robbins, 95.
2. S. B. Chrimes, *Lancastrians, Yorkists and Henry VII,* 78.
3. Jacob, 503.
4. Ibid., 345.
5. Jacob, 503.
6. Ibid., 326.
7. Chrimes, 78.
8. Jacob, 346.
9. Gairdner, II, 165, 174.
10. Ibid., 259, 261.
11. N. B. Lewis, from Jacob, 341.
12. Gairdner, II, 284–85.
13. Ibid., 295–97.
14. Ramsay, II, 173.
15. Gairdner, III, 13–14.
16. Ibid., 26–27.
17. Ibid., 75.
18. Ramsay, II, 220.
19. Jacob, 513.
20. Gairdner, III, 92.
21. Polydore Vergil, from Robbins, 358.
22. Ibid., 195.
23. Robbins, 209.
24. Ramsay, II, 236.
25. Ibid., 237.
26. C. L. Scofield, *The Life and Reign of Edward IV,* I, 138–39.
27. Ibid., 135.
28. Gairdner, III, 250.
29. Scofield, I, 143.

CHAPTER VIII

1. Jacob, 545.
2. R. S. Sylvester, ed., *The Complete Works of St. Thomas More,* II, 4.
3. Ramsay, II, 249–50.
4. Scofield, I, 178.
5. Ramsay, II, 295–96.
6. Jacob, 531.
7. Robbins, 196–98.

8. Scofield, I, 332–33.

9. Ibid., I, 354.

10. Sir John Fortescue, *The Governance of England,* ed. C. Plummer, 64.

11. Scofield, I, 541–42.

12. Robbins, 200.

13. Scofield, I, 569–70.

14. Ibid., I, 576.

15. Gairdner, V, 100.

16. J. Warkworth, *Chronicle,* ed. J. O. Halliwell (Camden Soc.), 21.

17. *The Great Chronicle of London,* ed. A. H. Thomas and I. D. Thornley, 220.

18. Scofield, I, 594.

19. Robbins, 200.

CHAPTER IX

1. Scofield, II, 161.

2. Ibid.

3. Chrimes, 96–97.

4. Cf. my essay "The Turbulent Career of Sir Henry de Bodrugan," *History, 1944,* 17 foll.

5. Gairdner, V, 195.

6. Scofield, II, 93.

7. Ibid., II, 209.

8. Jacob, 581.

9. P. M. Kendall, *Richard the Third,* 112.

10. Chrimes, 122.

11. Jacob, 588.

12. More, 10–13.

CHAPTER X

1. Jacob, 610.

2. A. F. Pollard, "The Making of Sir Thomas More's *Richard III,*" *Historical Essays in Honour of James Tait,* ed. J. G. Edwards, V. H. Galbraith, E. F. Jacob, 223.

3. Jacob is mistaken in saying (p. 613) that the Duke of York was at Stony Stratford. Indeed on p. 619 the little Richard of York is stated, correctly, to have been in sanctuary at Westminster with his mother. Fancy leaving these two statements unreconciled! The young Richard at Stony Stratford was Richard Grey.

4. More, 19–20.

5. *The Usurpation of Richard the Third,* ed. C. A. J. Armstrong, 99, 101.

6. More, 45.

7. Richard had a bastard of his own, but that was only natural.

8. Jacob, 618.

9. More, 47.

10. Jacob, 621.

11. More, 85; cf. L. E. Tanner and W. Wright, "Recent Investigations regarding the Fate of the Princes in the Tower," *Archaeologia, 1935,* 1–26.

12. Pollard, loc. cit., 225.

13. *The Great Chronicle of London,* ed. A. H. Thomas and I. D. Thornley, 234.

14. Armstrong, 113, 115.

15. More, 83 foll.

16. Kendall, 252.

17. Gairdner, 128.

18. Kendall, 258, 260.

19. Ibid., 252.

20. *Ingulph's Chronicle of the Abbey of Croyland with the Continuations,* trans. H. T. Riley, 490–91.

21. More, 90–91.

22. Gairdner, 132, 135–36.

23. Cf. my *Tudor Cornwall,* 110–11.

CHAPTER XI

1. Cf. my *Tudor Cornwall,* 112.

2. Riley, 495–96.

3. Gairdner, *Richard the Third,* 145, 164.

4. More, 87.

5. Riley, 496–97.

6. H. Ellis, *Letters,* Second Series, I, 149.

7. Riley, 500.

8. Gairdner, 201.

9. A. F. Pollard, *The Reign of Henry VII,* I, 4–5.

10. Gairdner, 237.

11. Polydore Vergil says "two thousand only." I follow his account of Henry's expedition, since Polydore Vergil was in a position to hear Henry's account of it from his own lips. Cf. *Polydore Vergil's English History. The Reigns of Henry VI, Edward IV, and Richard III,* ed. Sir Henry Ellis (Camden Soc.), 216 foll.

12. Cf. my "Alltyrynys and the Cecils," *Eng. Hist. Rev.*, 1960, 54.

13. Gairdner, *Paston Letters,* VI, 85.

14. Polydore Vergil, 223.

15. Ibid., 224–25.

16. Gairdner, *Richard the Third,* 246.

CHAPTER XII

1. Chrimes, 156.

2. *The Anglica Historia of Polydore Vergil,* ed. with a translation by D. Hay (Camden Soc.), 145. In using this translation I have occasionally emended words, e.g. for *pallidum,* "pale" rather than "sallow."

3. Francis Bacon, *The History of King Henry VII, Works,* ed. J. A. Spedding, R. L. Ellis, D. D. Heath, VI, 244.

4. Ibid., 240.

5. *The Reign of Henry VII from Contemporary Sources,* ed. A. F. Pollard, I, 217 foll.

6. Bacon, VI, 240, 242.

7. *Excerpta Historica,* ed. S. Bentley, 85–133, passim.

8. Loc. cit.

9. Bacon, VI, 243.

10. Polydore Vergil, 147.

11. Bacon, VI, 240–41, 244.

12. Pollard, II, 12.

13. *Plumpton Correspondence,* ed. T. Stapleton (Camden Soc.), 49.

14. Pollard, I, 35 foll.

15. J. D. Mackie, *The Earlier Tudors, 1485–1558,* 66.

16. Bacon, VI, 53.

17. Polydore Vergil, 15–17.

18. Bacon, VI, 45.

19. Pollard, I, 51.

20. *The Letters and Papers . . . of Richard III and Henry VII,* ed. J. Gairdner (Rolls Series), II, 55.

21. Cf. J. Gairdner, "The Story of Perkin Warbeck," in *The Life and Reign of Richard the Third,* 329–30.

22. Pollard, I, 213–14.

23. *The Complete Peerage. By G. E. C.,* Ed. G. H. White, XII, Part I, 451.

24. Mackie, 167.

25. Polydore Vergil, 127.

26. *A Relation of England,* trans. C. A. Sneyd (Camden Soc.), 27–28.

27. Cf. *The Complete Peerage,* XII, Part I, App. I.

28. J. Leland, *Collectanea,* ed. T. Hearne, V, 373–74.

29. *The English Works of Sir Thomas More,* ed. W. E. Campbell and others, I, 336.

30. Bacon, VI, 156.

CHAPTER XIII

1. For the following paragraphs I am indebted to C. L. Kingsford's authoritative *English Historical Literature in the Fifteenth Century.*

2. Ibid., 182, 183.

3. Ibid., 172–73.

4. Ibid., 129, 135.

5. Ibid., 110.

6. Pollard, I, 12 foll.

7. C. H. Firth, "The Ballad History of the Reigns of Henry VII and Henry VIII," *Trans. Roy. Hist. Soc.,* Third Series, II, 23; and cf. J. Gairdner, "The Song of the Lady Bessy," in *Richard III,* 345 foll.

8. Ibid., 26–27.

9. Kingsford, 190, 191.

10. *The Usurpation of King Richard III,* trans. C. A. J. Armstrong, 20, 24, 25.

11. Ibid., 17, 25–26.

12. A. F. Pollard, "The Making of Sir Thomas More's *Richard III,*" *Historical Essays in Honour of James Tait,* ed. J. G. Edwards, V. H. Galbraith, E. F. Jacob, 233.

13. Ibid., 225–26, 227.

14. *The Complete Works of St. Thomas More,* ed. R. S. Sylvester, II, c.

15. Pollard, 238.

16. Sylvester, lxxvi.

17. I have modernised from the original title-page "illustrious" for "illustre," "indubitable" for "undubitate."

18. *Dict. Nat. Biog.,* under "Edward Hall."

19. Kingsford, 271.

20. Ibid.

21. Ibid., 274.

22. *Holinshed's Chronicle as Used in Shakespeare's Plays,* ed. J. and A. Nicoll, 172.

23. M. McKisack, "Samuel Daniel as Historian," *Rev. Eng. Studies,* XXIII, 227.

24. S. Daniel, *The Civil Wars,* ed. L. Michel, 4.

25. E. M. W. Tillyard, *Shakespeare's History Plays,* 119.

26. The play is printed as an appendix to *The True Tragedy of Richard III,* ed. Barron Field. Shakespeare Soc., 1844.

27. Ibid., 165.

28. *The Letters of John Chamberlain,* ed. N. E. McClure.

CHAPTER XIV

1. C. F. Tucker Brooke, *The Tudor Drama,* 298.

2. P. Alexander, *Shakespeare's Life and Art,* 80, 81–82.

3. Edited, with an absurdly opinionated and ill-written introduction, in the Leavis manner, by A. P. Rossiter. Needless to say, on this important point he has nothing helpful to suggest.

4. J. D. Wilson, *King Richard II* (The Cambridge Shakespeare), xxvii.

5. Ibid., xviii.

6. A. S. Cairncross, *The Third Part of King Henry VI* (The Arden Shakespeare), xlvii–xlviii.

7. Cf. my *Shakespeare's Southampton,* 57.

8. G. Bullough, *Narrative and Dramatic Sources of Shakespeare,* III, 23.

9. Alexander, 83.

10. *The Poems of Richard Corbett,* ed. J. A. W. Bennett, 43.

EPILOGUE

1. G. Buck, *The History of the Life and Reign of Richard the Third* (ed. 1646), 11, 13, 20.

2. Ibid., 30, 34.

3. Horace Walpole, *Works* (ed. 1798), II, 107 foll.

4. Ibid., 145 foll.

5. Ibid., 221.

INDEX

A

B